Politics, Ethics and Social Responsibility of Business

Politics, Ethics and Social Responsibility of Business

K. V. Bhanu Murthy
Professor of Economics
Department of Commerce
Delhi School of Economics
University of Delhi

Usha Krishna
Associate Professor
Department of Commerce
Janki Devi Memorial College
New Delhi

Delhi • Chennai • Chandigarh

ISBN 978-81-317-3147-5

First Impression

Published by Dorling Kindersley (India) Pvt. Ltd., licensees of Pearson Education in South Asia.

Head Office: 7th Floor, Knowledge Boulevard, A-8(A), Sector-62, Noida, India.
Registered Office: 14 Local Shopping Centre, Panchsheel Park, New Delhi 110 017, India.

Laser typeset by Mukesh Technologies Pvt Ltd, Pondicherry.

Printed in India at Indian Binding House.

Contents

About the Authors

K.V. Bhanu Murthy is Professor of Economics, Department of Commerce, South Campus and Delhi School of Economics, University of Delhi. He is a Ph.D. in economics from the department of economics, Delhi School of Economics, in the area of industrialization strategy. His recent contributions are in the fields of banking and finance, environmental economics, agricultural market efficiency, international business, social responsibility and business ethics.

With an overall ranking at 97.8 percentile at the social science research network library (SSRN), the library has rated twelve of his papers among the world's top ten list. Of these, six are in the all-time top ten list. Two of his papers were adjudged to be the best at the 'National Conference on Emerging Issues in Financial Sector', held at Jaipuria Institute of Management (JIM), Noida, in 2009. His paper was also evaluated as the best at the 'Third National Conference on Capital Market' held at IBS Gurgaon, in 2009.

A recipient of the Siksha Ratan Puraskar from the India International Friendship Society in 2007 and the Best Citizens of India award from International Publishing House (IPH), New Delhi, in 2008, Professor Murthy has been a member of a Validation Committee that endorsed the world's largest savings and income survey conducted by Invest India Market Solutions and AC Nielsen in July 2007. He has written a book on environmental sustainability, which was published by Routledge, London, as part of a special series on environment in June 2006. He was bestowed with the eco-award for future scenarios by the World Society for Sustainable Development in 2002. Rated by allexperts.com as the best expert in economics in the world in 2000, Professor Murthy has over 30 papers and international conferences to his credit.

Usha Krishna received her post-graduate degree in commerce in 1973 and became the first woman to have completed the bachelor's as well as master's programme in commerce. She was awarded a Ph.D. in management by the faculty of management studies, Delhi University, in 1989 for her case studies on performance appraisal practices in Indian enterprises. Professor Usha Krishna began her teaching career at the early age of 21 as Assistant Lecturer in secretarial practice at Women's Polytechnic, New Delhi. She subsequently joined Delhi University as Lecturer in Commerce, before working with Shri Ram Centre for human resources and industrial relations for a period of five years. During this period she was part of a prestigious project on labour management relations in India, sponsored by the International Labor Organization. She was also a resource person for various executive development training programmes conducted by Shri Ram Centre for HR. She also had a brief stint teaching organizational behaviour and personnel management at Bombay University.

With a passion to educate, she has a rich experience spanning 37 years handling subjects like general management, human resource management, business communications, business organization and computer tools. She was instrumental in setting up a computer institute, the Cleveland Institute of Technology, in collaboration with Campus EAI Consortium, Cleveland, and Janki Devi College, which runs certificate courses in Web-based training. She has also been an honorary director at the New Delhi Institute of Information Technology, New Delhi, in 2005–2006. An established reviewer of books and articles in journals of national and international repute, Usha Krishna is currently Associate Professor in commerce at Janki Devi Memorial College, New Delhi.

Preface

Politics, Ethics and Social Responsibility of Business focusses on corporate social responsibility (CSR), an area of study that is interdisciplinary by nature. As a discipline, social responsibility of business was hitherto treated as a narrow subsidiary field of learning. This book brings CSR to the centre stage. Two other disciplines that form the basis of this subject are ethics and politics. Both these aspects have a bearing on the relationship between business and society, a topic of contemporary interest. The recent global financial crisis has clearly shown that if the politics and ethics of business are not addressed satisfactorily, it can lead to serious consequences that unsettle the natural scheme of events, the world over. In as much as business is a part of society, it draws resources from the society and satisfies the needs of the society. Its existence is validated by society's ethics and norms. The role of business cannot be understood without reference to politics in a society. Politics defines the idea of a 'good society' in terms of liberty, equality, justice, rights and recognition. Businesses play an important role in establishing such a 'good society'. Ethics draws on the philosophy of business, which defines the new concept of corporate responsibility.

This book looks at CSR from a new perspective and asserts that it needs to be understood as corporate responsibility. We feel that there is a need for business to review its philosophy since the very existence of business is validated by society's expectations from business. Therefore, politics and ethics remain the pillars from which business draws its strength, its existence and its role.

There are three aspects of corporate responsibility: corporate social responsibility, environmental accountability and good corporate governance. Corporate responsibility is determined by the integration of these three mutually inclusive aspects. Lack of either social responsibility or environmental accountability would mean irresponsible company or bad governance. Likewise, a responsible company would be one that follows the philosophy of ethical business practices and principles voluntarily. Unregulated business devoid of ethical standards of behaviour may result in disasters and scandals leading to temporary enactment and enforcement of legislations.

In terms of incorporating politics as a basis of social responsibility of business, the book articulates on how democratic values form the basis of a good society. It also discusses some lesser know aspects of the subject. For instance, it discusses the three models of management morality that help us to understand 'good and bad' behaviour. It also throws light on the importance of ethical decision making.

A common understanding is that while business is concerned with profit alone, politics, on the other hand, involves governance, conflict resolution and power—a role that has been traditionally left to the State. The book questions this understanding and shows how corporations have assumed enormous power and tended to act in unethical ways. Living in an age where companies are equivalent in wealth to countries and control much of the earth's resources and considering the fact that financial capital markets and business corporations are created by society, it is argued that business must serve the society and not just derive profit from it. It is concluded that CSR is meaningless unless the business meets the expectations of society. The book lays out the ethical basis of a business.

The book also throws light on some of the distinctive aspects of CSR, such as its definitions, tools and principles as well as standards of CSR. In addition, the concept of a responsible company that links up to the triple bottom-line of profits, people and planet, has been evolved. It also dwells upon current topics such as social exclusion, affirmative action and multiculturalism.

This book, though written for B.Com. (Hons) students of Delhi University, could be useful for students of higher-level courses as well. It could be of interest for management students as well as practicing managers and professionals, in general. It is made up of six units, spread across 30 chapters.

An overview of each unit and chapter is given below:

Unit I: 'Thinking Conceptually about Politics' consists of six chapters – Liberty, Equality, Justice, Rights, Recognition and Idea of a Good Society. The Idea of a Good Society incorporates the principles of liberty, equality justice, rights and recognition within itself. These also constitute the core of 'Politics'—the activity that determines the framework of society and how it is evolved and sustained. Chapter 1 discusses 'liberty' as the central theme of political life and clarifies its meaning and significance. Chapter 2 examines the concept of 'equality'. It discusses the two basic forms in which 'equality' is used in political philosophy—'foundational' and 'distributional'. Chapter 3 uncovers the meaning and essence of 'justice' with special reference to John Rawls' theory of 'Justice as Fairness'. Chapter 4 contains an analysis of the nature, characteristics, and principles of the doctrine of 'rights', while highlighting the significance of 'human rights', particularly in relation to the corporate world. Chapter 5 is about the importance of 'recognition'. Finally, Chapter 6 shows how the above-stated democratic values form the basis of a good society.

Unit II: 'Domain of Politics and Ethics' consists of three chapters, namely, Democracy, Welfare State, and Markets and Globalization. It is the power of politics that enables the actualization of a good society by regulating financial and economic sectors of the country. Hence, the domain of politics includes economic power, just as the political system necessarily has an economic system subsumed in it. Chapter 7 is about 'democracy'. By extending the framework of democracy to the Corporation, a new understanding of the corporate entity has been developed. It explains how a Corporation is a democratic entity and is a microcosm of society. Chapter 8 dwells on the notion of a 'welfare state'. There is a need for liberal democracy to move one step ahead by addressing social and economic issues that are not ensured by the mere provision of political rights. Chapter 9 is on 'markets and globalization'. Having seen that the domain of politics necessarily includes ethics, we proceed to analyze the ethical implications of 'markets and globalization' in this chapter.

Unit III: 'Business Ethics and Moral Reasoning' addresses concepts and issues in business ethics. Chapter 10 provides the basis of 'business ethics' in a novel way by bringing out the difference between business philosophy and the philosophy of business. While business philosophy refers to the vision of the company, the philosophy of business defines the role of business in society. Chapter 11 deals with the 'theories of moral reasoning', that is, the deontological and teleological approaches, which are the basis of standards of ethical conduct. Chapter 12 relates to 'issues and new developments' pertaining to the changing expectations of society from business and outlines the new developments in ethical theories. Chapter 13 is about ethical climate in organizations and its importance.

Unit IV: 'Politics and Ethics in Business' deals with the conceptual basis of responsibility in a new context where the Corporation or business is a microcosm of society. The modern notion of social responsibility of business is that 'regulation gaps and implementation deficits' have to be filled and balanced by diligent managers with pro-social behaviour and an aspiration to the common good. Chapter 14 is about the 'corporate code of ethics' based on the CII-UNDP document. Chapter 15 is about 'responsibility and accountability'. Corporate responsibility, it has been argued, arises from business ethics and has three dimensions—good governance, corporate social responsibility and environmental accountability. Chapter 16 is on 'environment' and asserts that environmental degradation is caused primarily due to industrial activity and indiscriminate consumption promoted by companies. In Chapter 17, aspects of 'leadership' qualities and attributes, and morality have been discussed. Chapter 18 explains 'workforce diversity'. The chapter shows that despite the benefits of diversity accruing to work groups, prejudice against women and minorities in matters such as recruitments and promotions remain a universal phenomenon.

Unit V: 'Corporate Social Responsibility' gives an overview of various issues related to the concept of social responsibility of business. Chapter 19 deals with the theme of 'corporate philanthropy' and its relation with CSR. Chapter 20 discusses 'corporate social responsibility', its meaning, its various conceptions and history, and its future goals. Chapter 21 discusses various 'CSR models'. Chapter 22 contains an analysis of the concerns and issues relating to the 'corporate social responsibility agenda', including drivers, historic and cultural factors as well as the CSR agenda in India. Chapter 23 presents the 'case for and against CSR' because though widely accepted, the concept, even today, has supporters as well as critics. Chapter 24 examines how business competitiveness and strategic planning for CSR go hand in hand.

Unit VI: 'Corporate Scandals and Issues in Business Ethics' explains the unethical consequences of business in a society and how the connivance between business and politics remains the biggest challenge for a civilized society. Chapter 25 on 'corporate scandals', explains the meaning, analysis, forms and the impact of corruption. Chapter 26 on 'whistle blowing', talks about the meaning, types and theories of the phenomenon, and case studies. Chapter 27 elaborates on the phenomenon of 'insider trading'. The chapter argues the controversial position that insider trading could in fact be beneficial to the economy. Chapter 28 aims at identifying the nature and forms of 'discrimination at the workplace' and also looks at other aspects of discrimination such as affirmative action programs. Chapter 29 deals with 'ethical issues in advertising', approaching the topic under the following headings: advertising message, quantum of advertising, inappropriate advertising, undesirable influences on the society. Chapter 30 is a chapter on 'consumer rights'. It affirms that in the present scenario, the consumer can exercise more choice for the satisfaction of his needs.

The book is expected to provide valuable insight into the factors that could have led to the recent global economic crisis, environmental disasters and climatic changes. Corporate responsibility is a futuristic concept that is much less understood by those who by their responsible actions could have averted the economic crisis and environmental disasters witnessed from time to time. In this context, the book is likely to appeal to a wide audience and prove to be of immense value for developing a proper perspective on issues crucial to the survival of human civilization.

Acknowledgements

We place on record our thanks to the various people who have proffered their writings to the creation of this book.

We acknowledge the contributions of our co-authors, friends and colleagues from Delhi University: Rana Sudhir Kumar (Associate Professor, Shriram College of Commerce), Dr Savita Hanspal (Associate Professor, Kamla Nehru College), Dr Ameeta Motwani (Associate Professor, Jesus and Mary College), Ms Sheela Dubey (Associate Professor, Gargi College), Ms Tanusree Jain (Lecturer, Ramjas College) and Ms Sonia (Lecturer, Bharti College).

We thank Dr Anil Kumar Singh and Dr Sarojini Singhal from Delhi University for their coordinated support. We are also indebted to a number of others who have been responsible for nurturing this subject at Delhi University in various ways.

We are grateful to our families for their forbearance in standing by us through this arduous endeavor. Thanks are due to the team at Pearson who handled the project. They were instrumental in bringing this book to fruition.

K.V. Bhanu Murthy
Usha Krishna

UNIT 1

Thinking Conceptually about Politics

Rana Sudhir Kumar

1.1 INTRODUCTION

The 'idea of a good society' incorporates the principles of liberty, equality, justice, rights and recognition within itself. These principles have been enshrined in the constitutions of most of the democratic nations of the world. These also constitute the core of 'Politics' – the activity by which the framework of society is evolved and sustained. 'The destiny of man presents its meaning in political terms', remarked Thomas Mann. Politicians, philosophers, academicians, businessmen and civil servants alike, entrusted with the task of creating a just society through maintenance or transformation of the human environment, recognize politics as the universal dimension of human life, which sustains the common world in which we live. Politics is what David Easton calls 'the authoritative allocation of values'. In other words, it is these principles that tell us what should be admired and what should be condemned. Only a 'good society' would be able to do that. A 'just' or a 'good' society, in turn, would be one which upholds the values of liberty, equality, justice, rights and recognition. This presupposes the existence of a democratic social order based on freedom of enterprise, welfare of the people, and above all, ethics and morality.

Chapter 1 discusses 'liberty', as a central concept of political life, clarifies its meaning and significance, and then elaborates on the important distinction, which is made between 'negative liberty' and 'positive liberty'.

Chapter 2 examines 'equality', recognized essentially as a principle of uniform apportionment, and attempts to answer the all-important question: equal in what? The two basic forms in which 'equality' is used in political philosophy – 'foundational' and 'distributional' are discussed in detail. Some of the more contemporary perspectives such as 'equality of capability', 'complex equality' and 'equality of status' are also examined briefly.

Chapter 3 attempts to uncover the meaning and essence of 'justice', explores its relevance as an ethical principle in business, and then examines, briefly, various theories of 'distributive justice' with special reference to John Rawls' theory of 'Justice as Fairness'.

Chapter 4 contains an analysis of the nature, characteristics, kind and basis of the doctrine of 'rights' and highlights the significance of 'human rights', particularly in relation to the corporate world.

Chapter 5 is a short essay on the concept of 'recognition'. Realizing the importance of taking 'differences' into account in democratic practice, an attempt is made to examine the various dimensions of the 'politics of recognition'.

Chapter 6 seeks to understand diverse systems, structures, processes and principles, which together could serve as the foundation of a 'good society'.

Chapter 1

Liberty

Rana Sudhir Kumar

"Liberty means responsibility. That is why most men dread it."
George Bernard Shaw

LEARNING OUTCOMES

This chapter examines the concept of liberty. After reading this chapter you will be able to:

- define liberty and understand its political and ethical significance.
- clearly distinguish between the 'negative' and 'positive' conceptions of liberty.
- know the ways in which freedom can be realised in society.
- learn how liberty affects and transforms life.

1.1 MEANING AND NATURE OF LIBERTY

The concept of 'freedom' or 'liberty' is a central one in the value system of most contemporary societies. Political thinkers customarily treat it with a degree of reverence that borders on religious devotion. Political philosophy and theory is replete with claims that humankind should break free from all forms of enslavement. Despite its popularity, confusion abounds about what the term 'freedom' actually means. Is freedom an unconditional good? How much freedom should the individuals or groups enjoy? Does freedom mean being left alone to act as one chooses? Is it some kind of fulfilment, self-realisation or personal development?

The Concise Oxford Dictionary defines 'liberty' as freedom from control, while the Chambers Dictionary defines 'freedom' as liberty, and 'liberty' as freedom to do as one pleases. The term 'liberty' comes from the Latin word *liber*, which means free. Liberty is sometimes regarded as the distinctive feature of liberalism. In modern liberal democratic societies, liberty is recognised as a supreme political value. Behind its political value, is the immense moral concern about man's quality of life. Human beings, as distinguished from other living beings, demand freedom and develop institutions to secure it. As a moral value, its virtue is that, attached to the idea that human beings are rationally self-willed creatures; it promises the satisfaction of human interests or the realisation of human potential. In short, liberty is the basis for happiness and well-being.

The inherent importance of liberty to human beings arises from the fact that they regard freedom of choice as an essential thing to human life. Human beings are constantly taking decisions about how they want to act. By clearing out a little space where we are able to make choices on our own, freedom allows us quite literally to become ourselves and invites us to stand up for what we make of our lives. The limitations on liberty arise from the fact that human beings are also social creatures, constrained in their choices by all kinds of social pressures.

According to Friedrich von Hayek, liberty means that each one of us, in some essential ways, is free from coercion by others. This is the basis on which we hold one another accountable in civil society. Where we are free only in principle, liberty may be intangible. Where we are free in actuality, liberty becomes tangible. It is in the tangible form that liberty allows us to become ourselves and makes us properly accountable for our lives as we choose to make them. When we take decisions freely, without coercion, we should be prepared to defend them. When we enjoy tangible liberty, we may justly assert our right not to be coerced by others.

In its broadest sense, liberty is the ability to think or act as one desires. A person is free to the extent that his/her actions and choices are not impeded by the actions of others. As a political and moral value, liberty becomes the force behind social change – it is the voice of the oppressed, it is the voice against injustice. In democracy, liberty is among the most fundamental purposes of governance. Douglas Rae of Yale University enlists five particulars which are absolutely essential to liberty in a modern democracy. They are:

1. the right to live in a place of one's own choice; subject only to constraints set by his/hers ability to pay and willingness to do so;
2. the right to move about freely without substantial risk of violent coercion and the fear it brings;
3. the right to educate one's children on terms approximating genuine equal opportunity, meaning that individual effort will be encouraged;
4. the right of a roughly equal opportunity to compete for good jobs; and
5. the right to participate on more or less equal terms in the politics which impose laws and other directives on oneself and one's family.

From the above discussion, it is evident that liberty has immense social, political and ethical significance. As such, the concept of liberty requires careful analysis. The most influential analytic approach to the understanding of liberty is the distinction between a 'negative' and a 'positive' conception of liberty, as expressed in Sir Isaiah Berlin's classic 'Two concepts of liberty' (1969).

1.2 NEGATIVE LIBERTY

The negative sense of the concept of liberty is contained in the answer to the question: 'What is the area within which the subject – a person or group of persons – is or should be left to do or be what he/she is able to be, without the interference by other persons?

Politically, it implies that individual freedom and state activity are antithetical. In short, liberty is the absence of restraint.

Negative liberty in the classical tradition comprises mainly the absence of two kinds of interference:

1. interference by the state or by the pressure of social conformism, with what the individual wants to do, at least within the widest possible area of action consistent with all others having the same freedom; and
2. invasion of one individual by other.

Negative liberty is 'simply the area within which a man can act unobstructed by others'. The concept of negative liberty found its first clear expression in the writings of Thomas Hobbes, who said in his *Leviathan* that 'Liberty, or freedom, signifieth, properly, the absence of opposition; by opposition, I mean external impediments of motion'. He said further, 'A freeman is he, that in those things, which by his strength and wit he is able to do, is not hindered to do what he has a will to do.' This view has been a marked feature of the thought of a number of classical liberal English philosophers such as Jeremy Bentham, James Mill, John Stuart Mill, Henry Sidgwick and Herbert Spencer and the classical and neo-classical economists. John Stuart

Mill was the most notable writer among these philosophers. In his essay *On Liberty*, Mill advocated for the liberty of the individual against legislative interference as well as against the pressure of public opinion. Mill believed that social progress depended upon giving to each individual the fullest opportunity for the free development of his personality. 'Over himself, over his body and mind, the individual is sovereign', says Mill. Accordingly, society has no right to impose any restraint over the individual because restraint as such is an evil thing.

The significance of 'freedom of choice' to the notion of 'negative liberty' is highlighted by Milton Friedman in *Capitalism and Freedom* (1962). Friedman explained that 'economic freedom' consists of freedom of choice in the marketplace – the freedom of the consumer to choose what to buy, the freedom of the worker to choose a job or profession, the freedom of a producer to choose what to make and whom to employ. This vital freedom is found only in free market capitalist economies, in which 'freedom' in effect means the absence of government interference.

Liberty conceived in 'negative' terms is linked very closely to the idea of privacy. In modern societies, privacy is a deeply respected principle and is regarded as a core liberal-democratic value. Privacy, says Andrew Heywood (2005), suggests a distinction between a 'private' or personal realm of existence, and some kind of 'public' world. Champions of negative liberty often regard this private sphere of life, consisting largely of family and personal relationships, as a realm within which people can 'be themselves'. It is an arena in which individuals should therefore be left alone to do, say and think whatever they please. Any intrusion into the privacy of a person is, in this sense, an infringement of his/her liberty.

The main political axiom of the negative liberty doctrine is that 'everyone knows his own interest best' and that the state should not decide his ends and purposes. It is based very firmly upon faith in the human individual, and, in particular, in human rationality. Free from interference, coercion and even guidance, individuals are able to make their own decisions and fashion their own lives. The result will be, as Bentham said, the greatest happiness of the greatest number, simply because individuals are the only people who can be trusted to identify their interests.

1.3 POSITIVE LIBERTY

Positive liberty means moral freedom, not absence of restraints on our freedom of action. Liberty without restraints would mean license, anarchy and chaos. It means the freedom to do things that are worth doing, to engage in self-development, to have a share in the government of one's society.

Positive liberty consists of 'being one's own master', says Isaiah Berlin. It is therefore equivalent to democracy – people are said to be free if they are self-governing and unfree if they are not. Thus, liberty is concerned with the question 'By whom am I governed?' rather than 'How much am I governed?'. In other words, positive liberty relates to the ideas of self-realisation and personal development. Positive liberty describes the capacity of human beings to act and fulfil themselves, and is therefore concerned with the distribution of material or economic resources. Unlike negative liberty, which is seen as justifying contraction of state power, positive liberty is linked to welfarism and state intervention. Liberty may be positive if it stands for effective power, self-realisation, self-mastery or autonomy, or moral or 'inner' freedom.

T.H. Green was among the first modern liberal philosophers who advocated the 'positive' conception of liberty. He defined liberty as the ability of people 'to make the most and best of themselves'. It consists not merely in being left alone but in having the effective power to act, shifting attention towards the opportunities available to each human individual.

Harold J. Laski is considered one of the greatest supporters of the concept of positive liberty. He believes in the dignity of the human personality. Liberty, says Laski, is the eager maintenance of that atmosphere in which human beings have the opportunity to be their best selves. It is a product of rights.

Laski refers to three different aspects of liberty:

1. Private or individual liberty: It means the opportunity to exercise freedom of choice in those areas of life where the results of an individual's efforts mainly affect him/her.
2. Political liberty: Political liberty according to Laski 'means the power to be active in the affairs of the state'.
3. Economic liberty: Economic liberty means simply that everyone has right to earn his/her livelihood. Citizens should be free from the constant fear of unemployment and insufficiency. Economic liberty also implies democracy in industry.

The concept of positive liberty has been eagerly adopted by modern social democrats, including Bryan Gould and Roy Hattersley, to provide a justification for social welfare. The welfare state enlarges freedom by 'empowering' individuals and freeing them from social evils, such as unemployment, homelessness, poverty, ignorance and disease, which adversely affect lives.

Liberty has also been portrayed in the form of self-realisation or self-fulfilment. Freedom in this sense is positive, because, says Andrew Heywood (2005), it is based upon want-satisfaction and need-fulfilment. Socialists have traditionally portrayed liberty in this way, seeing it as the realisation of one's own 'true' nature. Marx described the true realm of freedom as the 'development of human potential for its own sake'.

Another conception of positive liberty links it to the notions of personal autonomy and democracy. Rousseau, for example, described liberty as 'obedience to a law one prescribes to oneself'. In his view, freedom means self-determination, the ability to control and fashion one's own destiny. In other words, citizens are only 'free' when they participate directly and continuously in shaping the life of their community.

For Isaiah Berlin, the positive view of liberty assumes that freedom is not to be achieved by leaving individuals to get on with their lives. Rather, its point is to enable individuals to achieve self-mastery by the exercise of rational self-control over the irrational desires of the self. Freedom in a positive sense, for Berlin, entails overcoming obstacles to freedom which reside within individuals themselves.

Berlin's concepts of liberty have, however, not gone unchallenged. Gerald MacCallum rejects Berlin's distinction between two conceptions of freedom and maintains that freedom is a single value-free concept seen in one triadic relation. In MacCallum's formulation, liberty is always:

- of something;
- from something; and
- to do, or not to do, to become or not to become, something.

David Miller, in his account of liberty, steers a course between Berlin and MacCallum. Miller identifies three ways of formulating liberty: republican, liberal and idealist forms of freedom. According to the republican view, a person is free if he/she is a citizen of a free political community, that is independent and self-governing and plays an active role in the government, which means that the laws enacted reflect the wishes of the people. Freedom is realisable through public service and political activity. According to the liberal view, freedom is a property of the individual and precludes interference or restraint by others, and government secures freedom by protecting each person from interference by others. The idealist view shifts emphasis from social arrangements to the way a person actually lives and acts. Freedom is no longer the struggle to be free from external constraints but 'from elements within the person himself which thwart his desire to realise his own true nature – weaknesses, compulsions, irrational desires etc'.

1.4 CONCLUSION

Liberty, as David Miller points out, is a very important political value, but not of such importance that it should set absolute limits to the exercise of political authority. In a democracy especially, questions about the use of resources to promote liberty, freedom and social responsibility and rights that all citizens should enjoy will be openly debated, and in answering them, people will appeal to many different principles – to equality, to fairness, to the common good, to respect for nature, to the protection of culture and so forth. As societies change, new needs and new problems arise; for example, problems associated with free trade and barriers to trade among nations. World trade and its impact on the earth and its ecosystems, intellectual property rights, climatic change, food scarcity, water crisis and energy crisis makes us think, 'Did we use the liberty granted to us well?'. It has also resulted in common framework of international laws, without which, we will not be able to feel secure. According to David Miller, liberty remains the most important political value in any democratic setup.

Suggested Questions

1. What is the meaning of liberty? Explain its importance in relation to democratic values.
2. What is the concept of negative liberty? How does it lead to 'the greatest happiness of the greatest number'?
3. Which concept of liberty do you support – negative or positive – and why?
4. List five conditions essential to liberty in a modern democracy.
5. Explain MacCallum's formulation of liberty.
6. What is meant by 'freedom of choice'?

Bibliography

Ball, Allen, R. (1988). *Modern Politics and Government* (London: Macmillan).

Bellamy, Richard (1993). *Theories and Concepts of Politics: An Introduction* (Manchester: Manchester University Press).

Berlin, I. (1969). Two concepts of liberty. In: *Four Essays on Liberty* (Oxford: Oxford University Press).

Birch, Anthony, H. (2001). *The Concepts and Theories of Democracy* (London: Routledge).

Goodin, Robert, E. and Petit, Philip (eds.) (1993) *A Companion to Contemporary Political Philosophy* (Oxford: Blackwell Reference).

Held, David (1998). *Political Theory and the Modern State* (World View, Maya Polity).

Heywood, Andrew (2005). *Political Theory: An Introduction* (London: Palgrave Macmillan).

Leftwich, A. (1984). *What Is Politics?* (London: Basil Blackwell).

Minogue, Kenneth (1995). *Politics: A Very Short Introduction* (Oxford: Oxford University Press).

Shapiro, Ian and Hacker-Cordon, Casiano (1999). *Democracy's Edges* (Cambridge: Cambridge University Press).

Chapter 2

Equality

Rana Sudhir Kumar

'Men are equal; it is not birth but virtue that makes the difference.'

Voltaire

LEARNING OUTCOMES

After reading the chapter on Equality, you will be in a position to:

- identify 'equality' as a distinct political concept.
- understand why equality has a deep moral foundation.
- critically understand the basis of equality.
- know the various notions of equality.
- analyse the various forms of equality.
- appreciate the contribution of alternative models of equality.

2.1 MEANING AND SIGNIFICANCE OF EQUALITY

The idea of equality is perhaps the defining feature of modern political thought. In political theory, a clear distinction is made between 'equality' and ideas such as 'uniformity', 'identity' and 'sameness'. Equality, says Andrew Heywood, is not about blanket uniformity, but rather is about 'levelling' those conditions of social existence, which are thought to be crucial to human well-being. In popular parlance, 'equality' is considered synonymous with 'natural equality', which implies that all men are equal and should be entitled to identity of treatment and income. The protagonists of this view assert that all men are born equal and nature has willed them to remain so. The 'Declaration of Rights of Man and the Citizen' (1789) says, 'Men are born and live free and equal in their rights.' The American Declaration of Independence proclaimed, 'All men are created equal.'

Classical and medieval thinkers took inequality or hierarchy for granted because it was either natural or inevitable. However, the most modern political thinkers subscribe to the notion of equality in one or more of its various forms. According to Ernest Barker, 'the principle of equality means that whatever conditions are guaranteed to me, in the form of rights, shall also and in the same measure, be guaranteed to others, and that whatever rights are given to others, shall also be given to me.' Harold J. Laski says, 'Equality means that no man shall be placed in society that he can overreach his neighbours to the extent which constitutes a denial of the latter's citizenship.'

A core meaning of the term equality in a social and political context is that equality should be seen a basic presupposition of moral concern. On this basis, a fundamental presupposition of equality as a moral and procedural principle informs the plea that all persons are entitled to equal consideration save where a special case can be made for differential treatment. In more concrete terms, this has been translated into a concern that people should receive equal consideration before law. It has also led to a concern that voting rights are equal. Equality in these senses has now become a generally accepted norm in liberal democratic societies. More recently, there have been attempts to extend the concept of equality to include species other than human beings.

Equality is a highly complex concept, there being as many forms of equality as there are ways of comparing the conditions of human existence. For example, it is possible to talk about moral equality, legal equality, political equality, social equality, sexual equality, racial equality and so forth. The modern battle about equality is, therefore, fought not between those who support the principle and those who reject it, but between different views about where and how equality should be applied. Basically, equality is the principle of uniform apportionment, but it will remain meaningless unless we answer the question: equal in what? In what should people be equal, when, how, where and why? To answer that, we must examine various implications of the term, depending upon what is being apportioned.

Political philosophy attempts to answer these questions by using the concept of equality in two ways: foundational and distributional.

2.2 FOUNDATIONAL EQUALITY

The earliest notion of equality to have had an impact on political thought is what is known as 'foundational equality'. This notion of equality is based on the normative assertion about the moral worth of each human life. It implies that all people are equal by virtue of a shared human essence. Human beings are equal because they are born equal and are, therefore, approximately equal in strength. In practice, this implies that human beings are equal only in the sense that all human beings are invested with identical natural rights; however, these may be defined. Foundationally, equality can be identified in four forms.

2.2.1 FUNDAMENTAL EQUALITY OF PERSONS

Fundamentally, equality is seen as a levelling process. It also refers to the 'formal' equality of individuals based on the idea that all human beings are possessors of equal rights. Formal equality implies that, by virtue of their common humanity, each person is entitled to be treated equally by the rules of social practice. As such, as Andrew Heywood points out, it is a procedural rule, which grants each person equal freedom to act; however, they may choose and to make their lives whatever they are capable of doing, without regard to the opportunities, resources or wealth they start with. The most obvious manifestation of formal equality is the principle of legal equality, or 'equality before the law'. This means that the law should treat each person as an individual, without regard to their social background, religion, race, colour, gender etc. Legal equality is thus the cornerstone of the rule of law.

2.2.2 EQUALITY OF OPPORTUNITY

The idea of formal equality is said to have led naturally to the more radical notion of equal opportunities. The idea first found its expression in the writings of Plato, who proposed that social position should be based strictly upon individual ability and effort. Modern ideologies widely endorse the idea, and it is embraced as a fundamental principle by political parties of almost every shade of opinion. Social democrats and modern liberals, for example, believe that equal opportunity is the cornerstone of social justice. In essence, equality of opportunity means that everyone has the same starting point, or equal life chances. An individual should not be prevented by arbitrary obstacles from using his capacities, talents and so forth to pursue his own objectives and goals. This does not mean 'identical' opportunities, but simply that one is not denied his right to life, liberty and the pursuit of happiness, based on birth, colour, religion, gender and so forth.

The principle of equal opportunities is questioned by some on grounds that in reality it comes down to 'an equal opportunity to become unequal'. The reason is that the concept differentiates between two forms of equality, one acceptable and the other unacceptable. Personal talents, skills and hard work create an inequality which is considered either inevitable or morally 'right'. However, inequality created by social circumstances, such as poverty, homelessness and unemployment, is morally 'wrong', because, as Andrew Heywood says, they allow some to start the race of life halfway down the running track while other competitors may not even have arrived at the stadium. Equality, in this sense, leads to an unegalitarian ideal – a meritocratic society. In a meritocracy, success and failure are 'personal' achievements showing that while some are born with skills and willingness for hard work but others are either without skills or plain lazy. Such inequality is not only morally tenable but serves as an incentive to individual initiative by encouraging people to realise whatever talents they may possess. Equal opportunities mean the removal of obstacles that stand in the way of personal development and self-realisation, a right that should be enjoyed by all citizens.

2.2.3 EQUALITY OF CONDITION

Egalitarians hold that it would be a morally better state of affairs if everyone enjoyed the same level of social and economic benefits. Call this equality of condition or equality of life prospects. It makes an attempt to make conditions of life equal for appropriate social groups.

2.2.4 EQUALITY OF OUTCOME

Perhaps the most controversial face of egalitarianism is the idea of an 'equality of outcome'. As Andrew Heywood says that whereas equal opportunities requires that significant steps be taken towards achieving greater social and economic equality, far more dramatic changes are necessary if 'outcomes' are to be equalised.

A concern with 'outcomes' rather than 'opportunities' shifts attention away from the starting point of life to its end results, from chances to rewards. Equality of outcomes implies that all competitors finish the race in line together, regardless of their starting point and the speed with which they run. Equality of outcomes is commonly associated with the idea of material equality, an equality of social circumstances, living conditions and possibly even wages.

It is argued that equality of outcome is the most vital form of equality, since without it other forms of equality are a sham. Equal legal and civil rights are, argues Heywood, of little benefit to citizens who do not posses a secure job, a decent wage, a roof over their heads and so forth.

Equality of outcome can be justified on the grounds that it is a necessary condition for securing individual liberty. To the individual, a certain amount of material prosperity is essential if people are to lead full and happy lives. A high level of social equality is sometimes regarded as vital for social harmony and stability. R.H. Tawney has argued that social equality constitutes the practical foundation for a 'common culture', one founded upon the unifying force of 'fellowship'.

However, equality of outcome has been criticised on the grounds that it leads to stagnation, injustice and, ultimately, tyranny. Stagnation, writes Andrew Heywood, results from the fact that social 'levelling' serves to cap aspirations and remove the incentive for enterprise and hard work. Equality of outcome is, therefore, seen as 'unnatural' result which is achieved by massive interference and the violation of any notion of 'fair' competition. The drive for equality is carried out at the expense of individual liberty.

2.3 DISTRIBUTIONAL EQUALITY

As a distributional concept, equality is used to indicate an apparently desirable set of social conditions, for example – one person one vote, or an equal distribution of income, social opportunities and political powers among people. This means that in the political sphere, the possibilities for political participation should be equally distributed. All citizens have the same claim to participation in forming public opinion, and in the distribution, control and exercise of political power. Presently, therefore, most egalitarians, do not advocate an equality of outcome, but emphasise that the only things to be considered objects of equality are things serving the real interests of individuals. The opportunities to be equalised between people can be opportunities for 'objective welfare' (or simply, well-being), or 'subjective welfare' (i.e., preference satisfaction), or for 'resources'.

The most notable exposition of the 'welfare' and 'resourcist' conceptions of distributional equality is seen in the writings of Ronald Dworkin. He considers, mainly, two theories of distributional equality, 'equality of welfare' and 'equality of resources'.

2.3.1 EQUALITY OF WELFARE

This utilitarian theory holds that a distributional scheme treats people as equals when it distributes or transfers resources among them until no further transfer would leave them more equal in welfare. In this view, as Richard J. Arneson has pointed out, equality should always be sustained at the highest feasible level of welfare for all.

Besides enlarging freedom in the sense that it safeguards people from poverty and provides conditions for well-being, welfare serves as a redistributive mechanism that promotes greater equality and strengthens a sense of social responsibility. The concept of welfare equality is motivated by an intuition that when it comes to political ethics, what is at stake is the individual's well-being. However, as pointed out in the Stanford Encyclopedia of Philosophy, taking 'welfare' as what is to be equalised leads into major difficulties, which resemble those of utilitarianism. If one contentiously identifies subjective welfare with preference satisfaction, it seems implausible to count all individual preferences as equal, some – such as the desire to do others wrong – being admissible on grounds of justice. Any welfare-centred concept of equality grants people with refined and expensive tastes more resources – something distinctly at odds with our moral intuitions. However, satisfaction in the fulfilment of desires cannot serve as a standard, since we wish for more than a simple feeling of happiness. Such problems can be avoided, as pointed out by Rawls and Dworkin, if we aim at 'resource equality'.

2.3.2 EQUALITY OF RESOURCES

This theory holds that it treats people as equals when it distributes or transfers so that no further transfer would leave their shares of the total resources more equal. Accordingly, people should have equal chances to achieve whatever they might seek in life when each person commands equal resources such as:

leisure or free time,

income (a flow) and wealth (stock) and

freedom to use whatever goods one possesses in desired ways, within broad limits.

Dworkin's equality of resources is 'ambition-sensitive' and 'endowment-insensitive'. Unequal distribution of resources, says Dworkin, is considered fair only when it results from the decisions and intentional actions of those concerned. Dworkin proposes a hypothetical auction in which everyone can accumulate bundles of resources through equal means of payment, so that in the end no one is jealous of another's bundle. The auction procedure also offers a way to precisely measure equality of resources; the measure of resources devoted to a person's life is defined by the importance of the resources to others. In the free market, how the distribution then develops depends on an individual's ambitions.

2.4 EQUALITY OF CAPABILITY

The capability approach is a conceptual framework developed by Amartya Sen and Martha Nussbaum for evaluating social states in terms of human well-being (welfare). Amartya Sen proposes that citizens should be equal, not in their resources, but in their 'capability' for different 'functionings'. 'Capabilities' here mean 'substantial freedoms', such as the ability to live to old age, engage in economic transactions or participate in political activities. These are construed in terms of the substantive freedoms people have reason to value, instead of utility (happiness, desire-fulfilment or choice) or access to resources (income, commodities or assets). Poverty, in this view, is understood as capability deprivation. The emphasis here is not only how human beings actually function but on their having the capability, which is a practical choice, to function in important ways if they so wish. This approach to human well-being emphasises the importance of freedom of choice, individual heterogeneity and the multi-dimensional nature of welfare.

2.5 CONCLUSION

Questions about equality tend to generate ideological controversy. There is always a tendency to find an alternative model of equality that can be embraced as intrinsically morally desirable. Walzer, for example, endorses what he terms 'complex equality' by which he means a form of just society where inequalities in the several spheres of society do not invade one another. On this view, inequalities in one sphere are not repeated in others. Wealth may dominate the business world, but health needs would trigger treatment in the health sphere and education would be organised according to the learning needs and capacities of individuals rather than their wealth.

David Miller has urged that a more subtle view of political equality is required. He argues that a just society would be one in which all citizens would have 'equal status', an ideal which would be undermined if citizens of great wealth were to dominate society. He considers that all citizens have the right to a certain level of welfare if all are to enjoy an equality of respect in society.

Suggested Questions

1. Critically discuss the phrase 'all men are created equal'.
2. Analyse the four dimensions of 'foundational equality'.
3. 'Distributional equality could mean equality of welfare or equality of resources'. Explain with reference to a context.
4. Explain Amartya Sen's concept of 'equality of capability'.
5. What is the difference between 'equality of opportunity' and equality of outcome'?

Bibliography

Alkire, S. (2002). *Valuing Freedoms: Sen's Capability Approach and Poverty Reduction* (Oxford: Oxford University Press).

Axford, Barie, Browning, Gary, K., Huggins, Richard and Rosamond, Ben (1995). *Politics: An Introduction* (London: Routledge).

Ball, Allen, R. (1988). *Modern Politics and Government* (London, Macmillan).

Bellamy, Richard (1993). *Theories and Concepts of Politics: An Introduction* (Manchester: Manchester University Press).

Goodin, Robert, E. and Petit, Philip (eds.) (1993). *A Companion to Contemporary Political Philosophy* (Oxford: Blackwell Reference, 1993).

Heywood, Andrew (2005). *Political Theory: An Introduction* (London: Palgrave, Macmillan).

Minogue, Kenneth (1995). *Politics: A Very Short Introduction* (Oxford: Oxford University Press).

Watzer, M. (1983). *Spheres of Justice* (Oxford: Blackwell).

Chapter 3

Justice

Rana Sudhir Kumar

'Justice consists not in being neutral between right and wrong, but in finding out the right and upholding it, wherever found, against the wrong.'

Theodore Roosevelt

LEARNING OUTCOMES

After reading the chapter on Justice, you should be able to:

- understand the political and ethical importance of the idea of justice.
- know what elements constitute justice.
- explain the various theories of 'distributive justice'.
- evaluate Rawls' theory of justice as fairness.
- understand how Rawls' theory serves as a valuable tool for ethical decision making.
- apply principles of justice to the process of business allocation.

3.1 THE CONCEPT

Justice has been portrayed as the master concept of political thought. Since the time of Plato (427–347 BC) and Aristotle (384–322 BC), political thinkers have rendered the definition of a 'good' society as a 'just' society. Roman Emperor Justinian said that 'Justice is the constant and perpetual will to render to each his due.' Justice is the idea of a morally justifiable distribution of rewards or punishment and a matter of each individual person being treated in the right way.

In practical terms, justice, according to Kolb, is used in two senses:

1. to give man his dues and
2. setting right of wrong by either compensation or punishment.

In the first case, justice is concerned with the deciding of the principles of allocating rewards and opportunities; whereas in the second case, justice is related with the protection of the rights of people to whom justice might have been denied, by protecting their rights through the legal system.

3.2 CORE ELEMENTS OF JUSTICE

In an attempt to uncover the essence of justice, David Miller has referred to what he calls 'core elements' of justice. These core elements include the following.

3.2.1 NON-ARBITRARINESS

The primary concern of justice is that people must be treated in a non-arbitrary way. In business, for example, this element paves the foundation of corporate governance highlighting observance of ethical principles in the conduct of business practices.

3.2.2 CONSISTENCY

Justice demands that there must be consistency in how one person is treated over time, and there must be consistency between people. For example, if two people have the same qualities, or have behaved in the same way, they should receive the same benefits or the same punishments, as the case may be. The fact that justice requires consistency in treatment explains why acting justly is so often a matter of following rules or applying laws, since these guarantee consistency by laying down what is to be done in specified circumstances.

3.2.3 RELEVANCE

Justice requires relevance. If people are going to be treated differently from one another, it must be on grounds that are relevant to the treatment in question. For example, if two women, A and B, commit similar acts of killing somebody, but the reasons and circumstances in the two cases are totally dissimilar, the treatment in law to them will also be dissimilar. 'A' may go scot-free or even be commended for bravery as her act was probably committed in 'self-defence' and 'B' may get a stiff sentence for the same act but committed out of hatred, enmity or other malafide intent. This also implies that where there are no relevant grounds on which to discriminate, justice requires equality: everyone should be treated equally.

3.2.4 PROPORTION

The idea of proportion tells us that when people are treated differently for relevant reasons, the treatment they receive should be proportionate to whatever they have done, or whatever feature they have, that justifies the inequality. Many people believe, for instance, that if people work hard at their jobs, there are relevant reasons for paying them more. However, for justice, as David Miller says, there must be proportionality: if A works twice as productively as B, he/she should be paid twice as much as B, but not ten times as much.

3.2.5 PROCEDURE

Justice very often has to do not only with the treatment that people receive but also with the procedure that is followed in order to arrive at that outcome. In criminal justice, for example, it is important that guilty people are punished in proportion to their crime and that innocent people go free – that is what a just outcome requires – but it is also important that proper procedures are followed in arriving at a verdict, for instance that both parties are allowed to state their case. Procedures are important partly because they tend to ensure that the right verdicts are reached, and also because they show proper respect for the people who are standing trial. In some cases, justice is entirely a matter of procedure that is used to reach a decision – there is no independent standard that we can apply to the outcome. For instance, in the matter of allocation of official residences, to employees in an institution, the principle of allotment by seniority is generally considered a fair procedure. In a cricket match, for example, tossing is the fair procedure to decide who will bat or bowl first.

3.3 JUSTICE AS AN ETHICAL PRINCIPLE

Standards of justice do not generally override the moral rights of individuals. Justice is based on individual moral rights. The moral right to be treated as free and equal persons, for example, is part of what lies behind the idea that benefits and burdens should be distributed equally. Issues involving questions of justice and fairness are usually divided into three categories: distributive, retributive and compensatory.

3.3.1 DISTRIBUTIVE JUSTICE

The first and basic category is concerned with the fair distribution of society's benefits and burdens. Generally, distributive justice is comparative, in that it considers not the absolute amount of benefits and burdens of each person but each person's amount relative to that of others. The fundamental principle of distributive justice is that equals should be treated equally and unequals treated unequally. To gauge the efficacy of this principle, a number of models of distributive justice need to be examined:

3.3.1.1 Justice as Equality (Egalitarianism)

Each person should be given exactly equal shares of a society's or a group's benefits and burdens. Egalitarians base their view on the proposition that all human beings are equal in some fundamental respect and that by virtue of this equality; each person has an equal claim to society's goods. Critics, however, argue that there is no quality that all human beings possess in equal measure. Ignoring important characteristics like 'need', 'ability' and 'effort' in any scheme of distribution will result in a decline in society's productivity and efficiency.

3.3.1.2 Justice Based on Contribution (Capitalist Justice)

The advocates of capitalist justice argue that a society's benefits should be distributed in proportion to what each individual contributes to that society. However, using only effort or contribution as the basis of distribution ignores the intrinsic value of that contribution.

3.3.1.3 Justice Based on Needs and Abilities (Socialism)

The idea that material benefits should be distributed based on needs has most commonly been proposed by socialist thinkers, and is sometimes regarded as the socialist theory of justice. The socialist principle has the clear implication that material resources should be distributed to satisfy at least the basic needs of every person. The socialist principle has been criticized on the ground that, if explained, it would obliterate individual freedom. If a central government agency is going to decide what task one should do and what goods one can get, the socialist principle, it is argued, substitutes paternalism for freedom.

3.3.1.4 Justice as Freedom (Libertarianism)

The libertarian holds that no particular way of distributing goods can be said to be just or unjust apart from the free choices individuals make. Any distribution of benefits and burdens is just if it is the result of individuals freely choosing to exchange with each other the goods each person already owns. The major difficulty with the libertarian principle is that it ignores other freedoms, such as freedom from hunger, ignorance and disease. People have a moral obligation to take care of the needy and destitutes who cannot take care of themselves.

3.3.1.5 Justice as Fairness

After considering the above models of distributive justice, a comprehensive theory capable of drawing these considerations together and fitting them into a logical whole was required. John Rawls provides this approach to justice as 'fairness' which approximates to this ideal.

3.3.2 RETRIBUTIVE JUSTICE

This refers to the just imposition of punishments and penalties on those who do wrong. A just penalty is one that in some sense is deserved by a person who does wrong. A person who commits a crime upsets a moral equilibrium by making someone else worse off. The restoration of the moral equilibrium in cases of this kind is achieved by a punishment that 'fits the crime'. Retributive justice is therefore non-comparative.

3.3.3 COMPENSATORY JUSTICE

This concerns the just way of compensating people for what they lost when they were wronged by others. A just compensation is one that is in some sense proportional to the loss suffered by the person being compensated. The payment of compensation seeks to restore the moral equilibrium which gets upset by an accident or a wrong done. Compensatory justice is also non-comparative.

Retributive and compensatory justices are subject matter of law, distributive justice is concerned with 'just distribution' of resources for different interest groups, whether in the context of a nation or stakeholders in an organisation.

3.4 RAWLS' THEORY OF JUSTICE AS FAIRNESS

John Rawls in his book *A Theory of Justice* (1971) develops a rigorous analysis of what would constitute 'a just society'. The focus of Rawls' theory is on social justice that embodies fair terms of social cooperation. Opposing the utilitarian view, Rawls begins by describing justice as the foundation of social structure, and all political and legislative decisions must take place within the constraints that flow from the principles of justice. The primary domain over which justice operates, says Rawls, is the distribution of goods, where 'goods' is taken to include wealth, position, opportunity, skill, liberty and even self-respect.

3.4.1 RAWLS' METHOD

Rawls begins by asking us to imagine a situation in which free and equal persons, concerned to advance their own interests, attempt to arrive at unanimous agreement on principles that will serve as the basis for constructing the major institutions of society. He describes persons in this imaginary situation as self-interested agents.

Rawls' theory is based on the contractual view of society. Like Hobbes and Locke, he talks of a pre-social 'state of nature' in which people would decide consensually on the form of society they would agree to live in. In agreeing to form a society, they all seek to maximise satisfaction of their own interests such as rights, liberty, opportunity, income or wealth. They will be under a '*veil of ignorance*' which prevents them from knowing the full details of other's talents. Rawls calls the situation in which people find themselves as '*original position*', in which everyone has 'particular wisdom and general ignorance'. Rawls believes that the society chosen on these impartial grounds would be a just society and the concept of justice arrived at would be 'justice as fairness'.

3.4.2 RAWLS' PRINCIPLES OF JUSTICE

Rawls says that everyone will choose a kind of society which minimises his possible losses and makes sure that even the worse-off person is not too destitute. Rawls calls this the 'maximising principle' because it maximises people's minimum welfare.

Rawls says people would choose two principles of justice:

(i) each person to have an equal right to the most extensive basic liberties compatible with similar liberties of others

(ii) social and economic inequalities are to be arranged so that both are:

 (a) to the greatest benefit of the least advantaged, and

 (b) attached to positions and offices open to all under conditions of fair equality of opportunity.

Rawls tells us that principle (i) is supposed to take priority over principle (ii), should the two of them ever come into conflict, and within principle (ii), part (b) is supposed to take priority over part (a).

3.4.2.1 *Principle of Equal Liberty*

Principle (i) is called the 'principle of equal liberty'. Essentially, it says that each citizen's liberties must be protected from invasion by others and must be equal to those of others. It implies that it is unjust for business institutions to invade the privacy of employees, pressure managers to vote in certain ways, exert undue influence on political processes by the use of bribes, or otherwise violate the equal political liberties of society's members. The principle of equal liberty also prohibits the use of force, fraud or deception in contractual transactions. It also requires that just contracts should be honoured.

According to Rawls, the principle of equal liberty would be chosen because the parties to the 'original position' will want to be free to pursue their major special interests whatever these might be. In the original position, each person is ignorant of his or her special interests, and so each will want to secure a maximum amount of freedom to be able to pursue those interests.

3.4.2.2 *The Difference Principle*

Part (a) of principle (ii) is called the 'difference principle'. It assumes that a productive society will incorporate inequalities, but it then asserts that steps must be taken to improve the position of the most needy member of society, such as the sick and the disabled, unless such improvements would so burden society that they make everyone, including the needy, worse off than before. Because the difference principle obliges us to maximise benefits for the least advantaged, this means that business institutions should be as efficient in their use of resource as possible. The difference principle implies that markets should be competitive and that anti-competitive practices such as price-fixing and monopolies are unjust. Rawls says that the difference principle will be chosen because all parties would want to protect themselves against the possibility of ending in the worst position in society. By adopting the difference principle, the parties will ensure that even the neediest are taken care of.

3.4.3 The Principle of Fair Equality of Opportunity

Part (b) of principle (ii) is the principle of fair equality of opportunity. It says that everyone should be given equal opportunity to qualify for the privileged positions in society. This means that not only should job qualifications be related to requirements of the job but each person must have access to the training and education needed to qualify for the desirable jobs. According to Rawls, all parties to the original position will choose the principle of fair equality of opportunity because each will want to protect their interests in case they turn out to be among the talented. The principle of fair equality of oppurtunity makes sure that everyone has an equal opportunity to advance by using his or her abilities, efforts and contributions.

3.4.4 Critical Evaluation of Rawls' Theory

The main challenge to Rawls' perspective on distributive justice came from the neo-liberal theorist Robert Nozick. For Nozick, Rawls' theory involves an injustice in that the property of the better off might be redistributed by the state to benefit the worse off. The injustice would consist in the violation of the rights of the better off, who, for Nozick, would have gained their property through legitimate means.

In his book *Anarchy, State and Utopia* (1974), Robert Nozick spells out his 'entitlement' theory of justice, which is robustly individualistic. Individuals and individual rights are seen as being of primary importance, and the state is to be minimal, in that extensive interference is taken as diminishing individual rights. On the question of distribution, Nozick uses a Lockean argument: we acquire entitlements by mixing our own labor – which we own – with unowned resources. Provided this primary acquisition does not worsen the situation of others at that time, it is just. All inequalities resulting from the subsequent use and free exchange of holdings are just so long as the initial appropriation of resources is just. Nozick's objective was to identify a set of historical principles through which we can determine if a particular distribution of wealth is just. He suggested three 'justice preserving' rules, which are:

1. Wealth has to be justly acquired in the first place, that is, it should not have been stolen and the rights of others should not have been infringed.
2. Wealth has to be justly transferred from one responsible person to another.
3. If wealth has been acquired or transferred unjustly this injustice should be rectified.

Rawls' defenders claim that his theory does not clash with basic moral values such as freedom, equality of opportunity and the concern for the disadvantaged. His theory does not reject the market system and work incentives; it takes into account all other criteria of need, ability, effort and contribution. Rawls' 'original position' is defined so that its parties choose impartial principles that take into account the equal interests of everyone, and this is the essence of morality.

3.5 DISTRIBUTIVE JUSTICE AND BUSINESS

The question of distributive justice within societies with respect to businesses relates to how businesses allocate resources and rewards internally which in turn affects their impact on the larger society. It involves making choices about how to allocate and distribute profits; provide opportunities to their members and employees to gain access to organisational positions; and effectively use resources at their disposal. Businesses are just from this perspective to the extent they adhere to the traditional liberal principles regarding equal opportunities. By ensuring fair access to positions, businesses are likely to benefit from high-quality performances by highly motivated employees. They are also likely to reduce or eliminate potential resentment among workers, suppliers, managers and customers.

3.6 CONCLUSION

Fredrick Bird contends that businesses should act with justice because it is the right thing to do. Businesses should foster justice because by acting in this way they express and embody genuine respect towards others. When others are treated with respect, they are more likely to respond to invitations to cooperate and collaborate. Businesses should practice justice because in the process they are more likely to conduct their operations in ways that seem reliable and expected, rather than arbitrary.

Businesses should act with justice because, for the most part, that is how they expect others to act. A realistic ethic would help them find ways to attend to and limit possibilities for self-aggrandising conduct and to appreciate and encourage the possibilities for moral behaviour. Businesses should practice justice because it is in their own best interests. Just business practices help them realise their legitimate ends in several ways. A concern for just distribution reminds businesses to concentrate on allocating their resources in ways that best serve to realise their purposes, and conserve and enhance their overall assets.

Suggested Questions

1. What do you understand by justice and fairness? Explain the elements of justice.
2. Why is distributive justice important as an ethical principle in the context of business and society?
3. Organisations have vast resources at their disposal. What ethical principles should be guiding them to apportion the resources?
4. While 'retributive justice' and 'compensatory justice' are subject matter of law, distributive justice is concerned with 'just distribution' of resources. Explain various models of distributive justice.
5. Explain the two basic principles of justice as stated by Rawls.
6. Rawls' theory of justice may be termed as a theory of 'justice as fairness'. How fair is Rawls' theory of Justice?
7. On what grounds does Robert Nozick criticise Rawls' theory

Bibliography

Boatright, Joan, R. (2003). *Ethics and the Conduct of Business* (Australia: Pearson Education).

Bird, Frederick and Velasquez, Manuel (2006). *Just Business Practices in a Diverse and Developing World* (New York: Palgrave Macmillan).

Heywood, Andrew (2005). *Political Theory: An Introduction* (New York: Palgrave, Macmillan).

Miller, David (1976). *Social Justice* (Oxford: Oxford University Press).

Miller, David (2003). *Political Philosophy: A Very Short Introduction* (Oxford: Oxford University Press).

Nozick, Robert (1974). *Anarchy, State, and Utopia* (New York: Basic Books).

Rawls, John (1971). *A Theory of Justice* (Cambridge, MA: Harvard University Press).

Rosen, Michael and Wolff, Jonathan (1999). *Political Thought* (Oxford: Oxford University Press).

Shapiro, Ian (2003). *The Moral Foundations of Politics* (Connecticut: Yale University Press).

Velasquez, Manuel G. (2002). *Business Ethics, Concepts and Cases* (New Jersey: Pearson Education).

Chapter 4

Rights

Rana Sudhir Kumar

'In law a man is guilty when he violates the rights of others. In ethics he is guilty if he only thinks of doing so.'

Immanuel Kant

LEARNING OUTCOMES

After reading this chapter on Rights, you will be able to:

- understand why human beings have rights.
- classify rights according to their basis.
- distinguish between major categories of rights – 'negative' and 'positive' rights and 'legal' and 'moral' rights.
- realize the enormous significance of human rights.
- understand the role human rights play in the corporate world.
- appreciate the justification of consumer rights which will be discussed in a separate chapter later.

4.1 MEANING AND NATURE OF RIGHTS

Rights are important concepts in the world of ethical and political reasoning. We live in an age where it has become common for people in democratic societies to invoke the concept of rights in a political discourse. As Richard Bellamy observes, 'political debate is currently suffused by the language of rights. All the main political parties, most pressure groups and individuals of almost every ideological persuasion make their demands and define our identity as citizens in terms of rights.'

Ruth Abbey observes, 'be it in the arena of domestic politics, in relation between states or in the increasing intersections between intra- and interstate politics, players turn to the language of rights to find a way of expressing their claims for resources, recognition or simply for the entitlement to act upon their desires and achieve their aims without interference.' This reflects the fact that rights are the most convenient means of translating political commitments into principled claims.

Jeremy Waldron says, 'behind the idea of rights is the conviction that there are liberties and interests so basic that every society should secure them irrespective of its traditions, history or level of economic development'. Rights function as a way of highlighting important attributes such as free speech, free movement, property and life itself, which requires protection by law. Daniel Fischlin and Martha Nandorfy, while examining the current situation on human rights worldwide, have stated that 'rights give expression to how all humans participate fully in civil society, defining the idealised norms against which a society may be measured'. As expressions of the civic values that operate within any society, rights derive from the marriage of religious, philosophical and legal principles that address social justice in the context of worldwide struggles to combat oppression and inequity. They do so out of an underlying, deep-rooted respect for human life, dignity and diversity.

The expansion of the rights discourse in the modern era has seen rights coming to be thought of as primarily normative. Originally, a right, as Ruth Abbey points out as an entitlement that could be retrieved through legal means, was accorded to individuals in recognition of the normative gravity of the thing being promised or protected by the right. In the work of one of the seminal theorists of liberalism, John Locke, individuals are set to have a natural and inalienable right for life, liberty and property because these are seen as essential to human well-being. Making something right was, then, a sign of its moral significance. *The Stanford Encyclopedia of Philosophy* proclaims that 'rights structure the forms of our governments, the contents of our laws and the shape of morality as we perceive it. To accept a set of rights is to approve a distribution of freedom and authority, and to endorse a certain view of what may, must and must not be done.'

In general, a right is an individual's entitlement to something. A person has a right when he/she is entitled to act in a certain way or have others act in a certain way towards him/her. Rights also entitle us to make claims on other people either to refrain from interfering in what we do or to contribute actively to our well-being.

The concept of rights is essentially a concept about human relationships in society. If one person has a right to something, other members of his/her society have an obligation to respect this right. If it is a right of action, such as a right to engage in political dissent, fellow citizens and the government have an obligation to tolerate expressions of dissent. The social character of rights, says Anthony Birch, is an essential aspect of the concept. The existence of rights always implies obligations on the part of other citizens and frequently implies obligations on the part of the person or group holding the right. This aspect highlights certain important basic characteristics of rights:

- It is generally recognised that rights secure liberty by protecting the individual against the state and others.
- Rights safeguard the individual's private space ensuring that neither the state nor others can morally interfere without justification.
- It is generally recognised that the rights an individual enjoys are by virtue of being human, rather than being a member of a political community.
- Rights are an act of public language; they cannot be solely the product of an individual's mind.
- All rights may protect desirable values.
- A right ascribes a particular status or worth to the rights-bearer.

Conceptual discussions of rights invariably take their bearings from Wesley N. Hohfeld's classic study *Fundamental Legal Conceptions* (1919). Hohfeld identified four kinds of rights:

1. *Claim Rights*: Hohfield believed these rights to be the most basic and the only true rights. These depend for their existence on there being a duty on someone else. The classic example of a claim-right is a right generated by a contract and accompanied by correlative duties.
2. *Liberty or Privilege Rights*: These rights occur when someone has the right to do something in the sense that he/she has no obligation not to do it – for example, to dress as one pleases, to use the public highway etc. Here there is no correlative duty on the part of another.
3. *Power Rights*: Sometimes a right involves the exercise of power. A person is authorised or 'empowered' to do something either to secure the interests of others or to secure one's own interest. For example, a property owner has the power (a legal property right) to do as he/she pleases with his/her property.
4. *Immunity Rights*: Immunity rights are specific rights, when a person is protected from the actions of others. For example, the immunity enjoyed by the members of parliament for whatever they say inside parliament; or, such as the right of the very young, elderly and disabled people not to be drafted into the army.

4.2 BASIS OF RIGHTS

Whether a right is a right of action, a right of resilience or a right to be left alone, it is important to ask what is the basis of the right in question. Some rights derive from law, some from moral codes and some from tradition. It is essential, therefore, to classify rights according to their basis.

4.2.1 LEGAL RIGHTS

Legal rights are recognised and enforced as a part of a legal system. These rights are generally set forth in the constitution, and because they are enshrined in law, they are enforceable through the courts. Legal rights are limited, of course, to the particular jurisdiction within which the legal system is in force.

4.2.2 MORAL RIGHTS

Moral rights are entitlements which derive their authority from a code of morality shared by members of a community independently of the legal system. Such rights are enforced by the conscience of the individuals, the customs of the community or the pressure of public opinion. They may also be enforced by law, as pointed out by Anthony Birch, because moral codes underlie many laws, but in that case, the moral laws become converted into positive rights, which are more secure because they are enforced by the state.

Moral rights are normally contextual rather than universal; they are limited to people who share a common code of morality. In this sense, Andrew Heywood has opined that moral rights are more commonly 'ideal' rights, which bestow upon a person a benefit that he/she needs or deserves. Moral rights therefore reflect what a person should have, from the perspective of a belief system.

4.2.3 NEGATIVE AND POSITIVE RIGHTS

A large group of rights called *negative rights* is distinguished by the fact that its members can be defined wholly in terms of the duties others have not to interfere in certain activities of the person who holds a given right. Negative rights are usually characterised as *civil* or *political* in nature and held to include such rights as the right to freedom of speech, property, habeas corpus, freedom from violent crime, freedom of worship, a fair trial, freedom from slavery and the right to bear arms. *Positive Rights* do more than impose negative duties. They also imply that some other agents have the positive duty of providing the holder of the right with whatever he/she needs to freely pursue his/her interests. Positive rights are characterised as *social* or *economic rights* and held to include rights such as the right to education, health care, social security or a minimum standard of living.

4.2.4 CONTRACTUAL RIGHTS

Contractual rights and duties are limited rights and correlative duties that arise when one person enters an agreement with other person. Contractual rights and duties are distinguished by:

- the fact they attach to specific individuals and the correlative duties that are imposed on other specific individuals,
- contractual rights arise out of a specific transaction between particular individuals and
- contractual rights and duties depend on a publicly accepted system of rules that define the transactions.

Without the institution of the contract and the rights and duties it can create, modern business societies could not operate. The institution of contract provides a way of ensuring that individuals keep their word.

4.2.5 NATURAL RIGHTS AND HUMAN RIGHTS

According to Andrew Heywood, the idea of human rights developed out of the 'natural rights' theories of the early modern period. These theories were the result of a desire to establish some limits upon how individuals may be treated by others, especially by those who wield political power. John Locke had identified the right of 'life, liberty and property' as natural rights. Thomas Jefferson defined them as the right to 'life, liberty and the pursuit of happiness'. Such rights were described as 'natural' in that they were thought to be God-given and therefore to be a part of the very core of human nature.

Natural rights did not exist simply as moral claims but were, rather, in Heywood's view, considered to reflect the most fundamental inner human drives; they were the basic conditions for leading a true human existence. Natural rights theories, therefore, served both as psychological models and as ethical systems.

The 20th century saw a decline in religious beliefs leading to the secularisation of natural rights. These were reborn in the form of *human rights*. Human rights are rights to which people are entitled by virtue of being human. They are therefore *'universal'* rights in the sense that they belong to all human beings rather than to members of any particular nation, race, religion, gender or social class. Human rights are also *'fundamental'* in the sense that they are inalienable: they cannot be traded away or revoked. Human rights are sometimes said to be *'absolute'* and that they must be upheld at all times and in all circumstances.

Francis Fukuyama calls human rights as 'fundamental rights' that fall into three categories.

1. *Civil Rights*: These involve exemption from control of the citizen in respect of his/her person and property.
2. *Religious Rights*: These involve exemption from control in the expression of religious opinion and the method of worship.
3. *Political Rights*: These focus on exemption from control in matters, which do not so plainly affect the welfare of the whole community as to render control necessary.

Supporters of human rights argue that they constitute the basic grounds for freedom, equality and justice, and embody the idea that all human lives are worthy of respect. *The Universal Declaration of Human Rights* (1948) of the United Nations serves as the common standard for defining human rights and freedom.

4.3 HUMAN RIGHTS AND THE CORPORATE WORLD

According to Frederick Bird, as the 20th century drew to a close, international businesses were being evaluated increasingly in terms of their record on human rights. Companies operating in developing countries were expected to expose human rights, teach employees to honour them and conduct their operations accordingly. The language and rhetoric of human rights were incorporated into company codes and mission statements. Civil society organisations sought to expose practices that violated human rights.

Corporate concern for global human rights emerged in the 1990s as stories depicting the opportunistic use of child labour, payment of low wages and abuses in foreign factories helped reshape our attitudes about acceptable behaviour for organisations. At an annual human rights survey meeting, the executive director of Human Rights Watch introduced three guidelines that managers should consider to advance human rights.

1. companies need to establish an open dialogue between workers and management,
2. businesses should be aware of the human rights issues and concerns in each country in which they operate and
3. companies should adopt the prevailing legal standard but work to improve and embrace a 'best practices' approach and standard.

Suggested Questions

1. 'Rights empower and protect people and society.' Discuss.
2. Explain the concept of rights as per the classic study by Wesley N. Hohfeld.

3. What are the bases of rights?
4. How and why should companies ensure respect of rights?
5. What are human rights?
6. How are human rights important to the corporate world?
7. Enumerate the basic characteristics of rights.

Bibliography

Bellamy, Richard (1993). *Theories and Concepts of Politics: An Introduction* (Manchester: Manchester University Press).

Goodin, Robert, E. and Petit, Philip (eds.) (1993). *A Companion to Contemporary Political Philosophy* (Oxford: Blackwell Reference).

Minogue, Kenneth (1995). *Politics: A Very Short Introduction* (USA: Oxford University Press).

Chapter 5

Recognition

Rana Sudhir Kumar

'Good name in man and woman, dear my lord,
Is the immediate jewel of their souls:
Who steals my purse steals trash, 'tis something, nothing;
'Twas mine, 'tis his, and has been slave to thousands;
But he that filches from me my good name
Robs me of that which not enriches him
And makes me poor indeed.'

William Shakespeare

LEARNING OUTCOMES

After reading this chapter, you will be able to:

- understand the phenomenon of 'recognition' as a basic human need.
- analyse the 'politics of recognition' as a serious debate in political theory.
- define the various forms of recognition.
- learn about the multicultural perspective on recognition.
- identify the perils of 'misrecognition'.

5.1 INTRODUCTION

In a general sense, recognition is the act of recognising someone when you see him/her or identifying something when you see it. Recognition is also understanding and acceptance of a fact or situation. It also means official acceptance that something is valid or proper. In the field of international relations among nations, recognition is symbolised by establishing diplomatic relations, exchanging ambassadors and accepting the membership of others in the United Nations.

The concept of recognition is not new to political theory. Hegel in *The Phenomenology of the Spirit* had conceptualised recognition as the distinctive need of human beings. Recently, philosophers such as Charles Taylor, Axel Honneth and Nancy Fraser have hinged their political theories around recognition. The concept of recognition indicates, as Neera Chandhoke has pointed out, that we become conscious of ourselves when we see that others have become conscious of us. In other words, we recognise ourselves through and in the eyes of others.

5.2 MEANING OF RECOGNITION

Basically, the term recognition indicates that people need the approval and respect of others to develop self-esteem, self-confidence and self-respect. The recognition of the self, says Neera Chandhoke, through being seen or recognised by others, enters the constitution of self-identity in a fundamental sense. 'Human integrity', argues Axel Honneth, 'owes its existence, at a deep level, to the patterns of approval and recognition.'

Socially and politically, the idea of recognition has come to be associated with feelings people nurture in modern liberal democracies, wherein they pride themselves on being little more than equal citizens and therefore expect to be publicly recognised only as such. Democracy has ushered in a politics of equal recognition. Recognition of every individual's uniqueness and humanity lies at the core of liberal democracy, understood as a way of personal and political life. However, a question is often asked if democracy is letting citizens down, morally, when major democratic institutions fail to take into account our particular identities. Apart from ceding each of us the same rights as all other citizens, what does respecting people as equals entail? The answer lies in an understanding of what is known as the 'politics of recognition'.

5.3 POLITICS OF RECOGNITION

One of the liveliest debates engaging democratic theory concerns the relationship between civic equality and public recognition of cultural differences among citizens. Philosophers such as Taylor, Honneth and Fraser began using the phrase 'politics of recognition' to refer to the chorus of claims and aspirations voiced on behalf of groups defined by a sense of shared cultural, national, ethnic, racial, religious, gender or sexual identity. Recognition, says Paul Graham, is recognition of difference. However, as Elizabeth Kiss points out, mere tolerance of difference is not enough, nor is it sufficient for democratic societies to allow citizens to express different identities in the private realm. Equal moral and political status, and hence democracy, cannot be achieved unless social institutions and sensibilities become more attentive to and relative of cultural differences.

Proponents of the politics of recognition assert that democracy requires affirmative recognition of differences among citizens. However, why is such recognition necessary? Charles Taylor and Will Kymlicka have offered an account of culture as a basic or primary human good, arguing that human well-being depends on people's capacity to express their own, 'authentic' cultural identity and to experience an 'intact' culture. Cultures do shape people's basic beliefs about the sources of well-being, dignity and value, and hence actions which demean or destroy cultural practices can cause profound harm.

5.4 FORMS OF RECOGNITION

What forms should recognition take? Most theorists of the politics of recognition have argued for a need to take differences into account in democratic practices, but their proposed remedies have been avowedly utopian, such as Nancy Fraser's call for 'socialism in the economy plus deconstruction in the culture'. Others are vague on issues of institutional implementation, such as Iris Young's proposals for group differentiated democratic participation.

Democrats sceptical of the politics of recognition have suggested that all legitimate forms of recognition are already encompassed by individual rights of non-discrimination and free association. Groups subjected to cultural injustice are often discriminated against and denied rights of association and protection of these rights will go far towards remedying many cultural harms. Nevertheless, struggles for recognition typically involve claims, which go beyond demands for non-discrimination and free association. They involve more robust forms of state support, involvement or substantive changes in policy, legal doctrine or authoritative cultural narratives.

5.5 MULTICULTURALISM AND DIVERSITY

Multiculturalism simply brought about the realisation that plural cultures need to be respected and validated through explicit acts of recognition. Cultures, which have been marginalised, says Neera Chandhoke, should be revalued and revalidated in the public sphere through, for example, group representation. If minority cultures are either decaying because of what has been termed as 'benevolent neglect' or subjected to virulent attacks, they should be protected through special measures such as minority rights.

Steven C. Rockefeller and John Dewey have stressed on the liberal democratic value of diversity as crucial to recognition. Diversity is connected to the value of expanding the cultural, intellectual and spiritual horizons of all individuals, enriching our world by exposing us to differing cultural and intellectual perspectives and thereby increasing our possibilities for intellectual and spiritual growth, exploration and enlightenment.

5.6 MISRECOGNITION OR NON-RECOGNITION

In a very interesting discussion contrasting the politics of recognition with what she calls the politics of redistribution, Nancy Fraser identifies harms of 'misrecognition', which are logically distinct from, though in practice intertwined with, unequal distribution of political rights and economic resources. Harms of misrecognition are cultural or symbolic injustices 'rooted in social patterns of representation, interpretation and communication'. Examples of misrecognition include cultural domination, which Fraser defines as 'being subjected to patterns of interpretation and communication that are associated with another culture and are alien or hostile to one's own'. Non-recognition is the process of 'being rendered invisible via the authoritative representational, communicative and interpretative practices of one's culture'. And, disrespect is 'being routinely maligned or disparaged in public representations and in everyday life interactions'.

Fraser acknowledges that misrecognition tends to be closely intertwined with political and economic inequalities, and that efforts to remedy misrecognition will usually have a strong redistributive dimension, since they will depend on democratising access to 'the means of interpretation and communication'.

Fraser's analysis of misrecognition as a source of unjust inequality is illuminating. A society is not truly democratic if it imposes on some of its members, as the price of admission to equal protection and status, the requirement that they deny or hide a deeply felt identity, unless expression of that identity is itself incompatible with democratic equality. The clearest examples of misrecognition occur when people are socially disadvantaged if and only if they engage in, and identify with, socially stigmatised practices such as particular religious observances or sexual practices.

Misrecognition is a distinctive social harm, but it becomes a significant social injustice when it is linked to consequences in access to resources, opportunities, power and voice, and makes people vulnerable to deprivation and abuse. Iris Young has aptly emphasised that in a democratic politics of recognition, moral priority must be given to considerations of equal protection and opportunity. Recognition, Young rightly emphasises, is a means to equal protection and opportunity, not an end in itself.

5.7 CONCLUSION

Recognition brings honour, dignity and forges identity. With honour, dignity and identity comes a politics of universalism, emphasising the equal dignity of all citizens and the content of this politics has been the equalisation of rights and entitlements. Equalisation affects civil and voting rights and extends to the socioeconomic sphere as well. The politics of equal dignity is based on the idea that all humans are equally worth of respect. According to Kant, what commands respect in human beings is their status as rational agents, capable of directing their lives through principles. The basis of our intuitions of equal dignity is a 'universal human potential', a capacity that all humans share. This potential is what ensures that each person deserves respect.

The politics of recognition can teach democrats important lessons in humility, urging us to be vigilant about our prejudices and the ways that can blind us to the needs, vulnerabilities and legitimate aspirations of those different from ourselves. A politics of recognition encourages democrats to re-examine practices to see where they may stigmatise or place unjustified burdens on members of identity groups. It points towards a democratic ideal, which Bhikhu Parekh has called 'culturally mediated universalism'.

Humility is also in order, however, for proponents of a politics of recognition. Recognition claims are highly context-specific, and attempts to generalise from them to sweeping accounts of cultural or group 'rights to recognition' will almost certainly run afoul of basic democratic values.

Suggested Questions

1. 'We recognise ourselves through and in the eyes of others.' Explain this statement.
2. Discuss the politics and the forms of recognition.
3. 'Misrecognition is a distinctive social harm'. Do you agree? Give reasons.
4. What is the multicultural perspective on recognition?

Bibliography

Bhikhu Parekh (2000). *Rethinking Multiculturalism* (Basingstoke: Macmillan Press/Palgrave).

Iain Mackenzie (2005). *Political Concepts: A Reader and Guide* (ed.) (Edinburgh: Edinburgh University Press)

Ian Shapiro and Casiano Hacker-Cordon (1999). *Democracy's Edges* (ed.) (Cambridge: Cambridge University Press).

Neera Chandhoke (1999). *The Logic of Recognition*. http://www.India-seminar.com.

Chapter 6

The Idea of a Good Society

Rana Sudhir Kumar

'But the life that no longer trusts another human being and no longer forms ties to the political community is not a human life any longer.'

Martha Nussbaum

LEARNING OUTCOMES

After reading this chapter, you will be able to:

- understand what constitutes 'a good society'.
- explain the role of the state, the community and the market as partners in a good society.
- evaluate measures responsible for sustainability of the good society.

6.1 A GOOD SOCIETY

A good society is bonded by ties of affection and commitment rather than relationships as employees, traders, consumers or even as fellow citizens. A good society is based on the 'core' tenets of liberty, equality, justice, rights and recognition. These form the basic principles for the sustenance and evolution of a society.

The above-stated 'core' tenets serve as the moral foundation on which the three instrumental 'partners' of the good society, namely, the community, the state and the market are balanced. The interdependence and the role of the three partners in creating the fabric of a society are explained below.

6.2 THREE PARTNERS

6.2.1 Community and Society

Communities are the main social entities that are based on person-to-person relationship, while the market is based on person-to-thing relationships. Communities are based on two foundations:

1. bonds of affection that turn groups of people into social entities and
2. a shared moral culture from generation to generation.

While community bonding satisfies a profound human need, moral culture can serve to enhance social order significantly while reducing the need for state intervention in social behaviour.

A good society thrives on a diversity of cultures and ethnic groups that enrich people's lives through arts, music, dance, social contact, cuisine and so on. However, such a multi-cultural society cannot flourish without a shared framework based on the basic elements that satisfy basic tenets of democratic way of life and mutual respect.

6.2.2 State and Society

The importance of the state in the composition of a good society cannot be denied. The state raises the individual above religious, ethnic and other forms of communal consciousness and creates a regime of personal liberties and rights. It eliminates personalised rule and replaces it with an impersonal system of government in which the citizen is subjected only to the authority of the law.

The modern state establishes equality among its members, bypasses the social hierarchies of status, caste and class and nurtures their sense of dignity. It is the sole defender of its territorial integrity, provides the only legitimate system of authority within its boundary, regulates the economy, safeguards and transmits the national culture and is a symbol of the collective identity of its citizens.

Indeed, the state performs an important historical role in fashioning a good society, as it alone is able to provide a stable and democratic structure of authority, to establish the rule of law, to maintain order, to ensure social justice, to manage conflict and to give its citizens a collective sense of agency.

While the state promulgates laws and rules that impinge upon personal liberties, private property and markets, to the extent it is necessary to maintain a good society, the role of the state is not to abolish these laws and rules but to adapt them to changing conditions. In a good society, the state and the market become partners in according the people a basic sense of economic security.

6.2.3 Markets and Society

A good society should view the market as akin to nuclear energy: it can provide an enormous and growing bounty of products and services. It is generally recognised that the market is the best engine for production of goods, services and economic progress. While much attention has been drawn to social problems created by market forces, such as factory closures and loss of job security, overwork in some industries and idleness in others are happening. Such problems should not blind us to the basic merit of strong economic growth. The market has always operated within a social context, which has included a fabric of social values, laws and regulatory mechanisms. The social context of the market lies in markets drawing resources that belong to society and providing goods and services in return to society. However, in doing so there is a need for market to ensure both efficiency and equity. It has hitherto been assumed that markets would automatically ensure both. In fact, the operation of the market does not really balance the interests of the society and private producers. A good society should ensure such a balance. Another dimension of market and society is the need for an ethical framework that backs the working of the market without which a good society cannot be sustained.

6.3 SUSTAINABILITY OF A GOOD SOCIETY

Even though a lot can be expressed about the sustainability of a society, environment plays the decisive role in the continued existence of any society. Therefore, firstly, it should be recognised that a good society would be one where communities, the state and the market understand their duty to pass on the culture of 'sustainable environment' for future generations.

Secondly, there can be no two opinions about the fact that a good society must be a corruption-free society. Few issues concerning the proper balance between market and state are more important than preventing those with economic power and from concentrating political power. In numerous free societies, there is a growing stream of private monies into public hands – either in the form of personal bribing and favours or in the modern form of special interests 'contributing' funds to political parties, legislators or government officials in exchange for special treatment at the public cost. Few things are more corrosive than the corruption of public institutions. Such double-fisted concentration of power violates a profound precept of a truly democratic and good society, whereby all members are equal citizens, whatever their wealth differences.

Lastly, corporations, in particular, can serve to become microcosms of a good society by adopting a number of measures such as adopting a tradition of 'best' business practices, strict adherence to good corporate governance norms, incorporation of codes of ethics in their business programmes, integrating comprehensive corporate social responsibility (CSR) practices and contributing to environmental protection and sustainable development. Further, corporations need to respect diversity, behave ethically and responsibly and adhere to values that define a good society. It is evident, then, that the most important work of a society that aspires to be good is conducted by an amalgam of communities, state and the market.

6.4 CONCLUSION

A good society has a strong notion of common good, consisting in respect for a consensually grounded civil authority and basic rights, maintenance of justice, institutional and moral preconditions of deliberative democracy, a vibrant and plural composite culture and an expansive sense of community. According to John H. Dunning, the constitution of a good society can be summed up by reference to three interdependent, independent systems:

1. In its political life, it is constituted by a democratic republic based upon the consent of the people, the division of powers and the rule of law.
2. In its economic life, it is constituted by an inventive economy based upon personal initiative, personal property and markets.
3. In its moral and cultural life, it is constituted by a culture of self-government based upon the widespread practice of the virtues required of a free people: self-mastery, respect for others, law-abidingness, public spiritedness and the like.

Suggested Questions

1. Explain the concept of good society with the help of notions of community, state and markets.
2. What is a good society? What are the key issues for the sustainability of a good society?
3. 'A good society needs a partnership of community, state and markets.' Explain.
4. How does Dunning sum up the constitution of a good society?
5. 'It is not just important to have a good society; it is important to sustain it.' Explain.

Bibliography

Andrew Heywood (2005). *Political Theory: An Introduction* (New York: Palgrave Macmillan).

Bhikhu Parekh (2000). *Rethinking Multiculturalism* (Basingstoke: Macmillan Press/Palgrave).

John H. Dunning (2003). *Making Globalization Good* (USA: Oxford University Press).

Sudipta Kaviraj and Sunil Khilnani (2001). *Civil Society* (USA: Cambridge University Press).

T. Campbell (1981). *Seven Theories of Human Society* (USA: Oxford University Press).

Unit II

Domain of Politics and Ethics

Prof. K.V. Bhanu Murthy

INTRODUCTION

When we think about politics, the concepts that stand out are liberty, equality, justice, rights and recognition. We aspire towards a good society. The idea of a good society incorporates all these elements. However, there has to be a form of society that exists and actualises all these desirable features. Such a society must exist in reality. It should have a political form. It is the power of politics that enables actualisation. There is a strong connection between political and economic powers. Hence, the domain of politics includes economic power, just as the political system necessarily has an economic system subsumed in it. Therefore, the domain of politics involves the debate on political and economic systems that may enable actualisation. The power that could actualise such a system could be people's power or the power of coercion, either by monarchies or by other political forms of governance such as dictatorships. What we need to debate in the domain of politics is as to which political and economic system may satisfy our idea of establishing a good society and hence may vindicate people's power.

In previous lessons while thinking conceptually about politics, we have considered different ideas of liberty, equality and justice. The consensus favours a positive notion of liberty and equality that leads to a certain level of welfare for all. The preferred notion of justice is one that ensures distributional justice. And, finally the implicit choice of rights rests upon a positive notion of rights that ensures standard of living; right to education, right to health, right to social security etc. If these preferred notions are established in an actual society, we would be moving towards 'the idea of a good society'. A political and economic system having the above desirable features would be considered a good society. However, the mere establishment of such a system is not sufficient. It needs 'good' governance to allow the perpetuation of a 'good society'.

What is not stated explicitly in the preceding debate is that these preferences or choices towards certain aspects or certain types of notions or concepts that we have made, implicitly, while thinking conceptually about politics, necessarily imply an ethical framework. Each alternative that we have chosen implies that we have made ethical choices while arriving at the 'the idea of a good society', while having rejected other contending aspects.

The 'domain of politics' is always inclusive of ethics. Firstly, as stated, there are implicit ethical choices that society makes while establishing a certain kind of political and economic system. Secondly, there is a need for ethical judgement and moral reasoning as to whether the society so established by the wishes of the people is going in the right direction or not. The society, hence, needs to sustain itself by knitting a moral fabric of society that enables the continued existence of a 'good society'.

Thus, any debate on the 'domain of politics' cannot exclude 'ethics'. Therefore, we shall now study the 'domain of politics and ethics'. We shall first consider the political system and then the economic system.

THE CORPORATION IN THE DOMAIN OF POLITICS AND ETHICS

The system that satisfies all the desirable features of a 'good society' is the democratic system of governance. This system rests on certain democratic principles of governance. We shall consider these principles and extend them to the business corporation. A moot question is as to why we need to bring in the business corporation as a separate entity. Firstly, this is necessary because the corporation is a microcosm of society that incorporates the features of a 'good society'.

Secondly, while there have been many notions in 'the domain of politics and ethics', political theory and philosophy, as they stand today, have been shaped and stated, primarily, in terms of the *individual* as an entity. The individual is seen as a citizen, in relation to the stage. It is this realtionship which has, hither to, defined the 'domain of politics and eithics'. The emergence of powerful corporations alters this relationship radically. It forces us to reckon with a new entity that incorporates and exerts power. With advent of markets and the pervasion of globalisation, the modern state has lost much of its power (see next chapter Market and Globalisation for details). Therefore, the vacuum created by the decline of the state in being filled by the business corporation. The corporation has entered the 'the domain of politics and ethics' along with its power and its own ethics.

The following table can be used to assess this phenomenon. It gives the sales revenue of the top multi-nationals alongside the GDP of countries.

Table 1 Comparison of Selected Corporations and Countries: 1997 (GDP or Total Sales in $US Billions)

COUNTRY OR CORPORATION	GDP OR TOTAL SALES	COUNTRY OR CORPORATION	GDP OR TOTAL SALES
General Motors	164	Marubeni	124
Thailand	154	Greece	123
Norway	153	Sumitomo	119
Ford Motor	147	Exxon	117
Mitsui & Co.	145	Toyota Motor	109
Saudi Arabia	140	Wal Mart Stores	105
Mitsubishi	140	Malaysia	98
Poland	136	Israel	98
Itochu	136	Colombia	96
South Africa	129	Venezuela	87
Royal Dutch/Shell Group	128	Philippines	82

There are two chapters in this Unit. The first is about 'Democracy and Welfare State ' and the next is about 'Market and Globalisation'.

Chapter 7 is about 'Democracy'. While political theory may discuss democracy in greater depth, here the purpose is to gain basic knowledge of the evolution of democracy and the forms of governance. The purpose is to understand the types and processes of democracy. By extending the framework of democracy to the corporation, we have tried to understand how a corporation is a microcosm of a society.

Chapter 8 dwells on the notion of 'Welfare State'. The state bestows political rights upon individual citizens. This, however, does not mean that the democratic state ensures all that is needed. There is a need for the liberal democracy to move one more step ahead by addressing other social and economic issues that are not ensured by the mere provision of political rights.

Chapter 9 is on 'Markets and Globalization'. There are two terms associated with a liberal democracy – capitalism and markets as opposed to socialism and planning. The latter are associated with illiberal democracies. We have already seen that the domain of politics necessarily includes ethics. In this context, it is important to understand the ethical implications of 'Markets and Globalization'.

Chapter 7

Democracy

Prof. K.V. Bhanu Murthy

"Democracy does not guarantee equality of conditions - it only guarantees equality of opportunity."

Irving Kristol

LEARNING OUTCOMES

This chapter is about Democracy. By the end of this chapter you would be in position to gain in respect of the following things:

- You would know about the need for good governance.
- You would be informed about the evolution of democracy and the forms of governance.
- You shall know about types of democracy.
- An evaluation of the democratic process would then be possible.
- It should be possible to evaluate the relative merits of representative and direct democracy.
- It would be possible to examine democracy at the organizational level.
- Through the notion of democracy you would be in a position derive a broad concept of corporate responsibility.

7.1 INTRODUCTION

The debate over the domain of politics and ethics leads us to believe that the political system that we desire is democracy. A democratic system leads to the establishment of a 'good society', having all the preferred notions of liberty, equality, justice, rights and recognition.

7.2 WHY GOOD GOVERNANCE?

We have seen that there is shift away from the dominance of the state and towards the establishment of the economic power of the corporation. There is a need to take cognisance of this change. We need to understand implications of this change for 'good governance', sustenance of a 'good society' and its ethical implications. If we fail to do so, the aspirations of the people to establish and sustain a 'good society' would be compromised, which may be leading to chaos and anarchy.

Moreover, good governance is necessary for two more reasons:

1. It is necessary for the system of authority.
2. It is necessary to maintain sovereignty or independence.

It is to be seen as to how the emergence of these giant multinational corporations can affect the system of authority and sovereignty.

It can be seen that both these reasons are relevant for both the nation state and the corporation. While nation states could be eroded or overrun, corporations could collapse, split or be taken over. In addition, all this could happen without any financial reason in the case of a corporation. It might just be because of 'bad governance'. Therefore, the domain of politics includes ethics and good governance. For understanding this, we have to study the evolution and features of democracy.

7.2.1 EVOLUTION OF DEMOCRACY

Historically, the transition of anarchy and chaos towards the establishment of a 'good society' and democracy has been very protracted, bloody and painful. Therefore, it is also necessary to understand the historical development of democracy. It has been said that 'those who forget the past are condemned to relive it'.

The Parliament of England was the first major step towards a fully democratic system during the Middle Ages. Parliament gradually gained more decision-making and legislative powers.

The United States can be seen as the first liberal democracy, with a relatively wide franchise (although initially limited by property, gender, race restrictions and the existence of slavery) since the United States Constitution protected rights and liberties. The U.S. Constitution was adopted in 1789. Such liberal democracies were few and often short lived before the late 19th century.

Democracy as we understand and enjoy it today has not existed since the beginning. Even the right to form governments through the democratic method of voting has not been a universal phenomenon. Some countries in the developed world also did not bestow voting rights upon women before India had done so. Universal adult franchise is a relatively recent phenomenon. What were the forms of governance in the past?

7.2.2 FORMS OF GOVERNANCE

We shall now examine different forms of governance. Briefly speaking, the following are the forms of governance.

- Sortition, where everyone in the primitive communities such as tribal societies participates in governance and selects the leaders by sortition not by election.
- Monarchy, where the ruler have a pre-ordained position through the 'divine right', bestowed by God. Here, peoples' participation is not there either in the establishment of the government or in the processes of governance.
- Dictatorship, where there is no freedom and no participation of people in governance.
- Democracy, where people are involved both in the establishment of the government and in the processes of the governance.

In the decades following the Second World War, most of the Western democratic nations had a predominantly free-market economy and developed a welfare state, reflecting a general consensus among their electorates and political parties.

A number of liberal democracies currently stand at an all-time high and have been growing without interruption for some time. As such, it has been speculated that this trend may continue in the future to the point where liberal democratic nation states become the universal standard form of human society.

7.3 DEMOCRACY – ITS VARIETIES AND PROCESSES

Democracy (literally 'rule by the people', from the Greek words *demos*, which means 'people' and *kratos*, which means 'rule') is a form of government for a nation state or an organisation. Today, a democracy is often assumed to be a liberal democracy but there are many other varieties of democracy and the methods used to govern differ amongst these varieties. While the term democracy is often used in the context of a political state, the principles are also applicable to other areas of governance. The principles of democratic governance could extend to the 'organisation' or 'corporation' or 'business' as well. Therefore, the corporation or company is to be seen as a 'microcosm' of society. It should also have all the desirable features of a 'good society'. In the context of a corporation, democratic 'rule by people' would mean a demonstration of the will of the shareholders.

7.3.1 Varieties

The definition of democracy is made complex by the varied concepts used in different contexts and discussions. Political systems, or proposed political systems, claiming or claimed to be democratic have ranged very broadly. For example, Aristotle contrasted rule by the many (democracy), with rule by the few (oligarchy), and with rule by a single person (autocracy).

On the one hand, in the case of tribal assemblies, the system randomly selects leaders from the population. On the other hand, in the system that seeks consensus, we have a 'deliberative democracy'. Even what is usually seen as de facto dictatorships may claim to be democratic and hold sham elections to gain legitimacy (for example, the former German Democratic Republic).

7.3.1.1 Direct

Direct democracy is a political system where the people vote on all policy decisions, such as questions of whether to approve or reject various laws. It is called direct because the power of making decisions is exercised directly by the people without intermediaries or representatives. Here, the emphasis is on the process and procedure of democracy. Historically, this form of government has been rare because of the difficulties of getting all the people of a certain territory in one place for voting. Criticism is also drawn upon the use of this term for it implies the notion of voting, while it neglects other democratic procedures such as speech, media and civic organisations. That is, these critics argue that democracy is more than merely a procedural issue.

7.3.1.2 Representative

Representative democracy or polyarchy is so named because the people do not vote on most government decisions directly, but select representatives to a governing body or assembly. Representatives may be chosen by the electorate as a whole (as in many proportional systems) or represent a particular subset (usually a geographic district or constituency), with some systems using a combination of the two. Many representative democracies incorporate some elements of direct democracy, such as referenda. Our parliamentary system is a representative form of democracy.

7.3.1.3 Liberal

Liberal democracy is a representative democracy (with free and fair elections) along with the rule of law, a separation of powers, and protection of liberties (thus the name liberal) of speech, assembly, religion and property. Conversely, an illiberal democracy is the one where the protections that form a liberal democracy are either nonexistent or not enforced. The experience in some post-Soviet states drew attention to the phenomenon, although it is not of recent origin. Napoleon, for example, used plebiscites to ratify his imperial decisions.

As we have seen that in the modern context corporations also have a fair share of power and participate in the domain of politics and ethics; thus, elements of each of these varieties of democracy should be incorporated into the structure and functioning of a company.

7.4 DEMOCRATIC PROCESS

The history of democracy highlights two fundamental facets of democracy:

1. No individual was naturally superior to another. No one is born with 'divine rights'. Therefore, each person should enjoy equal political rights.
2. The interests of people are best safeguarded if they are themselves vested with the final political authority.

However, in an actual democracy, 'equal rights' cannot be acquired naturally. There has to be a process that ensures it. This points towards the need for a constitution and other legislations in general. Secondly, in practice the 'safeguard' of the interest of the people would be ensured only if their 'final political authority' or the 'say' or 'will' can actually be exerted. The democratic process and the role of people in that process determine it.

> Political decisions require 'Political *judgment* about what ought to be done in circumstances where there are several options open and there is a disagreement about which option is best.'
>
> (David Miller, pp. 41)

The three elements that required while undertaking such a judgement are:

1. factual information about what will happen if one or the other option is chosen
2. the information about the preferences of the people affected by the decision and
3. the moral principle; the basis on which the *fairness* of the decision is judged.

The hardest decisions involve the choice of all the above-stated elements. Those who argue in favour of representative democracy feel that ordinary citizen would not have the necessary information. However, it could be equally said of the representatives. They would have to rely on experts as well.

Regarding preferences, it might seem that democracy would have an obvious advantage. The preferences of people would be heard in a democracy. However, people's representatives tend to be influenced by the dominant majority rather than the minority. One problem with the democratic process is that sometimes the majority view may not be really the morally right view. Therefore, democratic decisions should often be based on the strength of preferences and not just on the number of votes. This forms the ethical basis of pluralism and tolerance of minority rights.

Another problem with the democratic process is that some people may be better organised even if they are the minority. For instance, in a democracy, the rich industrialist may able to lobby much harder because of their economic power.

Finally, regarding the moral judgement, it is felt by the opponents of direct democracy that ordinary people would not have the necessary competence to make such moral judgements. Yet it is a moot point of debate as to whether or not the representatives have a better claim to have such competence.

Admittedly, people, in general, do know have the inclination or time to gather all the necessary information or competence to be able to become effective participants in the democratic process.

Thus, while the debate about whether or not a representative democracy is better than a direct democracy could remain inconclusive in the impracticality of a direct democracy makes it a less pragmatic tool of the democratic decision-making process. In a large and complex society, it cannot be expected that all members would be able to participate effectively in the democratic process.

In general, a representative democracy with the necessary moral and ethical safeguards may prove to be better in establishing and sustaining a 'good society'. This emphasises the significance of ethics in democracy.

7.4.1 Implications for the Corporation

In the case of a company, there is a natural 'separation of ownership and control'. The investors, who are spread out, are owners of the company. They are the 'principals' and the managers, who are actually responsible for decision making, are their 'agents'. The managers have the control. Although, there is an annual general body meeting, in each company, most of the decision making is done by the managers. Therefore, perforce in the case of a company there can only be a representative democracy. The interest of owner-investor is in the company is not protected by the national constitution, while their political rights of the owner-investors are protected constitutionally. Nevertheless, their interest needs to be protected. Hence, the managers need to be made accountable towards the shareholders. Since the national constitution does not automatically ensure this, there is a need for an ethical framework that is beyond the legal obligations of the company towards its shareholders. This framework and process of democratisation is known as corporate governance.

7.5 A CORPORATION AS A DEMOCRATIC BODY

Ordinarily, the notion of a democratic body invokes the entity of a state; however, a corporation also incorporates democratic state-like features. Though there remains some philosophical debate as to the applicability and legitimacy of criteria in defining democracy, what follows may be a minimum of requirements for a state to be considered democratic. These requirements may be considered to be the premise of a company, which is also a democratic entity. The following features reflect the democratic character of a democratic state, which are being extended to the corporation.

A demo – a group that makes (political) decisions by some form of collective procedure – must exist. Non-members of the demos do not participate in the process. In modern democracies, the demos are the adult portion of the nation, and adult citizenship is usually equivalent to membership. In the case of companies, the demos are the body of shareholders.

A territory must be present, where the decisions apply, and where the demo is resident. In modern democracies, the territory is the nation state, and since this corresponds (in theory) with the homeland of the nation, the demos and the reach of the democratic process neatly coincide. In the case of a company, there is no such coincidence. The territory of a company may extend beyond the locality and the nation. The territory of a company is its 'domain'. Therefore, its immediate shareholders are not the only stakeholders. If the company draws its resources from the territory then those who provide the resources become 'remote stakeholders'. This raises an important question of accountability. The democratic processes of the company are restricted only to the shareholders and the 'board room' but its territory includes those who may be victims of the actions/decisions of the demo. The company 'demo' may decide to open a polluting unit in a residential area but might not themselves reside any where in the vicinity. The victims of pollution are neither shareholder nor are they 'remote stakeholders'. Nevertheless, the company is accountable towards the 'territory' or its 'environment'. Thus, in the case of a company, the domain of its politics includes its 'environmental accountability'.

A decision-making procedure exists, which is either direct, in instances such as a referendum, or indirect, of which instances include the election of a parliament. The procedure is regarded as legitimate by the demo, implying that its outcome will be accepted. If the shareholders in a company do not legitimise the decision making, if there is not enough transparency and if the shareholders do not accept the outcomes, there may be a 'market rejection' of the company by the shareholders. This points the fact that the 'domain of politics and ethics', of a company, includes 'corporate governance'.

Finally, in democracy, there has to be a binding or enforcement of the decisions. In a democracy, this is achieved by the enforcement of laws. Here, a peculiar situation has arisen. The corporation is a microcosm of society and has to have democracy within but it is also a part of the larger society and, hence, has to abide by the democratic system in which it resides.

7.6 DEMOCRACY – BEYOND THE STATE LEVEL

Thus, if we look beyond the level of the nation state, towards the corporation, it becomes clear that the corporation is a very significant entity in 'domain of politics and ethics'. We have earlier talked of how the manager of a corporation needs to be accountable towards the investor-owner. If we look beyond framework of the owner–manager relationship, there are other entities in society who are related to the company but may not be the shareholders, such as vendors and banks. The company has a responsibility towards such entities as well. Finally, the company or the business also draws resources from and produces for society. The existence of the company crucially depends on the society. This society need not be stakeholders in the ordinary sense. This obligation towards society in general arises out of the democratic system. It may not be a formal and legal obligation. Hence, it may not be legally binding upon business. The binding upon corporations towards society is ethical. This forms the primary basis of business ethics, which we shall be studying later.

Therefore, corporate responsibility includes– social responsibility, environmental accountability and good corporate governance. This arises in the pursuance of democracy and spells an agenda for 'corporate responsibility'. The agenda for corporate responsibility essentially deal with the concept of 'responsibility towards triple bottom line'.

The corporate responsibility to the 'triple bottom line' relates to people, profit and planet. Responsibility towards people is 'social responsibility', irrespective of whether they are stakeholders or not. The responsibility towards natural environmental or planet is termed as 'environmental accountability'. 'Corporate governance' would ensure that company is accountable towards the interests of shareholders/owners. An approach of balancing the objectives and goals for serving triple bottom line is termed as 'corporate responsibility'. It would be apparent that corporate responsibility is inherent and arises from the philosophy of business (see Unit III Chapter 10 for details). Any regulatory framework towards corporate responsibility cannot be substituted for this basic responsibility of business.

If we treat a corporation as a democratic body, it represents the 'voice' of its constituency or stakeholder. Among the stakeholders, we have immediate stakeholders such as shareholders. Other stakeholders are vendors or banks. Society in general is a remote stakeholder. The immediate stakeholders are a part of the decision-making and hence they have a voice. The next ring of stakeholders also has its means to be felt. The society, in general, is a remote stakeholder. It does not have a direct voice. The natural environment does not even have an indirect voice (Figure 7.1).

In the reverse order, the outer most ring needs the greatest attention. We need to evolve a system of accountability by which the corporate responsibility towards the environment can be enforced. On similar lines, the next ring also needs to be supported through enforcing responsibility on the business or corporation towards society in general. The entities in the central ring are within reach of the corporation and are often a part of the governance; therefore, in this case, their voice and the response of the corporation need to be strengthened.

In the light of the above argument, it becomes clear that the three strands of corporate responsibility do not have the same value based standing and they need to be viewed in hierarchical manner. It is obvious that

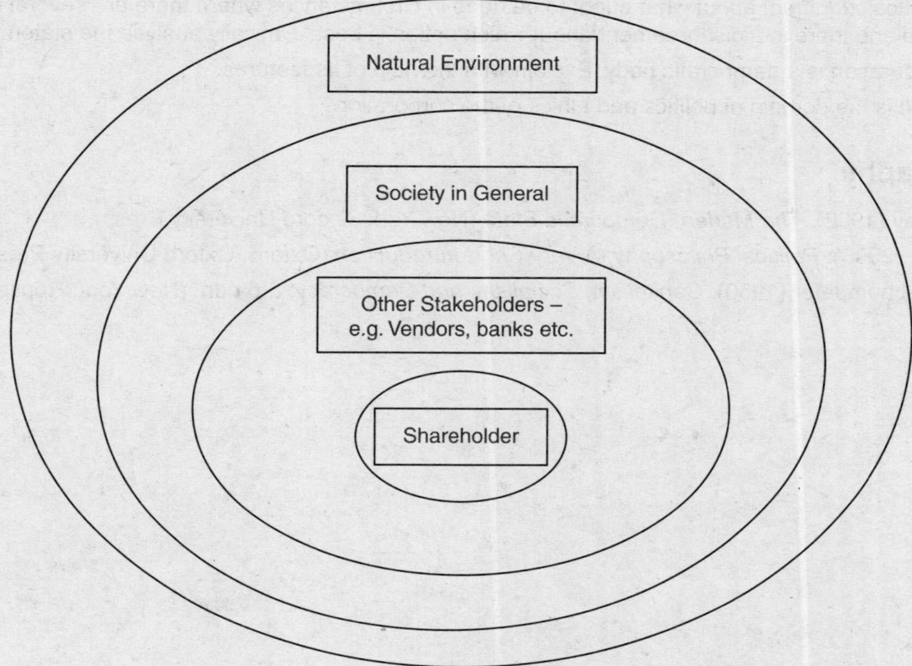

Figure 7.1 Domain of Politics and Ethics in relation to Corporate Responsibility.

the natural environment is most vulnerable and has no voice. Hence, the highest priority needs to be accorded to environmental accountability. In that order, corporate social responsibility needs to be placed second. The core that is corporate governance is central to the whole theme and yet may be accorded a lower priority in this sense.

7.7 CONCLUSION

The debate over the domain of politics and ethics leads us to believe that the political system that we desire is democracy. Ordinarily, the notion of a democratic body invokes the entity of a state; however, a corporation also incorporates democratic state-like features. Thus, if we look beyond the level of the nation state, towards the corporation, it becomes clear that the corporation is a very significant entity in 'domain of politics and ethics'. We have earlier talked of how the manager of a corporation needs to be accountable towards the investor-owner. The corporate responsibility to the 'triple bottom line' relates to people, profit and planet. Responsibility towards people is 'social responsibility', irrespective of whether they are stakeholders or not.

Suggested Questions

1. Why good governance is necessary? Explain the forms of governance.
2. Explain the different varieties of democracy. Discuss the relative merits of representative and direct democracy.

3. 'Political *judgment* about what ought to be done in circumstances where there are several options open and there is a disagreement about which option is best.' Critically analyse the statement.
4. Corporation is a democratic body. Explain with the help of its features.
5. What is the domain of politics and ethics of the corporation?

Bibliography

A. D. Lindsay (1962). *The Modern Democratic State* (New York: Oxford University Press).

David Miller (2003). *Political Philosophy: A Very Short Introduction* (Oxford: Oxford University Press).

Joseph A. Schumpeter (1950). *Capitalism, Socialism, and Democracy*, 3rd edn. (New York: Routledge).

Chapter 8

Welfare State

Prof. K.V. Bhanu Murthy

"An active welfare state must provide a floor below which no one should be allowed to fall, but its primary role must be to enable people to provide for themselves."

John Hutton

LEARNING OUTCOMES

This chapter follows the chapter on Democracy and tells us about the welfare state. Through this chapter:

- You would know about the three main interpretations of the idea of a welfare state.
- The basic developments in this respect would be known.
- An evaluation of the merits and demerits of such a system would be possible.
- You would understand that the link between social expenditure and economic performance is weak.

8.1 INTERPRETATIONS OF WELFARE STATE

The rationale for the existence and establishment of democracy, it has been shown, lies in the need for establishing political authority and sovereignty of the nation state. The state bestows political rights upon individual citizens. This, however, does not mean that the democratic state ensures all that is needed. A liberal democracy is one step ahead of a representative democracy in as much as it protects liberties (thus the name liberal) of speech, assembly, religion and property. However, a democracy is prone to other problems such as income inequalities, marginalisation of minorities, neglect of special interest groups such as women, the aged population and the unemployed youth. The establishment of political rights does not ensure social upliftment through the spread of literacy, removal of untouchability and so on. There is a need for the liberal democracy to move one more step ahead by addressing other social and economic issues that are not ensured by the mere provision of political rights. This points towards the need for establishing a welfare state.

There are three main interpretations of the idea of a welfare state:

1. The provision of welfare services by the state.
2. An ideal model in which the state assumes primary responsibility for the welfare of its citizens. This responsibility is comprehensive, because all aspects of welfare are considered; neither 'safety nets' nor minimum standards are enough. It is universal, because it covers every person as a matter of right.
3. The provision of welfare in society: In many 'welfare states', especially in continental Europe, welfare is not actually provided by the state, but by a combination of independent, voluntary, mutualist and government services. The functional provider of benefits and services may be a central or state government, a state-sponsored company or agency, a private corporation, a charity or another form of non-profit organisation.

8.2 ORIGINS

The English term 'welfare state' is believed to have been coined by Archbishop William Temple during the Second World War, contrasting wartime Britain with the 'warfare state' of Nazi Germany. In German, a roughly equivalent term (*Wohlfahrtsstaat*) had been in use since 1870. In French, the synonymous term 'providence state' (*État-providence*) was originally coined as a sarcastic remark used by opponents of welfare state policies during the Second Empire (1854–1870).

8.2.1 The Development of Welfare States

Modern welfare states developed through a gradual process beginning in the late 19th century and continuing through the 20th century. They differed from previous schemes of poverty relief due to their relatively universal coverage. The development of social insurance in Germany under Bismarck was particularly influential. Some schemes, such as those in Scandinavia, were based largely in the development of autonomous, mutualist provision of benefits. Others were founded on state provision. The term, however, was not applied to all states offering social protection. The sociologist T.H. Marshall identified the welfare state as a distinctive combination of democracy, welfare and capitalism.

Examples of early welfare states in the modern world are Sweden (Folkhemmet), Germany, the Netherlands and New Zealand in the 1930s. Germany is generally held to be the first social welfare state.

Changed attitudes in reaction to the Great Depression were instrumental in the move to the welfare state in many countries, a harbinger of new times where 'cradle-to-grave' services became a reality after the poverty of the Depression. In the period following the Second World War, many countries in Europe moved from partial or selective provision of social services to relatively comprehensive coverage of the population.

8.3 ARGUMENTS FOR AND AGAINST THE WELFARE STATE

The concept of the welfare state remains controversial and there is continuing debate over governments' responsibility for their citizens' well-being.

8.3.1 Arguments in Favour

Humanitarian – socialists believe the right to the basic necessities of life is a fundamental human right and people should not be allowed to suffer unnecessarily through lack of provision.

Democratic – the gradual extension of social protection is increasingly favoured by the citizens of mature economies, who have approved these as part of political election campaign promises.

Ethical – reciprocity (or fair exchange) is nearly universal as a moral principle and most welfare systems are based around the patterns of generalised exchange.

Altruism – helping others is a moral obligation in most cultures; charity and support for people who cannot help themselves are also widely thought to be moral choices.

Utilitarian – the same amount of money will produce greater happiness in the hands of a less well-off person than if given to a well-off person; thus, redistributing wealth from the rich to the poor will increase the total happiness in society.

Religious – major religions in the world emphasise the importance of social organisation rather than personal development alone. Religious obligations include the duty of charity and the obligation for solidarity.

Mutual Self-interest – several national systems have developed voluntarily through the growth of mutual insurance.

Economic – social programmes perform a range of economic functions, including the regulation of demand and structuring the labour market.

Social – social programmes are used to promote objectives regarding education, family and work.

Market Failure – in certain cases, the private sector fails to meet social objectives or to deliver efficient production, due to such things as monopolies, oligopolies or asymmetric information.

Economies of Scale – some services can be more efficiently paid for when bought 'in bulk' by the government for the public, rather than purchased by individual consumers. The highway system, water distribution, the fire department, universal health and national defence are some examples.

8.3.2 ARGUMENTS AGAINST

Moral (compulsion) – libertarians believe that the 'nanny state' infringes upon individual freedom, forcing the individual to subsidise the consumption of others. They argue that social spending reduces the right of individuals to transfer some of their wealth to others and is tantamount to a seizure of private property.

Religious/Paternalism – Some Protestant Christians also believe that only voluntary giving (through private charities) is virtuous. They hold personal responsibility to be a virtue and they believe that a welfare state diminishes the capacity of individuals to develop this virtue.

Anti-regulatory – the welfare state is accused of imposing greater burdens on private businesses, of potentially slowing growth and creating unemployment.

Efficiency – advocates of the free market believe that it leads to more efficient and effective production and service delivery than state-run welfare programmes. They argue that high social spending is costly and must be funded out of higher levels of taxation. According to Friedrich Hayek, the market mechanism is much more efficient and able to respond to specific circumstances of a large number of individuals than the state since public institutions of government are unable to collect knowledge to respond to specific circumstances as well as individual agents can.

Motivation and Incentives – the welfare state may have undesirable effects on behaviour, fostering dependency, destroying incentives and sapping motivation to work.

8.4 CRITICISM

The extreme criticisms of states and governments, and by extension the welfare state, are from anarchists, who believe that all states and governments are undesirable and/or unnecessary. They would tend to argue that the governmental practice of supporting people (paternalism) is a method of controlling and 'owning' those people, rather than an act of altruism.

Arguably, the idea of a welfare state receives most of its criticism in the United States, which has much more limited welfare services than many other developed countries. Some of this criticism concerns the idea that a welfare state makes citizens dependent and less inclined to work. This is unsupported by the economic evidence; there is no association between economic performance and welfare expenditure in developed countries. Similarly, there is no evidence for the contention that welfare state impedes progressive social development, show that on major economic and social indicators; the United States performs worse than the Netherlands, which has a high commitment to welfare provision.

Another criticism is that the welfare state allegedly provides its dependents with a similar level of income to the minimum wage. Critics argue that fraud and economic inactivity are apparently quite common now in the United Kingdom and France. Some conservatives in the United Kingdom claim that the welfare state has produced a generation of dependents who rely solely upon the state for income and support instead of working. They believe that the welfare state was created (in 1948 in the United Kingdom) to provide a carefully selected number of people with a subsistence level of benefits in order to alleviate poverty, but that it has been overly expanded to provide a large number of people indiscriminately with more money than the country can afford. Some feel that this argument is demonstrably false: the benefits system in the United Kingdom hands out considerably less money than the national minimum wage, and receipt of benefits is dependent on the regular submission of proof that the beneficiary deserves the money, either as a result of genuine incapacity or as a reward for seeking employment.

A third criticism of the welfare state is that it results in high taxes. This is sometimes true, as evidenced by places such as Denmark (tax level at 50.4% of GDP in 2002) and Sweden (tax level at 50.3% of GDP in 2002). However, these countries also have high wage economies and high GNPs; high taxes do not imply poor economic performance. In addition, they have a strong system of progressive taxation, which ensures that less burden falls on the poor and middle classes. Lowering taxes would not necessarily result in more spending money for the average citizen (since a lot of free services would no longer be free).

A fourth criticism of the welfare state is the belief that welfare services provided by the state are more expensive and less efficient than the same services would be if provided by private businesses. In 2000, professors Louis Kaplow and Steven Shafell published two papers, arguing that any social policy based on such concepts as justice or fairness would result in an economy, which is Pareto inefficient. Anything, which is supplied free at the point of consumption, would be subjected to artificially high demand, whereas resources would be more properly allocated if provision reflected the cost. A first response might be that the purpose of state-provided welfare is to respond to social needs, not necessarily to be cheaper overall. In a welfare state, the poor and lower-middle classes receive certain services free of charge, whereas in non-welfare states they would have to pay for those services, and could possibly not afford them. More fundamentally, although private provision can reduce unit costs, it often does so through adverse selection, or exclusion of disproportionately expensive cases.

The assumption that public provision of social services is more costly overall is often backed by examples of very large public institutions – such as the British National Health Service, which is the third greatest employer in the world. However, several studies have shown that national health care systems tend to be cheaper than equivalent provision through private care.

8.5 THE WELFARE STATE AND SOCIAL EXPENDITURE

On the one hand, welfare provision in the contemporary world tends to be more advanced in the countries with stronger and more developed economies. On the other hand, poor countries tend to have limited social services.

Within developed economies, however, there is very little correlation between economic performance and welfare expenditure. There are individual exceptions on both sides. However, the higher levels of social expenditure in the European Union are not associated with lower growth, lower productivity or higher unemployment, or with higher growth, higher productivity or lower unemployment. Likewise, the pursuit of free market policies leads neither to guaranteed prosperity nor to social collapse. Countries with more limited expenditure, such as Australia, Canada and Japan, do no better or worse economically than countries with high social expenditure, such as Belgium, Germany and Denmark.

8.6 CONCLUSION

Let us sum up the argument. The right types of notions of liberty, equality, justice, rights and recognition are necessary for the establishment of a good society. This involves ethical considerations and moral reasoning for choosing the 'right' type of notion. We shall understand more about this in Unit III but it is obvious that ethics and morality involve a judgement of what is 'right' and what is 'wrong'. The political system that we desire is a democracy, which can fulfil the 'idea of a good society'. However, even the process of establishment of such a political system in practice and to run it successfully needs ethics and morality. The fact that multinational corporations, in modern societies, play a very significant role in making or marring democracy complicates this picture. This is the most important argument that explains the relevance of all other topics that follow in the rest of the chapters.

Suggested Questions

1. Why do we need a welfare state? What are the different interpretations of a welfare state?
2. Argue the case for and against welfare state.
3. Critically view the welfare state and give your conclusions.
4. Write a note on social expenditure and welfare state.
5. Write a note on the growth of the welfare state.

Bibliography

Atkinson, B. (1995). *Incomes and the Welfare State* (Cambridge: Cambridge University Press).

David Miller (1989). *Market, State and Community: Theoretical Foundations of Market Socialism* (Oxford: Clarendon Press).

Goodin, R. *et al*. (2000). *The Real Worlds of Welfare Capitalism* (Cambridge: Cambridge University Press).

Takis Fotopoulos *Welfare State or Economic Democracy*? Retrieved on www.democracynature.org/dn/vol5/fotopoulos_welfare.htm.

Chapter 9

Markets and Globalisation

Prof. K.V. Bhanu Murthy

> "We must ensure that the global market is embedded in broadly shared values and practices that reflect global social needs, and that all the world's people share the benefits of globalization."
>
> *Kofi Annan*

LEARNING OUTCOMES

After studying about the market and globalization, you would gain in certain respects.

- It would be possible to understand the problems of an economy.
- You would know about the shortcomings of a market economy.
- The need for having controls would become clear.
- You would be better informed about how multinationals have grown.
- Lastly, the chapter would help you to appreciate what corporate responsibility means at the global level.

9.1 INTRODUCTION

In the previous chapter, we have highlighted the role of democratic decision making; however, the emphasis was on political decisions. If we agree that there is a strong connection between economic power and political power then it is important to know as to how basic economic decisions are taken and how this represents democracy. There are two terms associated with a liberal democracy – capitalism and markets as opposed to socialism and planning. The latter are associated with illiberal democracies. We have already seen that the domain of politics necessarily includes ethics. In this context, it is important to understand the ethical implications of 'market and globalisation'.

9.2 MARKET ECONOMY

We can define the *market economy* as the self-regulating system in which the fundamental economic problems (*what*, *how* and *for whom* to produce) are solved 'automatically', through the price mechanism, rather than through conscious social decisions. Therefore, the market is seen as an ethically superior system in two ways. Firstly, it resolves the basic economic problems of society to the maximum benefit or 'good' of the largest number. Secondly, it does so in a democratic manner – without curbing individual freedom.

The market solves the central problems in the following manner:

1. What to produce?
   Goods and services that are in greater demand would have a higher price and hence this represents the will of society. The high price reflects the democratic decision to allocate resources towards the preferred goods and services.
2. How to produce?
   There are three basic resources that need to be combined in certain proportions, namely, land, labour and capital. Each has its price or wage. The resource that has the highest price must be used the least, if scarce resources of society have to be put to the best use. Here, the high price of a certain factor of production is an indicator that it is a scarce resource. The market wage of such a factor would automatically restrain the use of such a factor of production. This is how the market carries out the democratic decision to employ society's resources in the best possible manner.
3. For whom to produce?
   This question must actually be reversed. Who produces? This is a better way to understand the third aspect of the market. After goods and services are produced, there is the question of how these must be distributed amongst those who are responsible for production. The resource that produces most efficiently deserves the highest wage. Therefore, who produces the best gets the most deserving share of what is produced.
   The three questions are simultaneously solved by the market. In the process, the fundamental economic decision is undertaken by an implicitly democratic process. What is this fundamental decision? The fundamental question is, 'How to put scarce resources to the best (most desired by society) use?' It is said that a market economy simultaneously solves the problem of equity (the third central problem) and efficiency. Ideally, the process carried out by the market mechanism is 'laissez faire' or 'hands-off'. It appears to be the best democratic process.

The welfare principle that eulogises the market is known as Pareto Optimality condition. It states that 'no one can be made better off without making someone else worse off' when economic welfare is optimised or at its best. Also, that it is the perfection of the market mechanism that leads to such an ideal state.

How does Pareto Optimality ensure the best or the most ethical solution?

1. The price of goods and services is such that a higher price will benefit the producer and a lower will benefit the consumer. Therefore, there is only one price, i.e., the *market price,* which is best for both producer and consumer; therefore, it is best for the society.
2. If more of a factor, say labour, is utilised then it implies that capital is under-utilised, which is bad for society. The resources are not best utilised; therefore, this is a loss for the whole of the society.
3. If one factor of production is paid more than its contribution, the factor is paid less. If Pareto Optimality holds then all factors are paid in relation to their contribution to society. Thus, society as a whole gains.

This portrayal of the market makes it appear as a very socially responsible mechanism that 'automatically' carries out all tasks that the society desires. And, that it does so without any ill effect or fallout or without any need for controls by the society.

9.3 WHAT IS MARKET FAILURE?

A welfare state does not answer the fundamental question that the market answers. However, a welfare state, generally speaking, is about the explicit democratic economic and social decisions that are not answered by the market such as unemployment, inequality, poverty, women's issues and minority problems.

The market economy is a broader term than capitalism. The market economy refers to the way resources are allocated, whereas capitalism refers to property relations. Although, historically, the market economy has been associated with capitalism, namely, private ownership and control of the means of production, a market allocation of resources is not inconceivable within a system of social ownership and control of economic resources.

The three major sources of problems in a market economy are:

1. externalities,
2. income inequalities and
3. imperfections.

This results in the market not operating in the most efficient and equitable manner. That is, this leads to the market not providing the best solutions. Hence, the market is no longer ethically superior.

Externalities are economic phenomena wherein the private benefits and costs do not match with social benefits and costs. The increased social cost, for instance, of pollution cannot be 'automatically' resolved by the market mechanism. As a result, the society has to pay a cost that should actually be borne by the companies. On this count, the market is not ethically superior because the rest of the society has to bear the 'social cost' of the unethical behaviour of business. Income inequalities cause biases in the private market mechanism. The three decisions of how, what and for whom can, in the presence of powerful and rich people in society, lead to a certain wrong choices that do not maximise the economic welfare. This means that it is not ethically superior. It is not working for the 'good' of the maximum people but is biased towards the rich. The basis of the welfare maximising Pareto Optimality condition is perfect competition. Under perfect competition, the price is so determined that it exactly represents the additional resource cost (marginal cost) of producing the additional unit of a commodity. There is no divergence between market price and social cost or cost to society. If there are market imperfections, such as monopolistic competition and monopoly (which is most often the case), the market does not provide optimal resource allocation and welfare. Once again, this points towards the fact that the market mechanism is not ethically superior. It does not provide the maximum 'good' to society.

The preceding discussion clearly brings out a conflict. The market is unable to do the maximum 'good' if it is allowed to function without any restriction ('laissez faire' or 'hands-off'). This is the problem of 'market failure'. A market operates through its basic entities – its businesses. The failure of the market to provide the 'best' (ethically superior) solution is hence due to the failure of its businesses. The lack of 'social responsibility' of the market, wherein it is unable to meet all the desires of society, is attributable to its entities. Clearly, the case, for 'social responsibility of business', arises out of 'market failure'. What are the implications of market failure for 'market and globalisation'? Globalisation is a phenomenon whereby the market principles and market mechanism are being universalised. Therefore, a straightforward implication of globalisation for business ethics is that market failure is also being universalised through globalisation. To reiterate this arises due to a conflict between the 'openness' of the market and economic freedoms and the inability of the market to provide an ethically superior solution to society. All these point out towards the need for control, on the market mechanism both domestically and internationally.

9.4 SOCIAL CONTROLS

The fact that in a market economy scarce resources are allocated 'automatically' does not mean that there are no social controls at all. Here, we should introduce an important distinction between the various types of social controls, which will help us to interpret the implications of the market and globalisation.

There are three main types of possible social controls on the market economy:

1. *Regulatory controls*: They have usually been introduced by the capitalists in control of the market economy in order to 'regulate' the market. The aim of regulatory controls is to create a stable framework for the smooth functioning of the market economy without affecting its essential self-regulating nature.

Such controls have always been necessary for the functioning of the system of the market economy. Some examples are regulations on investment, prices, trade etc. While, earlier, these controls were exercised by the national governments after globalisation such controls are now exercised by the various world bodies such as the World Trade Organization (WTO). These aim at regulating the world markets in the interest mainly of those controlling the global markets (multinationals or international businesses). Therefore, while it apparently seems that controls have been done away with for the 'global good', in fact the benefit accrues to these multinationals.

2. *Social controls in the broad sense*: Although they have them as their primary aim for the protection of those controlling the market economy against foreign competition, they may have some indirect effects that could be beneficial to the rest of the society as well. A primary example of such controls is the various protectionist measures aiming at protecting domestic commodities and capital markets (tariffs, import controls, exchange controls etc.). With globalisation, these controls have been removed. Ironically, however, the removal of such controls has lead to greater control by multinationals. Their power has increased.
3. *Social controls in the narrow sense*: They aim at the protection of humans and nature against the effects of marketisation. Such controls are usually introduced as a result of social struggles undertaken by those who are adversely affected by the effects of market economy on them or on their environment. Typical examples of such controls are social security legislation, welfare benefits, macro-economic controls to secure full employment, environmental controls etc. The need for such controls can never die down. It will be seen that while the first two controls have gone down and have moved in favour of multinationals, the third kind of control cannot be reduced. In fact, with globalisation, it can be seen, in what follows that the need for such controls is ever so greater.

Historically, we may distinguish three main phases in the process of marketisation:

1. the liberal phase, from the 1930s to the 1970s, which after a transitional period of protectionism, led to
2. the statist phase (growth of public sector), from the 1930s to the 1970s, which was succeeded by
3. the present neoliberal phase.

The above periodisation is directly relevant to the history of the welfare state. Its origins could be traced back to the protectionist period and its peak to the statist phase, while the present neoliberal phase marks its gradual collapse. Furthermore, as it is obvious from the above periodisation, the long-term trend, since the rise of the market economy, has always been one of the minimising social controls on the markets and, what is important from our point of view, of a parallel concentration of economic power. It could easily be shown, both theoretically and empirically, that there is a direct relationship between marketisation and concentration of economic power: the higher the degree of marketisation (i.e., the lower the social controls on markets, particularly social controls in the narrow sense) the higher the degree of concentration of power. Historically, it was only during the relative brief statist phase that this long-term trend towards marketisation was reversed, although even then it was social controls to protect labour, rather than the environment, that were introduced.

9.5 THE DECLINE OF THE WELFARE STATE AND GROWTH OF MULTINATIONALS

Although the welfare state reached its peak during the statist phase, the seeds of its decline were also sown during the same period. Thus, despite the expansion of statism at the *national* economic level, the marketisation process at the *international* level (in the sense of gradual lifting of controls on the movement of commodities and later of capital), which was interrupted after the Great Depression and the explosion of protectionism that followed, was resumed.

The subsequent developments lead to an international trend not only towards marketisation but also towards "globalization" of markets. The markets all over the world became one with the advent of globalisation. Globalisation has meant free flow of goods and services across borders; free interchange of technologies across companies and across borders; also the free flow of capital and funds across the whole globe; finally, it has meant a movement towards oneness across the globe in terms of economics structures, cultures, legal and political systems.

Such globalisation has lead to the growth of powerful multinationals (MNCs), who are often larger that the nation states. Global social controls have replaced national ones. International bodies such as the IMF, World Bank and WTO have gained greater control and power in the whole world. These conditions increase the power and reach of the corporation. These controls have meant a decline of government expenditure in keeping with the rise of markets against the presence of the state. The decline in government spending has lead to a decline in welfare spending. As marketisation and globalisation increase the negative fallout of the two also increases. Therefore, on the one hand, the role of the state has declined and the controls on the market have declined and on the other hand, the need for welfare measures has increased. The moot question is as who will fill in the gap? How can the ill effects of the market be removed in the absence of controls and with the decline of the state?

The answer lies in making the corporation responsible to take over some of the roles of the declining state. This implies that companies must become responsible towards society in respect of such responsibilities that the market does not carry out 'automatically' and that the state has been prevented from carrying or cannot carry out for want of resources. Secondly, in the absence of social controls companies may indulge in unethical practices. They may not 'automatically' demonstrate 'good governance'. In addition, finally there is an area of social concern that the market does on take into account, in any case – the environment. This spells out the new role of companies in the 'domain of politics and ethics'. The corporation must be socially responsible, must display good governance and must be accountable towards the environment.

9.6 IMPLICATION OF GLOBALISATION

9.6.1 GLOBALISATION

Since the Second World War, barriers to international trade have been considerably lowered through international agreements – GATT. Particular initiatives carried out as a result of GATT and the World Trade Organization (WTO), for which GATT is the foundation, has included:

- Promotion of free trade:
    - elimination of tariffs; creation of free-trade zones with small or no tariffs,
    - reduced transportation costs, especially resulting from development of containerisation for ocean shipping,
    - reduction or elimination of capital controls,
    - reduction, elimination or harmonisation of subsidies for local businesses,
    - creation of subsidies for global corporations,
    - harmonisation of intellectual property laws across the majority of states, with more restrictions and
    - supranational recognition of intellectual property restrictions (e.g. patents granted by China would be recognised in the United States).

9.6.2 ECONOMIC GLOBALISATION

Looking specifically at economic globalisation, it centres on the four main economic flows that characterise globalisation:

- goods and services – exports and imports,
- labour/people – net migration, inward or outward,
- capital – inward or outward direct investment and portfolio investment and
- technology – international research and development flows.

9.6.3 GLOBALISATION, MARKET AND INEQUALITY

Thus globalisation has meant an all-round opening-up of world markets. This has lead to a basic contradiction between two contradictory principles – freedom and inequality – between which only imperfect compromises can ever be made. A completely free market is in fact 'anarchic'. There is no control whatsoever. There is a confrontation between strong and weak entities such that competition ceases to exist, thus jeopardising the very principle of freedom. It in fact, results in the impoverishment and exclusion large parts of the country and large number of countries in the world. Beyond a certain threshold, the process breaks the bonds that hold society together and threatens the existence of 'good society'. And so, the argument goes, there must be a counterweight to market forces; the law of the market must be contained and regulated by political bodies, which endeavour to maintain a certain balance between unbridled economic freedom and unchecked inequality.

Several attempts have been made this century to strike such a balance. For a wide variety of reasons, most of these attempts have failed.

This explains why in the past few years all kinds of attempts to liberalise markets and weaken the ideological basis of political interventionism have made great strides. The globalisation of financial, technological and information flows, in these conditions, has created a highly volatile market that knows no frontiers, is prone to unpredictable developments and rapidly changing situations. In this globalised market, competition favours big transnational groups (while not preventing the emergence of new pockets of prosperity) and no international body seems able to control economic behaviour or arbitrate, politically or legally, the conflicts resulting from it.

9.6.4 GLOBALISATION AND CORRUPTION

The globalisation of corruption, siphoning off drug money and feeding international crime, is one dramatic symptom of this state of affairs which is corroding the foundations of democracy and undermining familiar religious, ethnic and national landmarks. It should come as no surprise that two very different trends are developing in response to this widespread corruption – the strengthening of democratic control mechanisms and recourse to the dictatorship of closed identities.

9.7 GLOBAL CORPORATE RESPONSIBILITY

Although in its original form globalisation was meant to be a remedy for the restricted growth of closed economies, in fact, it has created its own problems. Given below is a strong argument about how globalisation has actually lead to disparities and how this leads to a great social responsibility that business, especially big business has to bear.

The global economy is poised to enter into a new phase of growth and development in the next millennium that shall be unprecedented. It has been over a decade and a half since the process of globalisation has started. Already signs of this massive change to be are visible. These are apparent from the trends in income distribution, trade, environmental pollution and so on. However, what is most apparent about these trends is the extreme disparity on a global scale.

Globalisation has meant growth on an unprecedented scale. The features of globalisation are growth, trade and urbanisation. Table 9.1 shows how the patterns of global development have caused wide differences amongst low-, middle- and high-development countries, in respect of the main features of globalisation. This means that globalisation has brought about massive differences in development amongst these countries. More of trade implies, in addition, that countries consume much more that what they produce. Greater urbanisation leads to consuming goods that are environmentally unfriendly. Most often these are global goods whose consumption is promoted globally. The differences in consumption are much starker. For instance, energy consumption is 77 times and paper consumption is 240 times! These are the two most environmentally damaging consumptions. Most of the benefit of this development is going to multi-national corporations. They benefit from consumption as they benefit from production. In addition, they are the ones who consume scarce (non-renewable resources).

Table 9.1 Inequality in Consumption and Environmental Degradation Across HDI Classes (Human Development Report, 2000, UNDP).

DEVELOPMENTAL STATUS	LOW:MIDDLE:HIGH	ENVIRONMENTAL STATUS	LOW:MIDDLE:HIGH
GDP (per capita)	1:4:19	Consumption	1:3:14
Trade	1:10:200	Paper consumption	1:21:240
Urbanisation	1:2:3	CO2 (per capita)	1:6:23
		CO2 share	1:30:60
		Water consumption	1:5:7
		Energy consumption	1:15:77

While it may be true that there are other ways in which this responsibility can be understood Table 9.1 and argument puts into sharp contrast the differences between rich and poor countries and the implications for development and the environment. It must be realised that MNCs have a great corporate responsibility since they are responsible for this global disparity in development. Thus, they have a responsibility towards global environmental sustainability and economic development, more than others.

9.8 CONCLUSION

From all that has been discussed above certain things are clear.

> "The marketplace is thus a crossroads, a meeting place of some key issues of the late twentieth century. In reporting on this crucial phenomenon we have tried to shed light not only on the ways in which it has changed and is changing but also, and above all, on its contradictory aspects."
>
> Elnadi and Rifaat

The new trend of markets and globalisation raises many ethical questions that are economic in nature. They relate to the behaviour of businesses, especially, multinationol corporations. For understanding these issues, we must go into the basics of business ethics and moral reasoning. We shall continue with this theme in Unit III.

Suggested Questions

1. What are the central problems of an economy? What does the market mechanism solve the central problems?
2. What is market failure? How does it result in the market not leading to the 'best solution'?
3. What is the need for control? How did social control evolve?
4. How have multinationals become powerful?
5. What is globalisation of markets and what are its implications?
6. What kind of role is expected of multinationals in respect of corporate responsibility?

Bibliography

Baud, M. F. (1996). Market globalization, UNESCO Courier, November.

David Miller (1989). *Market, State and Community: Theoretical Foundations of Market Socialism* (Oxford: Clarendon Press).

Elnadi, B. and A. Rifaat (1996). The marketplace: past and present, UNESCO Courier, November.

Jha, R. and K. V. Bhanu Murthy (2006). *Environmental Sustainability – A Consumption Approach*, Chapter 1 (London: Routledge).

World Bank (1996). *From Plan to Market* (World Development Report).

Unit III

Business Ethics and Moral Reasoning

Prof. K.V. Bhanu Murthy

In the previous Units, we have studied 'Thinking Conceptually about Politics' and 'Domain of Politics and Ethics'. The gist of the argument is that we desire a good society and believe that a democratic society and a market economy would meet the bill. However, all along it is clear that there are ethical issues thrown up by this conception. Do markets provide the 'best solution' to the problems of an economy? Does democracy ensure ethically superior solutions? Is the role of multi-national corporations ethically wanting?

So far, we have been referring to business ethics in a general way. However, to arrive at a better understanding of business ethics, it is necessary to clarify certain concepts and definitions.

We may consider a basic definition to begin with:

'The study of what is ethically permissible or what is positively virtuous in regard to business activity' (Carroll (2002)).[1]

It draws upon moral theory and concepts and brings these to bear on problems and issues that arise in and for business.

While the interest in business ethics is age old, it has started in a serious way since the 1970s as an academic discipline. It is recognised as a separate branch of study today but the underlying issues and problems are not new. In our own context, a pertinent example is that of the Bhopal gas tragedy, which occurred two decades ago. The interest in business ethics has heightened because in the past twenty years, there has been a change in the way that business is conducted and in how society perceives business.

Business ethics is being enmeshed with moral reasoning, philosophy of business and corporate responsibility. Since we are largely concerned with modern corporations it also is related to management ethics.

In this Unit, we shall be studying the following related aspects.

Chapter 10 is a basic chapter about 'Business Ethics' – its nature and its evolution. The main emphasis is on business ethics, philosophy of business and the role of business in society. This is a core chapter that lays down our understanding about business ethics and corporate responsibility.

Chapter 11 tells us about the 'Theories of Moral Reasoning' that is, the deontological and teleological approaches. It explains complex phenomena such as these with the help of simplified diagrams.

Chapter 12 lays out 'Business Ethics – Issues and New Developments'. It deals with changing social expectations of society from business. It also talks of new developments in ethical theories.

Chapter 13 is about ethical climate in organisations and its importance. It discusses three models of management morality that help us to understand 'good and bad' behaviour. It also talks of the importance of ethical decision making and 'ethics in management'.

---

[1] Archie B. Carroll (2002) Ethics in Management (Chapter 12) in Fredrick, R.E. (ed.) A Companion to Business Ethics, (Blackwell: London).

Business Ethics and Moral Reasoning

Prof. K.V. Bhanu Murthy

In the previous Units we have studied Economic Concepts about Politics and Domain of Politics and Ethics. The gist of the argument is that we desire a good society and believe that a democratic society and a market economy would meet the bill. However, all along it is clear that there are ethical issues thrown up by this conception. Do markets provide the best solution to the problems of an economy? Does democracy ensure ethically superior solutions? Is the role of multi-national corporations globally wanting?

So far, we have been referring to business ethics in a general way. However, to arrive at a better understanding of business ethics it is necessary to clarify certain concepts and definitions.

We may consider a basic definition to begin with:

[illegible]

In this Unit we shall be studying the following related aspects:

[illegible]

Chapter 10

Business Ethics

Prof. K.V. Bhanu Murthy

"Being good is good business"

Anita Roddick, British founder of 'The Body Shop'

LEARNING OUTCOMES

This is the first chapter on ethics and morality. It lays down the basics. You learn the fundamentals.

- You will come to know the nature of business ethics as a study area.
- You will become acquainted with level of business ethics.
- In addition, you would come to know about the evolution of business ethics.
- An understanding would develop about various approaches to the area.
- You would be able to distinguish between philosophy of business and business philosophy.
- You would gain from an in-depth understanding of the relationship between society and business in the new context.
- The crucial link between business ethics and corporate responsibility will become clear.

10.1 NATURE OF THE STUDY OF BUSINESS ETHICS

The two concepts that are closely related are ethics and morality. Ethics is a discipline, which deals with what is good and what is bad and with moral duty and obligations. Morality is a system or doctrine of ethical conduct. The word ethics derives from the Greek word *ethos*, meaning character or custom. There are various areas of ethics such as business ethics and medical ethics. Character or custom is hence defined by its context. Ethics would have a different connotation in the context of business and a different connotation in the context of medicine. In the context of an organisation it connotes 'an organisational code conveying moral integrity and consistent values in service to public'.

Business ethics is a form of applied ethics that examines ethical rules and principles within a commercial context, the various moral or ethical problems that can arise in a business setting and any special duties or obligations that apply to persons who are engaged in commerce.

Generally speaking, business ethics is a normative discipline, whereby particular ethical standards are advocated and then applied. It makes specific judgements about what is right or wrong, which is to say, it makes claims about what ought to be done or what ought not to be done. While there are some exceptions, business ethicists are usually less concerned with the foundations of ethics (meta-ethics), or with justifying the most basic ethical principles, and are more concerned with scientific theories, engineering precision and practical problems and applications that might apply to business relationships.

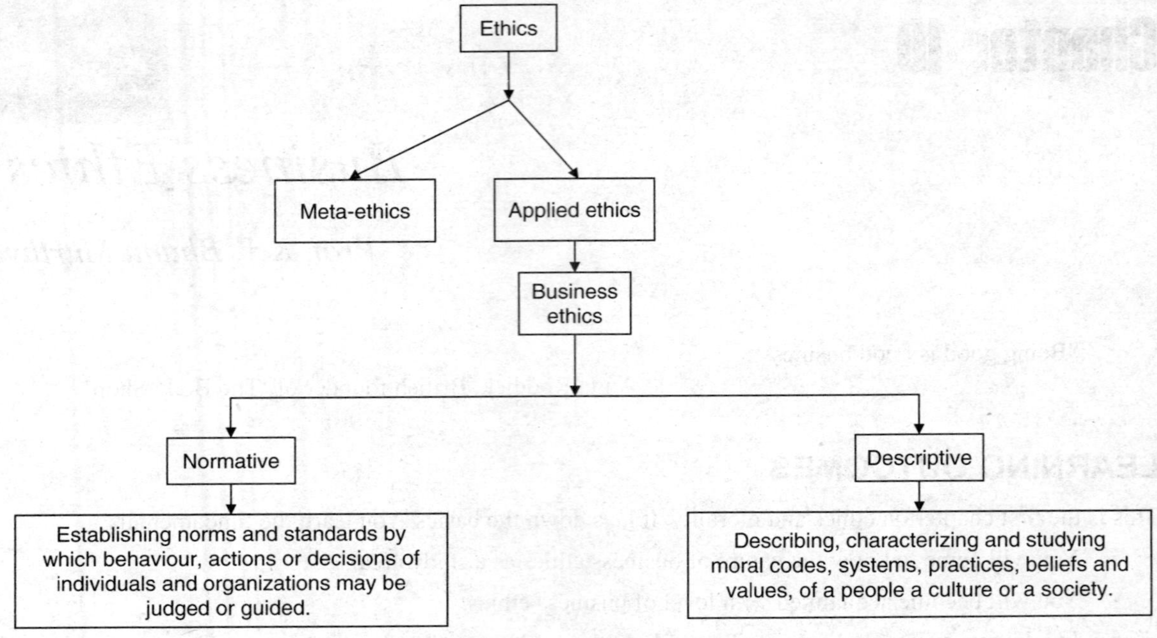

Figure 10.1 Antecedents of Business Ethics.

The limitation of descriptive ethics is that it deals with factual information that only explains what is happening and not what should happen, how it should be done and what are the standards for judgment. Normative studies look for solutions to problems through norms and standards.

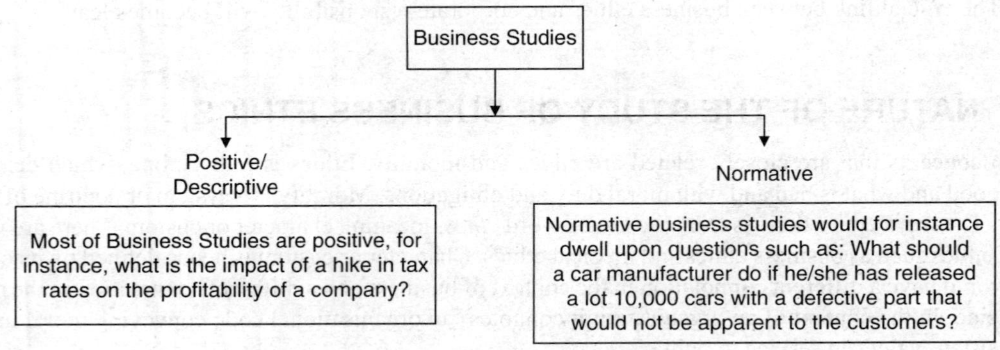

Figure 10.2 Types of Business Studies.

Some people believe that ethics need not be studied because it is an individual affair. However, business ethics could be a study of individuals or of corporations. Some of the individuals who have been in the news for the wrong reasons such as Harshad Mehta who indulged in a stock market scam or Abdul Karim Telgi who was responsible for fake stamp paper scam. On the other hand, there are companies such as Enron and WorldCom who were involved accounting scams and have lost their existence because of these malpractices. Thus, giants in business can fall overnight just because of unethical practices. When this happens, the consequences are *not individual*. Hence, it cannot be said that ethics is an individual affair and needs to be left to the individual.

Often their (un)ethical actions have led to a great loss to the society. It is often argued that the case for business ethics lies in ethical behaviour bettering the profits of the company. What is not emphasised is that a strong negative incentive exists for a company to pursue ethical practices. The cases of Enron and WorldCom amply make it clear that one single reason for a company to follow ethical practices is not profit but reputation. Their profits could not bail them out in the dire circumstances that lead to their debacle.

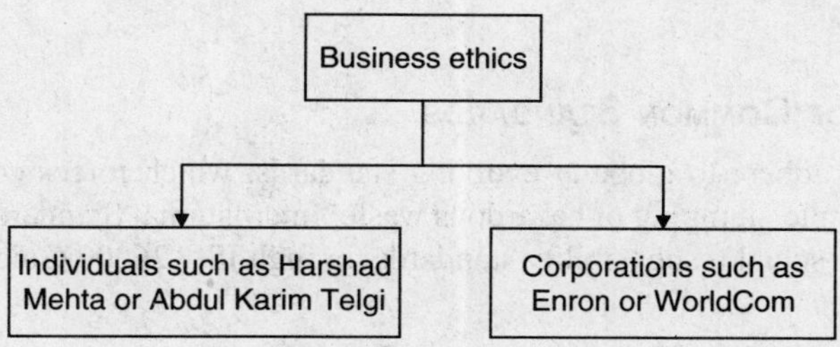

Figure 10.3 Ethics of Individuals and Corporations.

10.2 LEVELS OF BUSINESS ETHICS

There are levels of ethical practice and judgment. All these form a part of business ethics.

- Individual/personal,
- Organisational,
- Industry and
- Societal/country

Some examples of individual and company levels have been discussed above. In the case of industry, one pertinent issue is about pharmaceutical companies charging exorbitant prices for AIDS drugs.

At the country level, some of the hotly debated issues are non-implementation of child labour laws by developing countries. Businesses in India, Bangladesh and Sri Lanka often violate these laws and are able to produce cheap goods for export markets. On the other hand, the arms industry of developed countries often sells arms and ammunition to war torn developing countries that are at the brink of disaster.

10.3 EVOLUTION OF BUSINESS ETHICS

There are two views of history. The first view is that history has been created by the actions of individuals (kings, rulers etc.). The other view is that history has evolved on account of the real or 'material' circumstances. Individuals may rise to the occasion.

If we go by the second view, business ethics has arisen on account of certain trends that have taken place. Certain events have lead to the growth and development of business ethics as a discipline. The following trends have brought about this change.

10.3.1 DECLINE IN THE ROLE OF THE STATE

With globalisation and the new international economic order, the role of the government has declined in absolute as well as relative terms. This has directly affected certain social concerns such as health and education. There is a vacuum created because of this in the social sphere and businesses are bound to fill this vacuum.

10.3.2 IMPACT OF CONSUMER MOVEMENTS

Big businesses are under pressure due to social movements apart from the pressure of courts. Social awareness and social movements amongst consumers have increased. There are street plays and awareness programmes to awaken and enlighten consumers. 'Green Peace' is an excellent example of how a handful of spirited individuals can agitate through a social movement, to protect the environment, against big companies and bring them book.

10.3.3 EVOLUTION OF COMMON STANDARDS

There is peer pressure to adhere to globally evolving standards, which forces corporate bodies to eschew certain practices, for example, dumping of hazardous waste. International Standards Organization (ISO) is in the process of introducing social responsibility standards through ISO 26000 Guidance Standards[1]

10.3.4 ADVERSE IMPACT OF MULTI-NATIONAL CORPORATIONS

There is an increasing awareness of how multinational companies (MNCs) are capable of even manipulating the governments of domestic countries where they operate. There have been very infamous scandals associated with multi-nationals of repute, such as the Enron Corporation scandal. These are typical examples of unethical practices. Even the infamous Bhopal gas leak tragedy, caused by Union Carbide, a MNC, has brought to the fore the whole gamut of ethical questions related to business.

10.3.5 THREAT OF LEGAL ACTION

In recent times, the number of court cases against corporation by consumers has increased manifold. Exemplary legal action and heavy penalties have forced businesses to undertake self-regulatory policies and measures.

10.4 ETHICAL ISSUES AND APPROACHES

Philosophers and others disagree about the purpose of a business in society. For example, some suggest that the principal purpose of a business is to maximise returns to its owners, or in the case of a publicly traded concern, its shareholders. Thus, under this view, only those activities that increase profitability and shareholder value should be encouraged. Some believe that the only companies that are likely to survive in a competitive marketplace are those that place profit maximisation above everything else. However, some point out that self-interest would still require a business to obey the law and adhere to basic moral rules, because the consequences of failing to do so could be very costly in fines, loss of licensure or company reputation. The economist Milton Friedman is a leading proponent of this view.

> 'The Social Responsibility of Business is to Increase its Profits.'
>
> Milton Friedman

Other theorists contend that a business has moral duties that extend well beyond serving the interests of its owners or stockholders, and that these duties consist of more than simply obeying the law. They believe a business has moral responsibilities to so-called stakeholders, people who have an interest in the conduct of the business, which might include employees, customers, vendors, the local community or even society as

[1] As we shall be studying, social responsibility and business ethics are closely related.

a whole. They would say that stakeholders have certain rights with regard to how the business operates, and some would even suggest that this even includes rights of governance.

Some theorists have adapted social contract theory to business, whereby companies become quasi-democratic associations, and employees and other stakeholders are given voice over a company's operations (As discussed in the Chapters 7 and 8 of Unit II (i.e., "Democracy" and "Welfare State"). This approach has become especially popular subsequent to the revival of contract theory in political philosophy, which is largely due to John Rawls' *A Theory of Justice*, and the advent of the consensus-oriented approach to solving business problems, an aspect of the 'quality movement' that emerged in the 1980s. Professors Thomas Donaldson and Thomas Dunfee proposed a version of contract theory for business, which they call Integrative Social Contracts Theory. They posit that conflicting interests are best resolved by formulating a 'fair agreement' between the parties, using a combination of (a) macro-principles that all rational people would agree upon as universal principles and (b) micro-principles formulated by actual agreements among the interested parties.

Ethical issues can arise when companies must comply with multiple and sometimes conflicting legal or cultural standards, as in the case of multi-national companies that operate in countries with varying practices. The question arises, for example, ought a company to obey the laws of its home country, or should it follow the less stringent laws of the developing country in which it does business? To illustrate, US law forbids companies from paying bribes either domestically or overseas; however, in other parts of the world, bribery is a customary, accepted way of doing business. Similar problems can occur with regard to child labour, employee safety, work hours, wages, discrimination and environmental protection laws.

It is sometimes claimed that a Gresham's law of ethics applies in which bad ethical practices drive out good ethical practices. It is claimed that in a competitive business environment, those companies that survive are the ones that recognise that their only role is to maximise profits. On this view, the competitive system fosters a downward ethical spiral.

10.5 BUSINESS ETHICS AND PHILOSOPHY OF BUSINESS

Certain misnomers that have crept into the domain of the study of business ethics and social responsibility need to be examined before proceeding any further. The first relates to the fundamental basis of social responsibility and the second is about the relationship between business ethics and corporate social responsibility (CSR) or simply social responsibility.

It has become almost passé highlight a case for CSR by eulogising the benefits of social responsibility programmes for the bottom-line, that is, for profit. The justification for such an approach arises out of business strategy. In turn, business strategy relates to business philosophy. While having stated the premise of business philosophy it is important to distinguish between business philosophy and philosophy of business.

Business philosophy is a driving force of a particular business. For instance, the 'business philosophy' of Tata's might be to develop a business that is quality conscious and produces products that are within the reach of the common person. On the other hand, philosophy of business explains the moral principles that underlie business as a domain. It goes into the purpose of business and the ethical basis and consequences of business. Therefore, "business philosophy" relates to the vision of a company whereas 'philosophy of business' is an area of study. It is a sub-discipline of philosophy. 'business philosophy' may or may not include the ethical dimensions but 'philosophy of business' necessarily does. Peter Drucker and some leading management thinkers believe that it need not.

'There is neither a separate ethics of business nor is one needed.'

Peter Drucker

However, the 'philosophy of business' necessarily and clearly is concerned with the ethical foundations of business as a discipline[2]. It is in a similar vein to Hoffman and Moore (1982) that this paper seeks to 'clarify the nature, scope and purpose of business ethics.'

Philosophy of business is an area of knowledge that refers to an understanding of the moral and ethical basis of business. Just as medicine is an area of knowledge, business ethics is an area of knowledge. Philosophy deals with knowledge. It answers the question of what the role of a business is and as to what is the ethical basis of judgment of whether it is fulfilling its role or not. To draw an analogy, if the role of medicine is to cure, the question is as to whether it is right for medicine to produce artificial genetic material (genomic varieties of new forms of life, new species). Therefore, while business philosophy is a part of business policy or strategy, the philosophy of business is a part of applied philosophy. To answer Peter Drucker, since applied philosophy is different for each applied discipline, business ethics is a 'separate' study and needs to be so. Business philosophy is a way of conducting business so as to achieve the goals of a particular business. We have just said that philosophy of business is a distinct area of study. What is the study about? To emphasise that this issue is very much current and live, we quote a recent study.

> Understanding the rules and conventions of business is one of the main tasks for the philosophy of business. In one of its forms, this is known as 'business ethics'. The other main task understands how business is possible…
>
> Geoffrey Kempner (2006)

To which we need to add, 'What is the purpose of business?' Philosophy of business examines the purpose of business.

> A more complete definition of philosophy of business that we could give is:
>
> The philosophy of business considers the fundamental principles that underlie the formation, existence and operation of a business enterprise; the nature and role of a business as defined by society; and the moral obligation of business towards society.

10.6 BUSINESS AND SOCIETY

It is the perception about the nature of business and its relationship with society that defines the 'social responsibility of business'. It determines what the responsibility of business towards society is and hence, the setting up standards of such responsibility is based on philosophy of business since it is concerned with 'the fundamental principles that underlie the formation, existence and operation of a business enterprise'. The three inter-related aspects of the philosophy of business are:

1. nature of business,
2. its role in society and
3. its moral obligations towards society.

We first discuss the traditional notion of these aspects of business and then shall examine the shift in the paradigm. In the process, we shall take up the second misnomer by which it is believed that business ethics and social responsibility are unrelated things.

---

[2] See Hoffman and Moore (1982) Abstract: 'In his *What Is "Business Ethics"?* Peter Drucker accuses business ethics of singling out business unfairly for special ethical treatment, of subordinating ethical to political concerns, and of being, not 'ethics' at all, but 'ethical chic'. We contend that Drucker's denunciation of business ethics rests upon a fundamental misunderstanding of the field. This article is a response to his charges and an effort to clarify the nature, scope and purpose of business ethics.'

10.6.1 Nature of Business

Traditionally, business has been seen as a property institution rather than a social institution. In its conventional form, the primary motive of business was to earn profits. It was believed that business should earn profits at any cost. This implies that the domain of business as an entity was distinct and independent from that of the rest of society.

10.6.2 Role of Business in Relation to Other Entities

Traditionally, society expected business to produce goods and services as per the need of its members. Business as well as society expected the state or government to take care of other social and environmental concerns. Further, it was assumed that the managers would automatically meet the interest of shareholders.

10.6.3 Moral Obligation of Business

The conventional understanding is that a business is obliged to recompense factors of production, which it does through the market mechanism. The factor incomes are commensurate to their contribution to social product. The price paid for other resources, including natural resources, is equal to the cost of those in real terms. Hence, it is purported that a business automatically discharges its moral obligation towards society and does so in full measure.

The above argument leads to a position that business ethics is distinct and unrelated to social responsibility. The argument is that if business has effectively discharged its obligation towards society through the market mechanism then it has done so by *quid pro quo*. There is nothing wrong with such conduct. Its activities are in the interest of society and are demanded by society on the one hand, and it adequately compensates society, on the other hand. Therefore, no ethical question remains if business pursues its activities in the ordinary course. Hence, there is no such omnibus notion of business ethics that applies in general. It then reduces to how individual managers or entrepreneurs behave and this is governed by general ethics or individual ethics. It has nothing to do with business as a class. Thus, there is no scope for business ethics, as such. Any social activity or programme carried out by a business is hence, only voluntary, sans any moral obligation or ethical consideration. Therefore, business ethics is disparate from corporate social responsibility, as per the extant notion quoted above.

10.7 PARADIGM SHIFT

Over a period of the two decades since Drucker made his remarks about business ethics, there has been tremendous change in the paradigm, which is the result of two shifts. The first shift relates to the philosophy of business. The new perspective has broken down this compartmentalisation of business and society and by now, it has been realised that social and environmental issues can no longer be addressed entirely through a unilateral imposition by the state through a legal framework. In the light of this new development, the business had to gear itself to rethink to develop new theories and practices of management to align itself with this breakdown. Besides this, the phenomena of a rapid decline in the role of the state and withdrawal of the state from the social space have created a vacuum. As the needs and the imbalances in the society have not changed, the business has to emerge as the filler. The roles, relationships and realms of the three entities – the government, the business and the society – have changed. The first implication is that this imposes a corporate responsibility of businesses towards society. This is indicative of a paradigm shift in the philosophy of business.

By the existing philosophy of business, a business only had a responsibility towards its shareholder by earning profit for them. This was the understood as the role of business. Business was 'possible' because society desired this role of it.

Here, we wish to make a strong axiomatic enunciation, namely, if the philosophy of business is about 'how business is possible?' and about 'formation and operation of a business enterprise', then it automatically includes the premise of 'how business may not be possible' and how instead of 'formation and operation of a business enterprise' how a business may cease 'to operate'. The basis of the philosophy of business should naturally include its obverse. Hence, the philosophic basis of business does not arise out of 'business strategy' and is not buttressed by how CSR enhances profits. It lies in not only explaining, 'how business is possible?' but in explaining 'how businesses cease to operate?' or 'how businesses fail?' And, how this is not merely a question of finance or profit, for some of the most profitable concerns and giants at that have failed (Sims, 2003).

Hence, earlier businesses could be formed and could be operated successfully without including in their conduct anything that is a concern of society, beyond what is valued, created and delivered through the market. It was assumed that any responsibility that business had towards society is duly discharged through the market mechanism. Services, goods, raw materials and other resources that are drawn by business from society are adequately recompensed by the price established by the price mechanism. The prevailing philosophy was content with such a notion.

Now, the second implication of the paradigm shift is that businesses can no longer afford to do so. A business has to be responsible towards society. It has to be accountable to the environment. And, it has to be good to its shareholders. Without having such ethical conduct in business, it may cease to exist. The entire three dimensions arise out of business ethics, particularly out of the newfound role of business, and directly relate to business ethics. Thus, there is a need to incorporate in their 'business philosophy' all the three dimensions. There is a need to treat corporate responsibility as a package of three dimensions (a) good governance, (b) CSR and (c) environmental accountability. This implies that all three of them co-exist and can no longer be put in three watertight compartments. Business has been forced to accept corporate responsibility in its entirety, which means amalgamation of all the three dimensions taken together.

10.7.1 IMPLICATIONS OF SHIFTS IN PARADIGM

On the one hand, the above-mentioned shifts have resulted into a merging of business philosophy with business ethics, which were earlier distinct from each other and on the other hand, corporate responsibility is understood in its true sense; that is as a complete package. We now reconsider the renewed perception about the basis of business due to the shift in paradigm. The three interrelated aspects of the philosophy of business are:

1. nature of business,
2. its role in society and
3. its moral obligations towards society.

10.7.1.1 Nature of Business

There is a transformation in the nature of business. It cannot be continued to be viewed merely as a property. Internally, there are many dimensions of society that reside in the business, for instance, diversity across cultures and communities prevail amongst the employees. Secondly, there is scope for discrimination at the work place as there could be in the society, in general. This way business becomes more and more a microcosm of society. Externally, it has been pointed out that the decline of the state has lead to a vacuum in the social space.

10.7.1.2 Role of Business

This is no longer restricted to carrying out ordinary economic activity in pursuit of profit but to fulfil the gap uncovered by the state. Hence, the role is, at least, in part, that of a social institution. Therefore, the social responsibility of business has grown. Issues such as discrimination and diversity have nothing to do with profits. Yet it is an ethical norm of society that discrimination at the workplace is unethical. There is an expectation of society that a business would not indulge in discrimination. It is therefore indicative of a shift in the paradigm. Many more things can be pointed out in this direction that point towards a role of business that is socially responsible.

10.7.1.3 Moral Obligation of Business

Most importantly, this social obligation is not an undischarged or unfulfilled responsibility of business. It is apart from the obligation meted out to contracting parties such as vendors, employees or the government. For instance, if there is a natural calamity in an area adjoining of the business, there is an expectation of society that the business would participate in relief work. This has nothing to do with its ordinary economic activity where it might have discharged its obligation. Such a social responsibility arises out ethical considerations and not out of any consideration of profit. Therefore, the responsibility towards society is a moral obligation arising out of business ethics which in turn is steeped in philosophy of business.

10.8 BUSINESS ETHICS AND CORPORATE RESPONSIBILITY

Therefore, by our newfound understanding, it is necessary to visualise the relationship between philosophy of business, business ethics and the three elements of social responsibility of business, which could also be called as corporate responsibility.

Companies, which develop this understanding and accordingly build up their business philosophy, may not run the risk of scandals, failure and closure. It is for society to lay down the norms of business ethics that are expected of businesses. Such norms would be in keeping with the notion of philosophy of business and would clarify the social responsibility of business or simply corporate responsibility. It is then for the owners of businesses to have this realisation so as to guide the business philosophy in such a manner that there is no conflict of interest between profit making and doing ethical business. It is not for businesses to specify their own nature, role and moral obligation towards society but that of society to do so. It is for businesses to follow in right earnest in their own interest. It would be in the interest of the continued existence of business and their reputation that business is done ethically and in a socially responsible manner as defined above. Such a notion does not use profit as an argument for justifying social responsibility. It actually points out that in the event that a business fails to meet its 'social responsibility towards the people, planet and profit' it runs the risk of closure, which is a censure by society for not living up to the norms and standards of ethical behaviour that the society expects of a business. The societal reprisal does not arise on account of any wrong doing in the ordinary course of business but as a rebuff for not living up to the expectations of society in terms of its expected nature, role and moral obligation explained above.

10.9 CONCLUSION

Business ethics is a form of applied ethics that examines ethical rules and principles within a commercial context. It has both a positive and a normative aspect. It deals with the expectations of society from business and is based on philosophy of business. It specifies the ethical norms and standards and moral reasoning evolved by society in respect of the three pillars of corporate responsibility, namely, corporate governance, corporate social responsibility and environmental accountability.

It is an umbrella term under which the ethical rights and duties existing between companies and society is debated. The concerns include issues of leadership or governance, political contributions, corporate scandals, marketing strategies and human resource management. From the above exposition, it becomes clear that we can no longer separate. Corporate responsibility or social responsibility of business form business ethics. From now on, we should treat corporate responsibility as arising out of philosophy of business and as the overall responsibility of business towards planet, people and profit, while not being disparate from business ethics.

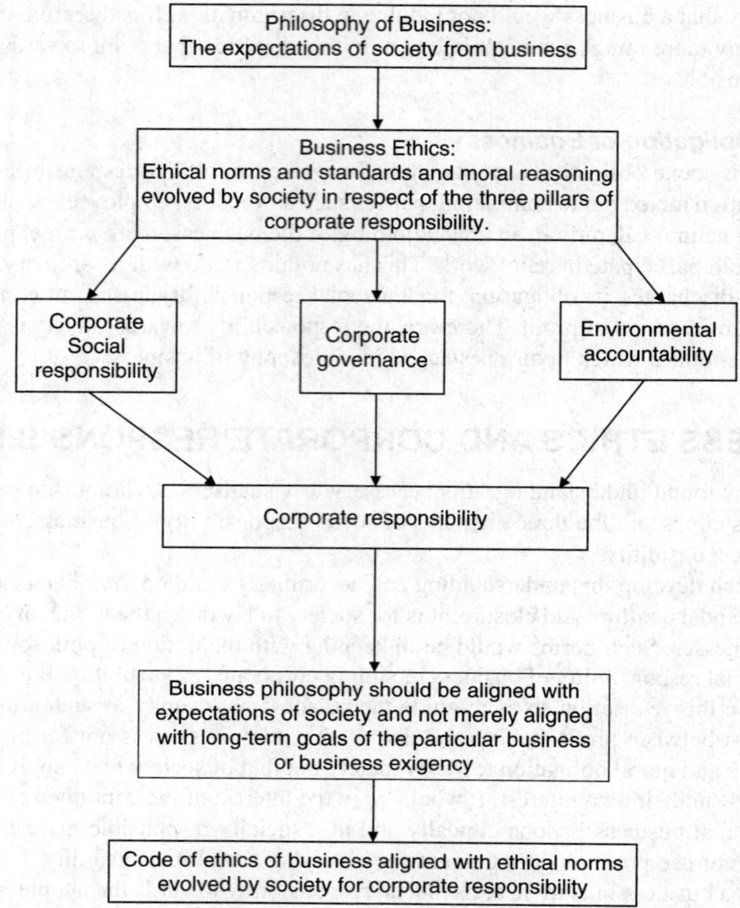

Figure 10.4 From Philosophy of Business to Company Code of Ethics.

Suggested Questions

1. 'There is neither a separate ethics of business nor one needed' - Peter Drucker. Critically analyse this statement.
2. 'It is the perception about the nature of business and its relationship with society that defines the 'social responsibility of business'.' Discuss.
3. What are the development in ethical issues and approaches to business ethics?
4. Distinguish between business philosophy and philosophy of business.
5. How can we explain the relationship between business ethics and corporate responsibility?
6. Explain the paradigm shift in the relationship between business and society

Bibliography

Bhanu Murthy, K. V. (2007) 'Business ethics and corporate responsibility – a new perspective', Papers and Proceedings of Workshop on ISO 26000 Guidance on Social Responsibility and the Implications for Developing Countries, 16–17 April, New Delhi.

Friedman, Milton (1970). The social responsibility of business is to increase its profits, *The New York Times Magazine*, September 13.

Hoffman, W. M. and Moore, J. M. (1982). 'What is business ethics? A reply to Peter Drucker'. *Journal of Business Ethics,* Vol. 1, No. 4, November.

Klempner (2006). 'On being a business philosopher', *Philosophies for Business*. E-journal, Issue 26, 5 February.

Sims, R. R. (2003). *Ethics and Corporate Social Responsibility: Why Giants Fall* (West Port, CT: Pragear).

Drucker, P. F. (1981). What is 'Business Ethics'? *The Public Interest* Spring, Vol. 63, PP 18–36.

Chapter 11

Theories of Moral Reasoning

Prof. K.V. Bhanu Murthy

"Right is right, even if everyone is against it; and wrong is wrong, even if everyone is for it."
William Penn

LEARNING OUTCOMES

The basics of moral theory shall be discussed in this chapter. There are certain things that you will gain from this chapter.

- You will understand the fundament basis of moral theory.
- You will be able to distinguish between two parts of moral theory.
- An evaluation of the two reigning theories of deontology and teleology will be possible.
- The value of moral reasoning theories for business ethics will be known.

11.1 INTRODUCTION

We have said that 'ethics is about what is right or wrong'. The statement is superfluous because 'right' includes 'wrong'. What is not 'right' is 'wrong' so it need not be stated separately.

Hence, ethics is about what is 'right'. However, this does not make it clear whether we mean 'right' about our actions or 'right' about the goals of our actions. This involves moral judgment.

11.2 MORAL THEORY

Moral theory involves two parts.

Textbooks speak of the above two parts as 'first part' and the 'second part' of moral theory. The confusion arises because the moment we say 'first' and 'second', it means that the first part comes before and 'takes precedence' over the second part. Therefore, we simply say that it has two parts without saying which is first or which comes second.

In almost all the debates in philosophy, the questions are not about whether two things co-exist or not, it is about which of the two things takes precedence over the other. For instance, does mind take precedence over matter; or matter take precedence over mind? Both mind and matter exist [1].

---

[1] The two schools of thought – idealism and materialism – differ on the basis of what takes precedence – mind or matter.

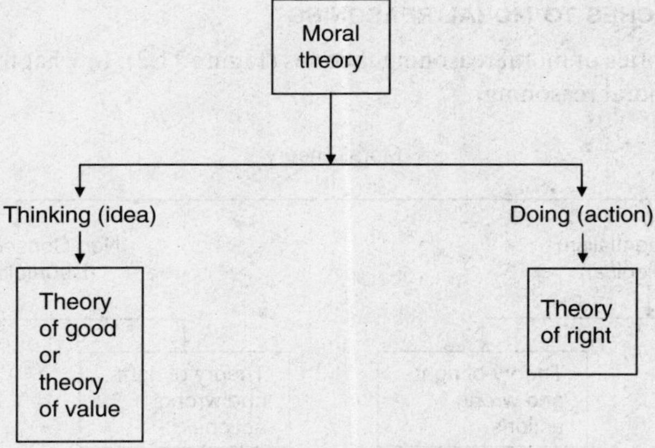

Figure 11.1 Moral Theory.

Therefore, we simply say that moral theory has two parts without saying which is first or which is second. Hence, moral theory involves two parts. One is the 'theory of good' and the second is the 'theory of right'. Moral theory is in general described in the context of 'thinking' and 'doing'. Alternately, it is about 'ideas' and 'actions'. If we do not think or act, there is no scope for moral judgement; there is no role of ethics or morality, since ethics and morality are about human behaviour which is thinking and acting.

When we say precedence, it could mean two things:

1. What happens first and what happens later? This is about 'ordering'.
2. What is more important and what is less important? This is about importance.

If we apply the 'ordering' connotation to moral theory what we mean is that our actions will always precede our goals. This is a tautology, which is a basic truth that needs no further proof.

However, the whole debate in moral theory is not about this tautology since there cannot be any further reasoning about a tautology [2]. The debate is about which of the two components – theory of good or theory of right – is more important.

Once we know what the debate is about it is easier to understand and reason.

We have earlier said that there are two parts:

1. What is right about our actions?
2. What is right about our goals?

When it comes to actions, we can say 'right' or 'wrong'. However, it would be odd to say 'right' or 'wrong' or 'ends' or 'goals'. It is always better to say 'good' or 'bad', when we talk of 'goals'. Goals are like dreams, so we have good dreams and bad dreams, not right or wrong dreams. Thus, one part of moral theory is about what is good. Obviously, what is good is valuable; therefore, one part of moral theory is the theory of good or theory of the valuable or simply the 'theory of value'. The second part of moral theory is about what should be done or what is right. What should individual organisations, institutions or companies do?

Hence, the debate in ethics is about whether we should do right because we think that it could cause some good or whether we should do right irrespective of the consequence of our actions. In other words, should our ethics depend upon the consequences of our actions? This brings us to the core of our debate in moral reasoning.

[2] By definition, tautology is one that does not have any further argument or reasoning. It is a basic assumption or basic truth.

11.2.1 TWO APPROACHES TO MORAL REASONING

There are two broad categories of moral reasoning theories (Figure 11.2). In what follows, we have discussed the two main theories of moral reasoning.

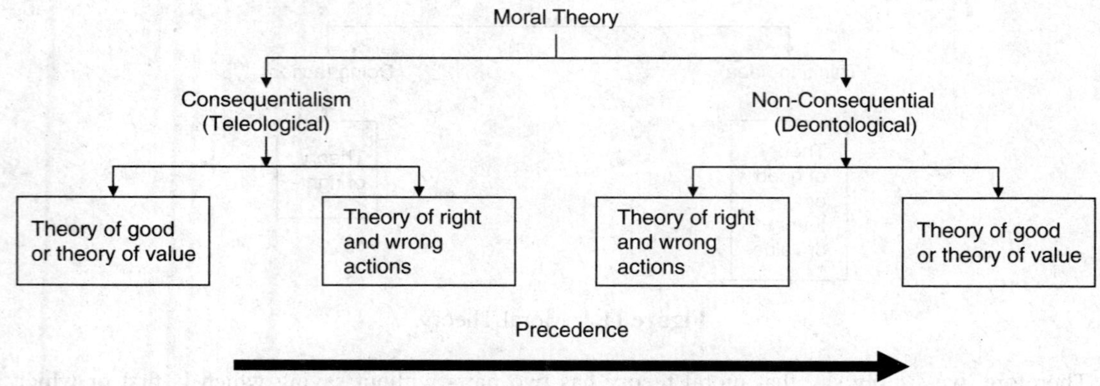

Figure 11.2 Approaches to Moral Reasoning.

11.2.2 DEFINITION OF CONSEQUENTIALISM OR TELEOLOGY

The idea or concept that rightness or wrongness of action is determined by goodness or badness of its results. The right action is the one that has the best consequences

The teleological approach is akin to consequentialism and derives from the Greek word *telos*, which means end or goal.

11.2.3 DEFINITION OF DEONTOLOGY

The concept or idea that actions are intrinsically right or wrong, regardless of their consequences.

The advantage with consequentialism is that it provides us with a moral standard in which the end justifies the means. With the establishment of norms and standards, consequentialism lends itself better as a pragmatic basis of corporate social responsibility. Deontology on the other hand, lays down an absolute or idealistic basis for ethical behaviour (Figure 11.3).

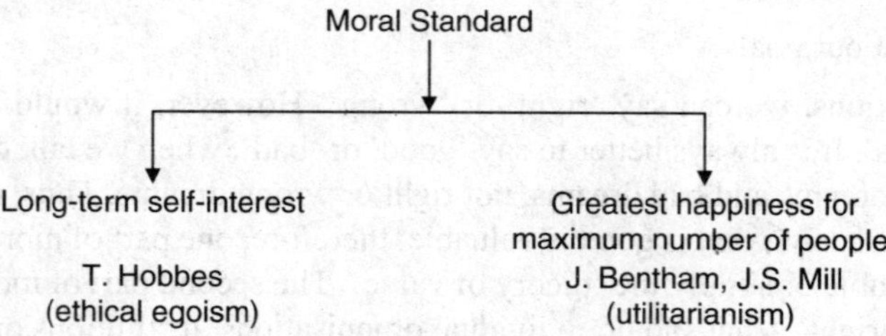

Figure 11.3 Moral Standards.

11.3 MORAL REASONING AND BUSINESS ETHICS

Business decisions, by their nature, involve ethical considerations because (1) most economic decisions are choices where the decision maker could have done otherwise, (2) every decision or action affects people and

(3) every decision or set of decisions is embedded in a belief system that presupposes some basic values or their abrogation. Thus, business management by nature involves moral reasoning. Since business decisions have consequences for both the business and the society at large moral theory applies the behaviour of business. Business ethics hence involves the application of moral reasoning or moral theory to business situations and decisions. If there no conflict exists between the business and society, there would be no need to apply moral reasoning to determine good or bad though or actions by business. But more often than not there is a conflict regarding the location of a business, the price and quality of goods, the return to the investor or owner, the impact on the environment and so on.

The above study shows that the conflict between social interest and individual interest is founded in different kinds of moral standards and not between different moral reasoning approaches. Therefore, corporate social responsibility, whether pursued by self-interest or social interest, essentially is in the realm of consequentialism, either as ethical egoism or utilitarianism. With non-consequentialism, there is no expected outcome and therefore there is no scope for standards or benchmarks for measuring or evaluating moral conduct in the pursuit of business. The ethical behaviour cannot be measured objectively by others if the ethical basis of business is founded in non-consequentialism. It is, therefore, more pragmatic to determine business ethics as a study in consequential moral reasoning.

11.4 CONCLUSION

There are two parts of moral theory: theory of right and theory of good. Accordingly, there are two approaches to moral reasoning: consequentialism and non-consequentialism. The difference between these approaches lies in the importance that each approach gives to the two types of moral theory. These approaches help in laying down moral standards and ethical behaviour. Business ethics can be better understood with the help of consequentialism because it lends itself to moral judgement standards.

Suggested Questions

1. What is ethics and moral reasoning?
2. With the help of the two parts of moral theory, explain the difference between consequential and non-consequential approaches to moral reasoning.
3. Discuss the appeal to theory of right.
4. How can we justify consequentialism?
5. For evaluating ethical behaviour of business which moral theory is better and why?

Bibliography

Nancy (Ann) Davis (1993). Contemporary deontology (Chapter 17). In: Peter Singer (ed.), *A Companion to Ethics* (Maldem, MA: Blackwell).

Phillip Pettit (1993). Consequentialism (Chapter 19). In: Peter Singer (ed.), *A Companion to Ethics* (Oxford: Blackwell).

Ronald R. Sims (2003). *Ethics and Corporate Social Responsibility: Why Giants Fall?* (Westport, CT: Greenwood).

Chapter 12

Business Ethics Issues and New Developments

Prof. K.V. Bhanu Murthy and Dr Usha Krishna

> "The term 'business ethics' is used in a lot of different ways, and the history of business ethics will vary depending on how one conceives of the object under discussion."
>
> Richard T. De George

LEARNING OUTCOMES

This chapter furthers the thought process of understanding the basis of business ethics. It tells us about some new developments in the area. You will learn the following things from this chapter.

- You will be generally informed about business.
- You will be made aware of the new expectations of society from business.
- The different areas of business ethics shall be known to you.
- You would gain from knowledge of some new developments in business ethics.

12.1 OVERVIEW OF BUSINESS ETHICS

Business ethics is an umbrella term under which the ethical rights and duties existing between companies and the society are debated. Interest in business ethics as an academic discipline has came into prominence with number of corporate scandals that have cajoled the consciousness of policymakers, social scientists and activists equally. The underlying reasons for these have primarily been the unethical business practices. In some cases, the unethical nexus between political leaders and business leaders has resulted in the death knell of companies. On the one hand, institutionalisation of ethical climate in organisations and on the other hand, regulatory mechanisms may be the panacea to the damage caused due to scandals in the world today. The significant issues in business ethics include 'ethical management of enterprise' in relation to its stakeholders in particular and natural environment in general. The topics for study concern leadership or governance, political contributions, corporate scandals, marketing strategies, human relations and rights of employees, consumers, etc. While making decisions at enterprise level managers face many ethical challenges arising out of contradictions in the interests of employees, consumers, shareholders and financiers. Managers may also face the dilemma related to contrast between individual values versus organisational values. The solution the challenges is being attempted by the development of normative framework of business ethics. Thus, the study of business ethics has assumed significance for students of business as well as practitioners.

12.2 BUSINESS ETHICS AND SOCIETY

The underlying reasons for the recent scandals relate to moral degradation of leadership. Political interference in the business, demanding favours from business in return for business leaders demanding protection for unethical business practices. It may be the simple explanation to the reasons behind the scams that occurred in recent past resulting in short-term personal gains for individuals but great loss for the society. Apart from the scams, corruption, lack of transparency, unethical practices and unholy nexus between immoral agents are other fallouts to the above.

Multinational corporations are powerful enough to dodge smaller governments, dump obsolete technology, dump wastes and indulge in unethical trade by bribing the petty politicians of a country. This changing equation between the society and business has changed the expectations of society from business. This has necessitated that corporations be more responsible towards society, environment and planet.

The business too does not want to lose reputation, and has come forward to do what it takes to prevent loss of business. There are attempts to deal with the issue of quality, transparency, accountability and governance by proper development of guidelines. However, all such efforts are in infancy, and have fuelled interest in business ethics. The current interest in business ethics does not stem from the obvious unethical practices per se but from the changing expectations of the society from business. Some of these are explained in the box below.

Box 12.1 Changing Social Expectations of Society from Business.

- With globalisation and the new international economic order, the role of the government has declined in absolute as well as relative terms. There are changing social expectations from business. It is expected to take over some of the social programmes that hitherto have been assumed to be the responsibility of governments.
- Big businesses are under pressure from consumer groups to justify their ethical profiles to public at large. Consumers have become vocal not only in exercising their rights but also in demanding that business must explicitly state their policies, business processes and practices.
- There is need for countries to agree on common standards of labour, environment, quality etc. and to adhere to globally evolving standards. It forces corporate to eschew certain practices, for example, dumping of hazardous waste and pollution control. The managements need to spell out their codes of conduct.
- There is an increasing awareness that multinational corporations are capable of even manipulating the governments of domestic countries where they operate. What is the extent to which they should get involved in the politics of other countries?
- The corporations operating in different countries cannot afford to lose the business due to behaviour that may be called unethical. In addition, exemplary legal action and heavy penalties have forced businesses to undertake self-regulatory policies and measures. Firms are expected to explicitly state what practices or policies should be banned and why. The biggest conflict managers' face arises not from their own ethics and values but the ambiguity concerning what is ethically 'defensible' or 'appropriate'. The managers' ethical dilemma further accentuates when they have to balance their commitments to investor, workers, employees and communities.

12.3 BUSINESS ETHICS IN MANAGEMENT

The ethical challenges and issues in managing a company have been explained below in a brief manner.

12.3.1 BUSINESS ETHICS AND ACCOUNTING

Creative accounting and earnings management are euphemisms referring to accounting practices that may or may not follow the letter of the rules of standard accounting practices but certainly deviate from the spirit of those rules. They are characterised by excessive complication and the use of novel ways of characterising income, assets or liabilities. The terms 'innovative' or 'aggressive' are also sometimes used.

The term as generally understood refers to systematic misrepresentation of the true income and assets of corporations or other organisations. 'Creative accounting' is at the root of a number of recent accounting scandals, and many proposals for accounting reform – usually centring on an updated analysis of capital and factors of production that would correctly reflect how value is added.

Newspaper and television journalists have hypothesised that the stock market downturn of 2002 was precipitated by reports of accounting irregularities at the Enron, WorldCom and other business entities in the United States.

12.3.2 ETHICS OF HUMAN RESOURCE MANAGEMENT

The ethics of human resource management (HRM) covers those ethical issues arising around the employer–employee relationship, such as the rights and duties owed between employer and employee.

Discrimination issues include discrimination on the bases of age (ageism), gender, race, religion, disabilities, weight and attractiveness; also sexual harassment.

A large number of issues are enlisted here.

Issues surrounding the representation of employees and the democratisation of the workplace: union busting, strike breaking etc.

Issues affecting the privacy of the employee: workplace surveillance, drug testing etc.

Issues affecting the privacy of the employer – whistle blowing.

Issues relating to the fairness of the employment contract and the balance of power between employer and employee. Non-payment of minimum wages.

Indentured servitude is one type of slavery. Typically, the employer provided little or no monetary pay, but was responsible for accommodation, food, other essentials and training. Upon completion of the term of the contract, the labour sometimes received a lump sum payment.

Occupational safety and health (OSH) is another dimension of HRM. The primary view of, and in the view of many, the most prominent reason for establishing OSH standards is moral – an employee should not have to expect that by coming to work life or limb is at risk, nor should others be adversely affected by their undertaking.

12.3.3 ETHICS OF SALES AND MARKETING

Marketing which goes beyond the mere provision of information about (and access to) a product may seek to manipulate our values and behaviour. To some extent, society regards this as acceptable, but where is the ethical line to be drawn?

Pricing strategies: price discrimination and cartelisation are some of such methods. The OPEC countries are often accused of such behaviour of cartelisation.

Anti-competitive practices: these include but go beyond pricing tactics to cover issues such as manipulation of loyalty and supply chains. Foreclosure of raw materials and critical inputs: Cola companies often corner bottles of a competitor. They give incentives to vendors asking them not to stock the competitor's product.

Specific marketing strategies: green wash. Policies that make their products appear to be environmentally friendly. There are many so-called 'natural' cosmetics that are in fact chemical based.

Social issues in marketing include: Content of advertisements – sex in advertising, for instance. Children and marketing: marketing in schools that encourage anti-social trends such as gambling. Pokemon card is one such example. Black markets and grey markets are another dimension. A black market price pinches those who need a product the most. It could be a medicine during an epidemic. Grey markets encourage the sale of stolen or poor quality goods or by circumventing legal provisions such as taxes.

12.3.4 Ethics of Production

This area of business ethics deals with the duties of a company to ensure that products and production processes do not cause harm. Some of the more acute dilemmas in this area arise out of the fact that there is usually a degree of danger in any product or production process and it is difficult to define a degree of permissibility, or the degree of permissibility may depend on the changing state of preventative technologies or changing social perceptions of acceptable risk. The case of pesticides in Colas, in recent times, in India clearly enunciates this issue.

Defective, addictive and inherently dangerous products and services: Tobacco products, such as cigarettes and gutka, are example of such products.

Ethical relations between the company and the environment: pollution of water and air and waste disposal are typical issues of environmental ethics.

Ethical problems arising out of new technologies are another area of concern. For instance, genetically modified food raises the issue of whether we should tamper with nature for the sake of profit. In the case of mobile phone, radiations cause and health problems.

Product testing ethics: animal testing is very common in developing medicines. In fact for obtaining the raw material of many cosmetics many animals are tortured.

12.3.5 Ethics of Intellectual Property, Knowledge and Skills

Knowledge and skills are valuable but not easily 'ownable' objects. Nor is it obvious as to who has the greater rights to an idea: the company that trained the employees or the employees themselves? The country in which the plant grew or the company which discovered and developed the plant's medicinal potential? As a result, attempts to assert ownership and ethical disputes over ownership arise.

Intellectual property issues: arise when there is a patent infringement, copyright infringement or a trademark infringement. An example of patenting issues is that of Indian products such as basmati rice being patented by the United States.

Employee raiding or poaching: the practice of attracting key employees away from a competitor to take unfair advantage of the knowledge or skills they may possess.

Bioprospecting: it is exploring the forest wealth for commercial use with any partnership or joint venture arrangement is ethical. However, biopiracy such as patenting neem and haldi in unethical because India has a natural and cultural right over them.

12.3.6 International Business Ethics

While business ethics emerged as a field in the 1970s, international business ethics did not emerge until the late 1990s, reflecting the international developments of that decade. Many new practical issues arose out of the international context of business. Theoretical issues such as cultural relativity of ethical values receive more emphasis in this field. Other, older issues can be grouped here as well.

12.3.7 Issues and Subfields Include

Ethical issues arising out of international business transactions; for example, the fair trade movement and transfer pricing. In the case of fair trade, it has been seen that farmers often are unable to obtain fair prices because of unfair competition from multinationals.

The way in which multinationals take advantage of international differences, such as sweatshop where in the production of clothes workers work in inhuman conditions. In addition, in the case of services (Y2K problem), employees from the low-wage countries are exploited by multinationals.

12.4 NEW DEVELOPMENTS IN ETHICAL THEORIES

There has been an explosion of new developments in ethical theory in recent years, partly based on increasing dissatisfaction with these traditional approaches and partly due to newer attempts to develop new theories that are more directly relevant to business practices. These new theories include feminist theory, stakeholder theory, social contract theory, ethics and nature and pragmatism. These are discussed in the following sections.

12.4.1 FEMINIST THEORY

Feminist philosophy to business ethics is also called the ethics of care. The word feminine should not be taken too literally. Feminist philosophy focuses on traits of character that are valued in close relationships; traits such as sympathy, compassion, fidelity and friendship. Along with this focus, this philosophy rejects such abstractions as Kant's universal moral rules and Bentham's Utilitarian calculations. Feminist theory connotes 'moral impartiality' instead of fostering respect for all individuals, in fact negates respect for concrete individual by impersonally viewing them as anonymous and interchangeable. The concern for the individual in feminist philosophy is not a focus on the individualism of atomic agents, but rather on relationship and the caring, compassion and concern these relationships should involve. This philosophy points out that the feminine 'voice' or perspective is by and large radically different from the male voice of abstract rights and justice, which has dominated the development of moral theory. Feminist thought rejects the notion of rights involving contracts among free, autonomous, and equal individuals in favour of social cooperation. The model used to describe this kind of relationship is often that of the parent–child relationship. The focus on relations leads feminist philosophy to the importance of the need to be attuned to other perspectives.

12.4.2 STAKEHOLDER THEORY

Friedman gets the credit of evolving stakeholder concept. The concept has been widely employed to describe and analyse the relationship between a corporation and society.

As per this theory, management is accountable beyond shareholders to society. It may include 'any individual or group who can affect or is affected by the actions, decisions, policies, practices or goals of the organisation.' A stakeholder, therefore, has some kind of stake in what business does and may affect the organisation in some fashion. Stakeholder theory stands for the principle that corporations should heed the needs, interests, and influence of those affected by their policies and operations. The typical stakeholders are considered to be consumers, suppliers, government, competitors, communities, employees and stockholders. Stakeholder management involves taking the interests and concerns of these various groups and individuals into account in arriving at a management decision, so that they are all satisfied at least to some extent.

12.4.3 CRITICISM

This theory originally assumed that stakeholders are isolatable, individual entities and their interests can be taken into account in decision-making process. However, it has been recognised that it is very difficult to isolate each stakeholder as a separate group. The corporation cannot be isolated from its employees, suppliers, consumers and so on.

Larger market forces and business environment have a large impact on a firm than stakeholders.

Stakeholder theory does not take into cognisance the feminist theory insights.

12.4.4 Social Contract Theory

The old contract business and society were based on the view that economic growth was the source of all progress, social as well as economic. The engine providing this economic growth was considered profits by competitive private enterprise. The basic mission of business was to produce goods and services at a profit, and in doing this; business was making its maximum contribution to society and being socially responsible.

However, the emerging social responsibilities concept has changed the expectations society had from business earlier. The changing contract between business and society is based on the view that the single-minded pursuit of economic growth produced detrimental side effects that imposed social costs on society. The pursuit of economic growth, some believed, did not necessarily lead automatically to social progress but, instead, led to a deteriorating physical environment, an unsafe workplace, discrimination against certain groups and other social problems. It reflects changing expectations regarding the social performance of business. Today the terms of contract between society and business are, in fact changing in substantial and important ways. Business is being asked to assume broader responsibilities to society than ever before and to serve a wider range of human values. Business enterprises, in effect, are being asked to contribute more to quality of life than just supplying quantities of goods and services. The social contract notion prescribes greater responsibilities on multinational corporations in terms of host countries and home country.

The social contract is a set of two-way relationship. The relationship between business and society and the changes in this contract that have taken place over the past several decades are a direct outgrowth of the increased importance of the social environment of business. The 'rules' of the game have changed, particularly through the laws and regulations that have been passed relating to environmental pollution and discrimination.

The concept of social responsibility of business has its origin in contract between business and society through the changing expectations regarding the social performance of business.

12.4.4.1 The Natural Origin of Business Values

This theory is based on the origins of the ethical dimensions of business in its social context and was developed by William Frederick. He developed the hypothesis that the original values of business, which include economising, growth, and systematic integrity, are rooted in the first and second laws of thermodynamics. The values, which constitute the first cluster of values, are listed under the general category of economising values that support prudent and efficient use of resource. This value cluster is, in turn, intertwined with two other sets of value clusters, called ecologising and power-aggrandising respectively. The tensions and conflicts between these three sets of value clusters, by nature are seen as evolutionarily inevitable. This means that the values, by which humans gain a living, allocate and wield power, and establish communal relations with each other are anchored partially in nature and partially in socio-cultural processes.

The theory contradicts the traditional approach of abstract rule application of universal moral principles. The intimate and inextricable interrelation between three sets of values roots business in a social context with which it is associated. The theory negates the notion of profit as a primary business value while stressing the moral legitimacy of the economising function. It also distinguishes between expansion and authentic growth.

12.4.4.2 Pragmatism

Rosenthal and Buckholz have proposed the pragmatism theory. Pragmatism is an approach to business ethics that incorporates and systematises the various trends to be found in contemporary business ethics perspectives. Pragmatic philosophy develops a deeper, unifying level for moral pluralism to explain why and how we reconstruct rules and traditions and choose among various principles in an ongoing process of dealing with change and novelty, thus new understanding of what is to think morally.

In place of the traditional understanding of moral reasoning as abstract and discursive, it is now understood as concrete and imaginative. It does not work downwards from rules to their applications, but works upward from concrete moral experience and decision making toward guiding moral hypotheses. Normative claims are hypotheses grounded in the domain of the diversity of contextually emergent valuing, and established, guided and revised by concrete, imaginative reason utilising experimental method. Pragmatism also rules out absolutism in ethics without falling into relativism. This philosophy offers an epistemic basis for norms of any kind as based not in abstract rationality but is rooted in the existence of diversity. Within this pragmatic context, growth cannot be understood in terms of a fixed end. It rather involves the enrichment of experience in its entirety. Thus, growth is ultimately answerable to the moral dimensions of concrete human existence, whether this be growth of self, growth of community or growth of the corporation. In sum, pragmatism is pluralistic, it involves attunement to concrete situations in contrast to rule applications, and that it overcomes atomic individualism within relational view of the self and community.

12.5 CONCLUSION

Business ethics is an umbrella term under which the ethical rights and duties existing between companies and the society is debated. The ethical challenges and issues lie in the areas of accounting, marketing, production, intellectual property rights and so on. There has been an explosion of new developments in ethical theory in recent years.

Suggested Questions

1. What are the reasons for the renewed interest in business ethics?
2. What do you understand by stakeholders' theory?
3. 'Feminist thought rejects the notion of rights involving contracts among free, autonomous and equal individuals in favour of social cooperation.' Discuss feminist theory.
4. 'With the exception of feminist theory and pragmatism theory, all other theories are less ethical in nature.' Do you agree with this comment?
5. Explain the 'theory of natural origin of business values'.
6. What do you understand by the social contract theory?
7. What are the various issues of business ethics? Discuss briefly.
8. 'It is important for managers to be ethical decision makers.' Elaborate why.

Bibliography

George, R. T. de (1999). *Business Ethics* (Upper Saddle River, NJ: Prentice Hall).

Hartman, L. (2004). *Perspectives in Business Ethics* (Burr Ridge, IL: McGraw-Hill).

Rogene, A. Buchholz and Sandra, B. Rosenthal (2002). Social responsibility and business ethics (Chapter 25). In: Fredrick, R. E., *A Companion to Business Ethics* (Oxford: Blackwell).

Chapter 13

Ethics in Management

Dr Usha Krishna

"An integrity strategy is characterized by a conception of ethics as the driving force of an organization."

Lynn Sharp Paine

LEARNING OUTCOMES

After having learnt all the theoretical aspects of business ethics, we shall now look at the implementation of ethics at the organisational level by managers. In this chapter, you will learn the following things.

- You will develop an understanding about the ethical climate in the organisation.
- You shall come to know the about the ethical models of management morality.
- Finally, you will learn about ethical decision-making processes.

13.1 INTRODUCTION

This chapter will give you basic understanding of ethical climate in organisations and its importance. Now you know that ethical climate is necessary for ethical decision making. In the next section, you will be given an understanding of evaluating the ethical climate with the help of Carol's models of management morality. It depicts the degree of morality among managers. With the help of this model, you will realise why there is passive approach towards ethical issues in organisations. Out of the three types of managers, an amoral manager consists of a larger section than moral and immoral managers put together. You will notice that ethical climate cannot be established unless the large numbers of amoral and immoral managers are motivated towards ethical behaviour. By the end of this chapter, you will have gained the ability to test an ethical decision through an 'ethical check'.

13.2 INSTITUTIONALISING ETHICAL CLIMATE

Managers must act ethically because they are responsible to the organisation as well as to the society. Ethics are the standards for right conduct or morality. Ethical behaviour is the personal behaviour of the managers that should be in conformity with the rules or standards for right conduct. Social responsibility refers to the ethical behaviour of organisation. Ethical behaviour means showing respect to laws and conformity to standards. It also assumes that ethical balance is maintained in case of the interest of different stakeholders. The role of top management is important while providing leadership in creating ethical climate. It is the top management who is responsible for institutionalisation of ethical climate within the organisation. In the following discussion, we will enumerate the role of top management and the steps for ensuring a healthy ethical climate.

It is imperative that managers as leaders should strive towards institutionalising the ethical climate. The following strategic processes must be established for creating systems of adherence to ethics through reward and punishments.

The second most important factor in shaping the ethical climate is the behaviour of top management. There should be no duality in what you 'say' and what you 'do'.

Thirdly, institutionalising ethical processes creates the right climate for perpetuation of ethical social norms in organisations. Other than social norms, ethical climate includes: written codes of conduct, organisational value system, ethical decisions making, effective two-way communication system, rewards for ethical actions and penalty for unethical actions.

Whistle blowing should be encouraged as a mechanism to dissuade unethical practices in the organisation. Protection should be given to those who are honest and ethical and punishments should be awarded to the guilty on ethical standards.

13.2.1 IMPORTANCE OF ETHICAL CLIMATE

Ethical climate is shaped through ethical decisions. Every decision of managers affects one or the other system of organisation including human resources. When it comes to decisions such as rewards and punishments, such decisions must be made without any prejudice and as per the rules. The persons affected by the decision must perceive the decision to be ethical, impartial and person or gender neutral. It is quite likely that majority of the decisions taken by the managers may follow the rules but sometimes, the parties affected by that decision do not perceive the decision to be impartial. In order to prove that a decision has been fair and ethical, managers have to prove to the affected parties that they have adhered to ethical norms and stand by their conviction. If people perceive that the decisions are not accordance with rules, they will distrust the management and take recourse to law. In order to prevent spending time, money and energy for legal actions, ethical decision making is important.

13.3 ETHICAL MODELS OF MORALITY

Carroll has presented three models of management morality that help us to understand 'good and bad' behaviour. These three models or archetypes – immoral management, moral management and amoral management – serve as useful base points for comparison.

The immoral or unethical behaviour has been the focus of attention as far as the media is concerned. However, very little attention has been given to the distinction that may be made between those activities that are immoral and those that are amoral.

A major goal in considering the three management models of morality is to develop a clearer understanding of the full gamut of management behaviour in which ethics or morality is a major dimension. It is helpful to see through example the range of ethical behaviour that management may intentionally, or unintentionally, display. Let us consider the two extreme positions first.

13.3.1 IMMORAL MANAGERS

To start with, let us take immoral management as a decision-making style or behaviour. This model is perhaps most easily understood and illustrated. Immoral management is a style that not only is devoid of ethical principles but also implies a positive and active opposition to what is ethical. Immoral management is discordant with ethical principles. The management's motives are full of priority to selfish interest over organisational interests. Immoral management regards the law or legal standards as impediments it must overcome to accomplish what it wants. The operating strategy of immoral management is to exploit opportunities for personal gain. The key question of immoral management would be 'can I gain from this decision or action, or can we make money with this decision or action, regardless of its consequences or impact on stakeholders?' Examples of immoral management are easy to identify, as they involve illegal actions or fraud. Usually media brings such acts to the attention of masses.

13.3.2 MORAL MANAGERS

Moral management strives to be ethical by conforming to high standards of ethical behaviour. It adheres to professional code of conduct, abides by law and aspires to succeed but only within the confines of sound ethical principles. Moral management strives to operate at a level well above what the law requires. Moral management requires ethical leadership. It is an approach, which strives to seek out the right thing to do. Moral management would embrace what Lynn Sharp Paine has called an 'integrity strategy'. An integrity strategy is characterised by a conception of ethics as the driving force of an organisation. Ethical values shape management's search for opportunities, the design of organisational system and the decision-making process. Ethical values in the integrity strategy provide a common frame of reference and serve to unify different functions, lines of business and employee groups.

Examples of moral management are Infosys, Tata Group and Dr. Reddy's Laboratories.

Infosys has the most transparent business governance procedures in place. Tata Group is the most humane employer that has contributed for the development of communities. Dr. Reddy's Laboratories have aimed at the care of public health by research and development of generic medicines.

13.3.3 AMORAL MANAGERS

There are two kinds of amoral managers: 'unintentional' and 'intentional'. Unintentional amoral managers are neither immoral nor moral but are not sensitive to, or aware of, the fact that their everyday business decisions may have harmful effect on other stakeholders. They go through their organisational lives not thinking that their actions have an ethical facet or dimension. Alternatively, they may just be careless or insensitive to the implications of their actions on stakeholders. These managers may be well intentioned, but they do not see that their business decisions and actions may be hurting those with whom they transact business or interact.

Intentional amoral managers simply believe that ethical considerations are for their private lives, not for business. These people reject the idea that business and ethics should mix. Though most amoral managers today are unintentional, there may still exist a few who simply do not see a role for ethics in business or management decision making.

The problem today is not of immoral managers but amoral managers. These amoral managers are basically good people, but they essentially see the competitive business world as ethically neutral. Until this group of managers moves towards the moral management ethic, we will continue to see businesses and other organisations criticised as they have been in the past several decades.

13.4 ETHICAL DECISION MAKING

13.4.1 IMPORTANCE OF ETHICAL DECISION MAKING

We have alluded to the importance of ethical decision making but it is useful to treat it briefly as a distinct topic. There is a special reason for managers to improve their ethical decision-making choices:

- The costs of unethical workplace conduct,
- the lack of awareness of ethically questionable, managerial role-related acts,
- the widespread erosion of integrity and exposure to ethical risk,
- the global corruption pressures that threaten managerial and organisational reputation and
- the benefits of increased profitability and intrinsically desirable organisational order.

13.4.2 PRINCIPLES OF ETHICAL DECISION MAKING

The useful principles of ethical decision making include:

- the principles of justice,
- the rights,
- the utilitarianism and
- the golden rule.

The basic idea behind the principles approach is that managers may improve the quality of their ethical decision making if they factor into their proposed actions, decisions, behaviours and practices, a consideration of certain principles of ethics. A practical approach to ethical decision making that is to ask three questions to an individual. It is called 'ethical check'.

Obviously, nay to the above questions must make the manager reconsider his or her decision.

'Ethical climate' in an 'unethical business model' makes hardly any sense.

Presently, there is a debate going on in America whether it is ethical to make use of food grains for producing ethanol. Ethanol is used for producing oil. There are more than thirty distilleries that have come up in America for producing ethanol since 2005 after the rise in the prices of gasoline. The use of ethanol reduces the cost of gasoline considerably but the prices of food grain will escalate. As a business model, it is very good that consumers will get oil at cheaper rates. However, there is a grave danger associated with the production of ethanol, which can result in food shortages and increased hunger around the world. If we let this business to continue for the coming decades, more and more people will start such distilleries with the sole objective of earning profits. Judging it on ethical basis, business model that reduces the price of petrol at the cost of escalating grain prices is not an ethical model of business. There are many such unethical business designs operating such as tobacco, arms and alcohol. What are your comments on unethical model of business claiming to be socially responsible?

13.5 CONCLUSION

What we discussed is the nature of ethics and the importance of ethical climate. Why there is need to institutionalise ethical climate. We examined the role of top management in this process of institutionalisation. If ethical climate manifests in the form of over all moral and ethical behaviour of managers in the organisation, there will be balanced decisions made without raising controversies and conflicts among various interest groups. We discussed the three models of morality among managers – amoral, immoral and moral managers – to show that ethical decision making is necessary for ethical climate. We discussed the importance and principles of ethical decision making. Finally, a practical approach to ethical decision is through 'the ethical check'. It is needless to say that ethical climate is relevant for an ethical business model. It makes no sense where 'unethical business model' exists.

Suggested Questions

1. What do you mean by ethics and morality in context of business?
2. What it the importance of ethical climate for an organisation?
3. 'Amoral managers lead to an erosion of the ethical climate in an organisation'. Explain.
4. Explain three models of management morality. Why is it important to institutionalise ethics in organisation?

5. What steps should be taken by the top management to shape the ethical climate in organisations.
6. What are the principles of ethical decision making?
7. Ethical decision making must pass the test of 'ethical check'. Explain.
8. Write a note on management ethics.

Bibliography

Archie, B. Carroll (2002). Ethics in management (Chapter 12). In: Fredrick, R. E. (ed.), *A Companion to Business Ethics* (Oxford: Blackwell).

Bentley College (1999). *Developing Strategies for Ethical Business Conduct* (Waltham, MA: Center for Business Ethics).

Johnson and Phillips (2009). *Absolute Honesty: Building a Corporate Culture that Values Straight Talk and Rewards Integrity* (New Delhi: Prentice Hall of India).

Sir Allan Davis (1986). *Twelve Steps for Implementing a Code of Business Ethics* (London: Institute of Business Ethics, London).

Unit IV

Politics and Ethics in Business

Prof. K.V. Bhanu Murthy

BACKGROUND

Traditional approach to the role of business ignores politics in business. The role of business was supposed to be purely economic. Therefore, the responsibility of the corporation is purely economic. This meant that it should be concerned with profit alone. In other words, corporate responsibility in management theory and practice is implicitly built upon the neoclassical concept of a strict division of labour between political and economic actors and domains. Politics concerns governance, conflict resolution and power. That is the role of politics to institute the norms, rules and structures that permit orderly economic and social activity. This role has been left traditionally to the State. Therefore, politics is associated with the State and economics with business. Since the State is supposed to play its role without any self-interest, it is believed that the State is discharging a moral obligation towards society. Therefore, the State is carrying out its social responsibility. In doing so, it is accountable to the different stakeholders and society at lange. There are laws and structures that make it accountable. The actions of the State are directed towards 'good governance'. Its politics and power are directed towards working for the common 'good' and doing so in an ethical manner although there are situations of ethical conflict.

SOCIAL RESPONSIBILITY OF BUSINESS

The social responsibility of business is considered restricted to the social process of production (economic activity, including trade) and the social process of distribution; that is of dividing the fruits of production among the stakeholders, namely, the factors of production. Subsequently, business firms have to obey the law — this has always been a precondition and has been accepted as a minimum social responsibility of businesses.

Laws are promulgated based on the moral judgements and ethical values of the society. If smuggling is considered unethical, it leads to the setting up of laws against smuggling. However, as the system of law and the enforcement apparatus of the state are often incomplete, there is probably a possibility of regulation gaps and implementation deficits. This is much more possible in the case of giant corporations which possess immense 'power'.

MODERN NOTION

The modern notion of social responsibility of business is that 'regulation gaps and implementation deficits' have to be filled in and balanced by diligent managers with pro-social behaviour and an aspiration to the common good. This therefore, arises out of the ethics of corporation or business. Managers are the 'agents' of the owners of business (who are the principals). The owners gain from the business. They reap profits. They gain from the presence and actions of a socially responsible state. They gain from its power and political actions and programmes. If the state does not invest effort and funds in social projects such as health, literacy and social security, business would suffer on account of social problems and unrest. Similarly, if the state does not preserve the natural environment (against pollution) and if it does not preserve natural resources (especially those which are non-renewable), then businesses would suffer. Their workers would be unhealthy and inefficient and their energy cost would increase in the long run.

GLOBALISATION, POLITICS AND ETHICS IN BUSINESS

With globalisation, it seems, the negative consequences of businesses have intensified. Paradoxically, today, business firms are not just considering the 'bad guys', causing environmental disasters, financial scandals and social ills. They are at the same time considering the solution. This is because most often state agencies are unable, overtaxed or unwilling to contribute to the social good. In such a situation, business has to adopt a much greater social role. Therefore, it not just the matter of more or less investment by business firms in corporate social responsibility (CSR) projects. With globalisation, a *paradigm shift* is necessary while thinking about business ethics and corporate responsibility. Normally, the assumption has been that firms operate within a more or less properly working political framework of rules and regulations that are defined by the power and politics of the government. With globalisation, this assumption does not hold anymore. The global framework of rules is fragile and incomplete. Moreover, the role of the state has been severely undermined. Secondly, with globalisation and the growth of global business, the organisation of business has become a 'microcosm' of society. Corporations have grown to become 'giant' political and 'social' entities. Therefore, business firms have an additional political responsibility to contribute to the development and proper working of governance. All this throws up issues of ethical and social concerns within and outside the organisation which need to be handled with proper leadership and organisational change.

This unit consists of the following chapters which follow from the above perspective:

Chapter 14 emphasises the 'Corporate Code of Ethics' based on the CII-UNDP document. Industry has undertaken the leadership to formulate code of ethics for all in order to make the earth safer and business sustainable.

Chapter 15 focuses on 'Responsibility and Accountability'. It relates the two aspects to a third, that is, governance. Corporate responsibility: it has been seen arises from business ethics and has three dimensions:

1. Good governance,
2. Corporate social responsibility and
3. Environmental accountability.

Chapter 16 throws light on 'Environment'. The primary cause of environmental degradation is industrial activity, indiscriminate consumption promoted by companies, wastes and effluents and emissions by companies. It is therefore the primary responsibility of businesses, in particular, to find solutions.

Chapter 17 focuses on 'Leadership'— the Qualities and Attributes of Leaders, Leadership and Morality. Leaders are the ultimate accountability for everything that happens.

Chapter 18 throws light on 'Workforce Diversity'. It has been proved that diversity benefits workgroups. Despite these benefits, prejudice towards women and minority is universally reported in matters of recruitment, promotions etc. Though most countries have enacted laws that prevent such discrimination, yet it has not been rooted out and remains as a hot topic of debate, 'social exclusion'.

Chapter 14

Corporate Code of Ethics

Dr Usha Krishna

'We cannot wait for governments to do it all. Globalization operates on internet time. Governments tend to be slow moving by nature, because they have to build political support for every step. Therefore, industry has to undertake the leadership to formulate code of ethics for all, in order to make the earth safer and business sustainable.'

Kofi Annan

LEARNING OUTCOMES

This chapter is about operationalisation of ethics through a written code of ethics. There are many things to learn over here.

- First, you would know the rationale for having ethical codes in business organisations.
- Second, you would be made aware of types of codes.
- Then, you shall develop an understanding of the processes in developing such codes.
- Finally, you would also come to know the steps for institutionalising codified behaviour.

14.1 INTRODUCTION

Codes of ethics are accepted standards of behaviour for individuals at corporate level. An automobile manufacturer in South Africa enacted the first set of codes of conduct for its employees in the year 1977. Many companies adopted these codes of conduct, commonly known as 'Sullivan Principles'. Subsequently, OECD made an attempt to collect the codes of conduct from 247 companies to find its scope. As per their study, the companies issued codes of conduct in the areas of environment management, labour standards, consumer rights, anti-corruption, bribery, human rights, science and technology etc.

Before proceeding further, let me first clarify the terms ethical codes', 'social codes' and 'codes of ethics or conduct' that have been used interchangeably in this chapter. Codes are stated principles of social norms and are written as part of company policies. Codes of ethics help and guide managers/employees, not only towards righteousness of action, commitment to ethics, adherence to procedural and moral actions, but also towards minimising the chances of unfair practices, frauds and scandals.

The rationale behind developing codes is that the government takes a very long time to frame rules and regulations for industry with respect to social and environmental codes. So, as mentioned by Kofi Annan (former UN Secretary General) businesses need to act on their own in this respect. Such codes are also used as a shield to pre-empt imposition of penalties and fines on industry for wrongful actions that is damaging for the 'triple bottom line'. Moreover, most importantly, ethics should not be driven by rules and legality. It needs to be prompted, formalised and implemented through self-recognition and self-will.

14.2 TYPES OF CODES OF ETHICS

Codes of ethics may be discussed under two heads namely, (i) general codes (international conventions) and (ii) specific operational codes.

14.2.1 General Codes

There are some international treaties that bind the signatories to concerns such as fair business practices, pollutant to pay for environmental degradation, respect for human rights, respect for rule of law of each nation, recognition of democratic rights and duties, respect for accepted labour conventions, protection of consumer rights and safeguarding the interests of multiple cultures and rights of community.

14.2.2 Specific Codes

These codes guide the organisations to behave in a manner that is in conformity with the above general principles as well as codes related to sustainable business practices; fairness to the consumers by providing quality products at reasonable prices; protecting the stakeholder concerns by thoughtful and ethical decision making; accountability towards business partners and general public; integrity and transparency in business transactions; be vigilant for the business process of supply-chain and customer satisfaction. Business practices emanating from these principles are focused on business competitiveness through corporate social responsibility (CSR) management in the following areas:

- Stronger financial performance and profitability (e.g. through eco-efficiency),
- Improved accountability,
- Enhanced employee commitment,
- Decreased vulnerability through stronger relationships with communities and
- Improved reputation and branding.

14.3 NATURE OF CODES OF ETHICS

According to J. Bhagwati (2004), codes of ethics deal with the questions involving what corporations *should do* and what corporations *should not do*. As said by him, the nature of codes of ethics may be explained as social norms or voluntary and/or mandatory codes. While *voluntary codes* specify what organisations *should do*, *mandatory codes* must clearly spell out what *they should not do*.

14.3.1 Social Norms

Social norms are the behavioural norms for managers. We can say that social norms are an outcome of what managers accept as standards of individual behaviour, whereas codes of conduct are norms of corporate behaviour. These codes can be further classified into two categories namely voluntary and mandatory.

14.3.2 Voluntary Codes

A voluntary code of conduct is an important element of CSR commitments on the part of businesses. The objective of the creation of voluntary codes of conduct for companies is to establish public trust in their business practices by demonstrating commitment and efforts to meet the type of behaviour that corresponds to societal expectations. Globalisation, health, safety and environment protection are the issues that have necessitated the acceptability of international standards voluntarily.

14.3.3 MANDATORY CODES

These codes refer to the rules and regulations with respect to social, environmental and economic areas. Managers of one country/region are required to follow rules and regulations of respective country/region. For instance, bribery has been declared as a criminal offence in the United States, the managers of US firms should indulge in bribery neither in their own country nor in other countries. However, that has not been the practice. There is a tendency to accept/offer bribe where corruption exists. What should be the nature of mandatory codes and how these can be applicable to international communities and thereby multinational companies functioning in different countries is going on. International laws on labour, human rights, intellectual property rights (IPR) and environment are some areas, where mandatory codes have been put in place.

14.4 CSR PRINCIPLES, PROCESSES AND CODE OF ETHICS

CSR does not require companies to comply merely with laws and regulations on social, environmental and economic areas. Compliance with laws sets the official level of CSR performance. CSR is aimed at involving the private sector commitments that extend beyond this foundation of compliance with laws. Laws act as the tools which determine the extent to which industry should be responsible and could be accountable to stakeholders. These tools have been clustered into the four groups:

1. Principles,
2. Codes of conduct,
3. Approaches for developing management processes and
4. Monitoring, communicating and benchmarking.

There is a sequential relationship among these four clusters that clears doubts over multiple codes and related CSR principles and practices. As has been stated, CSR principles began with the Sullivan and OECD principles. The standardisation of products, services and management processes was in the interest of organisations. For doing this independent certifying authorities evolved the procedures for certification and accreditation. The organisations implemented codes of conduct for products, services and certification of management systems. Each country possesses its own national standardisation system. The central or the most representative national standard bodies participate within the regional or international bodies. Most of the technical standards are drafted by standard bodies, conforming to recognised procedures, and for voluntary implementation. Unless a law or other similar measure requires conformance to a cited standard: in this case, the standard becomes mandatory. However, in some countries, standards are mandatory.

Product certification attests that a product complies with the safety, fitness for use and/or interchangeability characteristics defined in standard(s), and in specification(s) supplementary to standards, where they are requested by the market. Standards for management systems apply to the processes that an organisation employs to realise its products or services — they do not apply to the products or services themselves.

The companies standardised their management processes through quality assurance such as ISO 9000, environmental certification such as ISO 14000 and similar certifications on health and safety, in order to ensure quality and competitiveness. The other measures included transparency in governance through accountability, and reporting. Figure 14.1 shows the Relationship between codes of ethics, CSR principles, processes, and reporting.

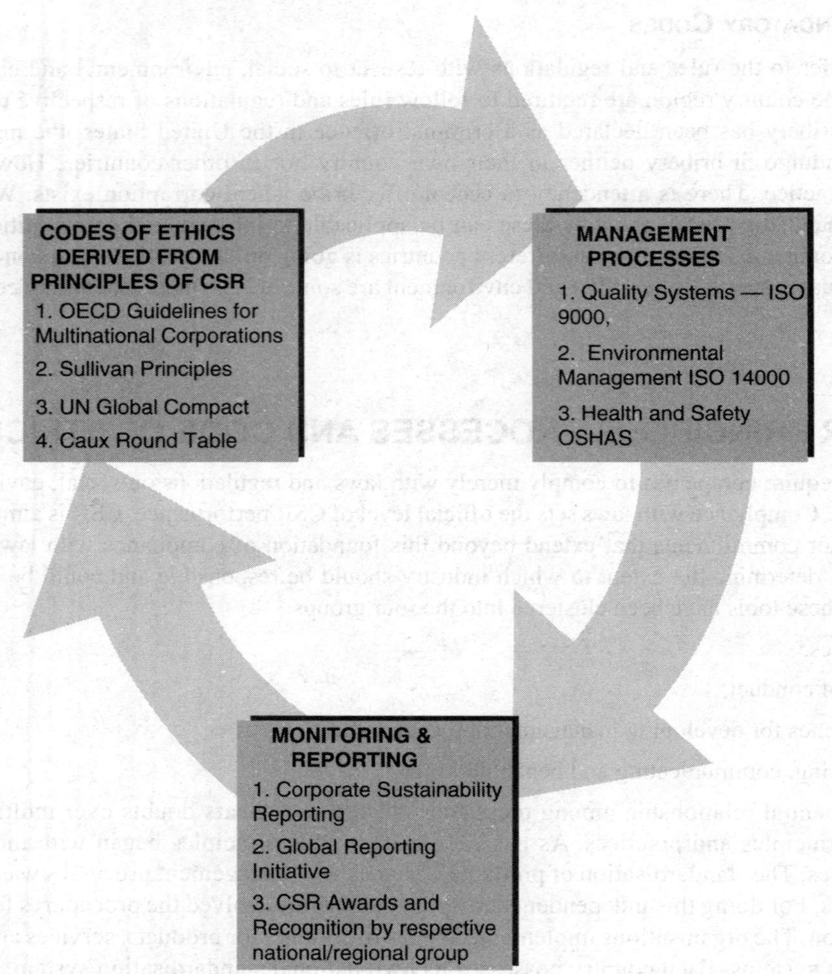

Figure 14.1 Relationship between codes of ethics, CSR principles, processes and reporting.

14.5 STEPS FOR INSTITUTIONALISING ETHICAL NORMS AND BEHAVIOUR

As we have explained in Unit III, ethics are the acceptable norms of behaviour for employees in organisations. If an organisation institutionalises ethics, its fall is unlikely. The institutionalisation of ethics indicates getting ethics formally and explicitly into daily business life. Moreover, an ethical organisation is meant to include its stakeholders. Business leaders can institutionalise ethical principles through demonstration of ethical values and principles themselves and encouraging rest to do the same. The process for institutionalising ethics within an organisation is as follows.

14.5.1 WRITTEN CODES, POLICIES OR GUIDELINES

Code of ethics is a written statement of codes of ethics with respect to company policies on governance, environment, consumers, and csr relations with stakeholders.

14.5.2 ETHICAL COMMITTEES

Ethical committees should be assigned the role of communicating ethical behaviour, training employees in ethics and revising what is stated in the codes of ethics.

14.5.3 DISSEMINATION OF POLICIES TO STAKEHOLDERS, NOT JUST MANAGEMENT

It is the duty of the company to disseminate the policies through employees to all stakeholders, as the ethical climate cannot be achieved without their support. Policies need to be widely circulated among employees in writing to ensure that these are clearly understood.

14.5.4 REINFORCEMENT

Ethical climate cannot be ensured without the continuous support of executives. Therefore, there is a need to reinforce it by constant efforts of the company to communicate with employees through magazines, articles, posters, bulletin boards, training and motivational talks by the top management and experts in respective fields.

14.5.5 TRAINING

Two types of training programmes are necessary for ensuring practice of policies. One relates to the interpretation of policies and the other to the communication of policies. These efforts will help executives apply ethical codes and policies in everyday work situations.

14.5.6 GRIEVANCE MECHANISM

Employees should be encouraged to report unethical behaviour to ethics committee/officers. Encouraging employees to air their grievances in case they feel that they have not been treated in fair and just manner includes protecting them from any backlash. For instance, if whistle-blowers are not given any protection by the organisation they will be too scared to report any matter unless they are powerful enough to take on those involved in scam. The policies must ensure full support to those who wish to report/complain against unethical behaviour meted out to them or a group of people, by elaborate grievance mechanism in place.

14.5.7 MONITORING

Contentious issues that raise conflicts and encourage people to justify unethical and immoral acts should be resolved. Ethics office or board of ethics, in charge of enforcement of ethics should monitor the cases, policies and issues with prudence. Prudence means, 'What we think, say, or do should be truthful and fair, promote goodwill for the company, and benefit stakeholders.'

14.6 SOCIAL CODE FOR BUSINESS BY CONFEDERATION OF INDIAN INDUSTRY AND UNITED NATIONS DEVELOPMENT PROGRAMME

Social Code for Business

Company affirms the interdependence of its enterprise with the well-being and self-reliance of the community. This can be done by adopting an article of association on CSR that advocates harmonising economic progress with social and environmental considerations.

Company has a specific written policy statement on CSR, which is in the public domain. *(Contd.)*

The company has an explicit strategy on social and environmental issues that can be seen in the form of an annual work plan mainstreamed with its business process.

The company has included CSR as part of its corporate communications including newsletters and there is reporting on CSR in the company's annual report.

The company has a senior executive under the CEO responsible for CSR and managerial level officers tasked specifically with social and environmental work. The CEO reviews the CSR programmes twice a year.

The company ensures equal access to employment and promotion opportunities across gender and cultures through policies and programmes.

The company has allocated specific resources to CSR activities and has monitoring system to track implementation process and impact.

The company demonstrates its CSR by providing an able environment for employees to volunteer which includes recognition and accounting for volunteer time.

The company is committed to document its learning experiences in terms of human achievements, contribution to the community and the learning for all stakeholders for sharing with local governments and development agencies.

The company is also known for the partnerships it builds with various development players in the field to synergise all available opportunities to bring about holistic development of the local community.

The companies also expand the scope of learning from each other in their role of being good corporate citizens by way of exchanging data, views, implementation procedures and even exchange of expert personnel whenever necessary.

14.7 CONCLUSIONS: LIVING ETHICAL NORMS

Code of ethics is a written statement of policy that shapes the ethical climate of an organisation. It is the responsibility of top management to provide ethical standards for all managers. It is common to find codes of all kinds written down on paper. The employees hardly know about them. Top management should spend some time in sharing their values with the employees. Apart from this, it is important to live the ethical norms by encouraging moral behaviour and discouraging immoral/amoral ones. Unless the commitment of top management is there, ethical climate of the company cannot be efficient. There have been cases where top management overlooks or fails to penalise unethical behaviour and lands into public criticism and legal problems. President and CEO of Siemens, Peter Loscher, faced similar situation when Siemens involved in allegations of bribes to foreign governments and unions. After that incident, the CEO had to reinvent company's ethical climate and value system by upholding 'zero tolerance to corruption'. Management cannot expect the employees to be ethical and loyal to them without themselves being so. In order to make ethics reality, ethical behaviours of employees must be rewarded with career progression and other incentives.

Suggested Questions

1. Explain the rationale for developing code of ethics for multinational companies.
2. Are codes of ethics mandatory or voluntary? Explain.
3. What is the relationship between CSR principles, management processes and code of ethics?
4. 'Ethical norms of human behaviour need to be institutionalised.' Explain with reasons.
5. What are the salient features of CII-UNDP social code for business?

6. Why is it necessary for organisations to involve and engage stakeholders in framing, communicating and monitoring codes of conduct?
7. What is the role of top management in institutionalising ethical climate in the enterprise?
8. What are the types of codes of ethics in the context of social responsibility of business?

Bibliography

Bhagwati Jagdish (2004). *In Defense of Globalization* (USA: Oxford University Press).

Knowledge @ Wharton, Wharton Business School. retrieved from http://knowledge.wharton.upenn.edu/.

Lee, L. Morgan (1977). Business ethics starts with the individual, *Management Accounting* (March).

Theodore Vincent Purcell and James Weber (1979). *Institutionalizing Corporate Ethics: A Case History* (New York: The Presidents of the American Management Association).

The Wall Street Journal (1999). Lockheed Martin's corrective actions after being fined for violating U.S. anti bribery laws, *The Wall Street Journal* (October).

Chapter 15

Responsibility and Accountability

Prof. K.V. Bhanu Murthy

'We are made wise not by the recollection of our past, but by the responsibility for our future.'

Winston Churchill

LEARNING OUTCOMES

In this chapter, we shall discuss a very complex relationship between 'responsibility', 'accountability' and 'governance'. The focus shall be on gaining insights in the following ways.

- You will develop a critical appreciation of the three key concepts.
- You would be able to evaluate the difference between informative and coercive aspects of accountability.
- A critical understanding of the nexus between accountability and governance will be gathered.
- Therefore, you would know about the new concept of corporate responsibility.

15.1 INTRODUCTION

'Responsibility', 'accountability' and 'governance' are the key terms within business ethics. This is obviously so for 'responsibility and governance'. We discuss about corporate 'social responsibility' and 'governance' in this chapter. It is less obvious with respect to 'accountability'. Accountability is not usually differentiated from the former two and is sometimes used as a synonym for them.

15.2 BASIC FRAMEWORK

According to John Kaler,[1] accountability is not on a par with responsibility or governance but it connects responsibility with governance. The connecting role differentiates accountability from responsibility and governance. Neither responsibility nor governance can be properly understood except with reference to accountability. Moreover, the relationship between these two concepts can be best understood through an understanding of their mutual connection to accountability.

Governance is a relatively straightforward concept. It acquires complexity only with the involvement of responsibility along with accountability.

[1] Kaler (2002). The initial discussion is based on Kaler.

15.2.1 RESPONSIBILITY

We can look at responsibility in two ways. In one sense, responsibility is used as 'duties owed'. This is what we mean when we say 'people having responsibilities' or 'people being responsible'. Police personnel are responsible for law and order. Preventing crime is their duty.

The 'duties-owed' dimension of responsibility can be contrasted with 'casual' effect of responsibility. The 'casual effect of responsibility' works in the following ways: By discharging responsibility, people are presumed to bring about a situation of some kind. The situation can be of positive or negative nature — something that happened or something that failed to happen. In terms of consequences for those who are affected, these two situations can be called 'good' or 'bad'. When the consequences of discharging responsibility is 'good', then 'credit' or 'possible reward' can be assigned to the agency discharging the responsibility. When it is 'bad', it can result in 'blame' or 'possible punishment'. Bringing about a bad situation indicates a failure to fulfil responsibility, whereas bringing about a good situation constitutes a successful fulfilment of responsibility.

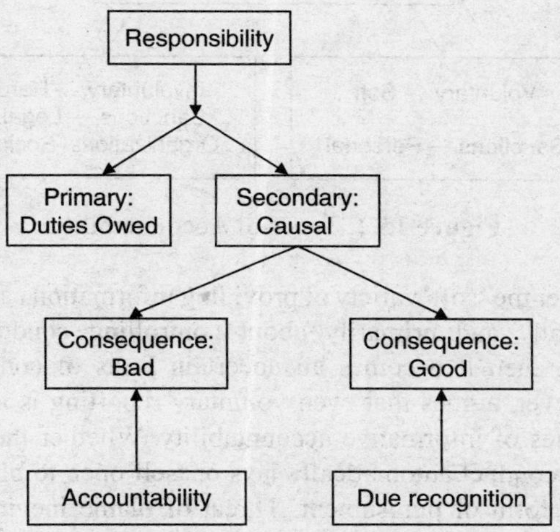

Figure 15.1 Responsibility.

Among these two dimensions of responsibility, that is, 'duties owed' and 'casual', the former is primary and the latter is secondary. Accountability comes in only in the context of the second dimension or the 'casual' dimension of the term responsibility and that too predominantly in the context of 'bad' consequences of the discharge of responsibility. Bad consequences attract accountability, whereas positive or 'good' consequences of the discharge of responsibility call for 'due recognition'. These dimensions of responsibility are depicted in Figure 15.1 it should be obvious that the above framework draws from the consequentialist approach to moral reasoning.

15.2.2 ACCOUNTABILITY

The word 'accountable' and 'answerable' are virtually synonymous: To be 'accountable' is to be 'answerable'. Accountability thus involves providing answers through reporting or other devices or giving an account. In the corporate or business context, accountability gets connected to financial auditing and reporting as well as accounting in general. Business ethics has linked accountability to auditing and reporting of a social, ethical or environmental sort, as well as to the whole notion of transparency in business reporting and information providing. The above factor constitutes the 'informative' approach to understanding accountability.

While providing information, a business entity is being accountable for its conduct with respect to carrying out its responsibility. In other words, being accountable is providing answers to questions about how well or badly the entity has carried out its responsibilities. As pointed out earlier, accountability is primarily concerned with the latter ('how badly') rather than with the former ('how well'). Kaler quotes a scholar and a source to define accountability. The quotations are: "to account for something is to explain or justify the acts, omissions, risks and dependencies for which one is responsible to people with legitimate interest" and "to be accountable for one's activities is to both explicate the reasons for them and to supply the normative grounds whereby they may be justified".

Accountability in terms of explaining or justifying conduct can be voluntary or involuntary as illustrated in Figure 15.2. In the former case, it is discharged only when the agent wants it to do so and on his/her own right. In the latter, there may be legal, organisational or social requirements or sanctions for discharging it. The former is called 'soft' accountability and the latter is called 'hard' accountability.

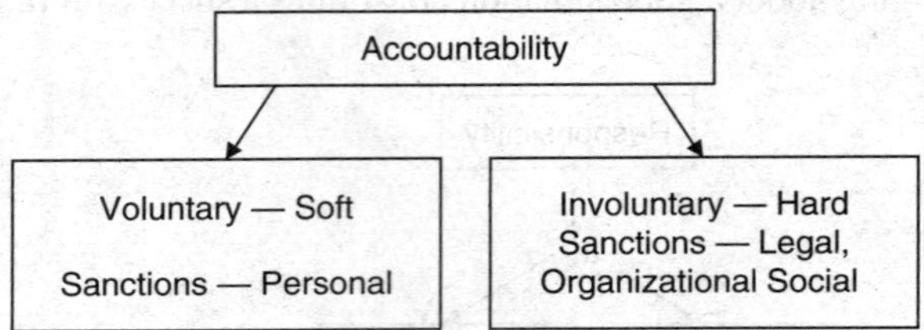

Figure 15.2 Types of Accountability.

The question arises as to whether the 'soft' variety of providing information can alone be called accountability. Accountability is fundamentally and primarily about controlling conduct or preventing misconduct. If accountability is voluntary, then it becomes an uncertain basis of controlling conduct or preventing misconduct. The author, however, argues that even voluntary reporting is accountability because coercive aspect is implicit in all varieties of informative accountability. Whether they are compelled to or not, the very act of reporting on one's conduct automatically lays oneself open to blame, should the answers reveal misconduct. Blame itself is a form of punishment. Threat of blame inevitably accompanies reporting of conduct, voluntary or involuntary, and blame is a powerful instrument of social control.

'Informative accountability' is accountability only because of the implicit coercive element in it is provided by blame. Since the element of blame always accompanies the process of providing information, informative accountability — whether hard or soft — is very much an exercise in accountability.

However, coercion can be applied *suo moto* without the requirement of going through a process of providing information. In the words of Kaler, 'there are perfectly ordinary and acceptable uses of the words 'accountable' or 'answerable' that rely on the fact of coercion and nothing more'. When we say that people are being accountable to other people, we mean that people to whom they are accountable are in a position to inflict punishment on those who are accountable, in case the latter are deemed to be guilty of misconduct. Thus, apart from informative accountability, there is a 'purely coercive' variety of accountability which need not be accompanied by provision of information. This coercive variety can operate quiet independently of the informative variety of accountability. In fact, the former has a better claim to the title of accountability.

The coercive is generally a more flexible form of accountability than the informative. Firstly, unlike the informative, it does not depend upon punishment by way of blame. To apply coercive accountability, only two conditions are required to be fulfilled. Firstly, the people who are held accountable are vulnerable to punishment by others for what is seen as their misconduct. Secondly, people who enforce accountability should have the willingness and the ability to inflict punishment on those who are accountable. The punishment can take the form of fines, imprisonment, beating, confiscation of property, deprivation of income, loss of office, demotion in office etc.

Another difference between the coercive variety of accountability and the informative variety is that the latter is generally the product of some kind of organisational framework within which accountability occurs. The obligation to report, and provide accounts or balance sheets. is generally within the organisational framework of a company, a corporation or an institution. Coercive accountability, on the other hand, can operate through an organisational structure as well as independently. The example of the former is when shareholders decide to vote a director out of office. The example of the latter is when a perception of misconduct by company managers leads to a loss of customers, reluctance to provide investment, move towards greater regulation, efficiency sapping, damage to morale due to campaign launched against the company by public interest groups, and so on. These are all instances of accountability that are coercive rather than informative, that go beyond blame and directly inflict substantive punishment. They are also very much extra-organisational, that is, the punishment comes from quarters outside the organisation which is supposed to be held accountable. It is then argued that nothing prohibits these two forms of accountability, that is, informative and coercive, being combined. In fact, they are very often combined in business as elsewhere. In organised companies, coercive accountability generally follows the exercise of informative accountability. For instance, before dismissing a director for misconduct, shareholders would like to have a report on his/her conduct.

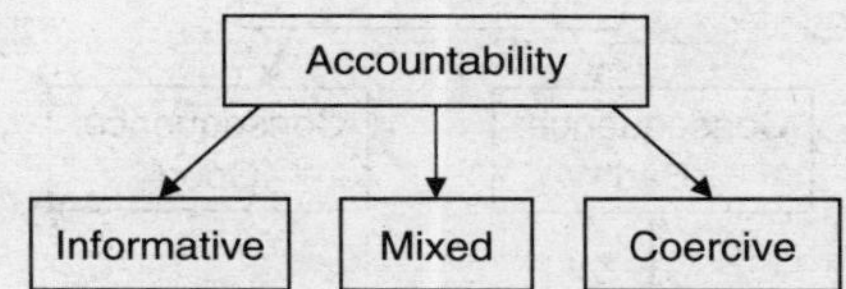

Figure 15.3 Approaches to Accountability.

There are three approaches to accountability namely informative, coercive and a combination of the two. This is shown in Figure 15.3. As already explained, informative approach can be both soft (voluntary) and hard (compulsory). It is a weaker version of accountability because it realises on the element of blame implicit in the report revealing or inability to discharge responsibility. Informative accountability is generally discharged in an organisational framework. Coercive variety is generally hard. It can be both weak and strong. It is generally exercised extra-organisationally, but its exercise through an organisation is not ruled out. The combined variety not only has most of the elements of coercive variety but also has the elements of informative variety.

15.2.3 GOVERNANCE

Governance has been defined as 'the system by which the companies are directed and controlled'. Governance in general, as distinct from corporate governance in particular, is a system of 'directing and controlling' more or less formally structured groupings of people, be they states, communities, companies, universities, social clubs etc.

Since governance is related to a 'system', it is not concerned with directing and controlling of decision making on particular issues and occasions. It is rather concerned with established structures for decision making, for determining who has what sort of decision-making power in relation to what sort of issues. Thus, governance is directing and controlling in a systematic sense of the term. This definition of governance also applies to corporate governance because companies are undoubtedly the most formally structured system.

Governance, as a system for 'directing and controlling', does not by itself involve responsibility and accountability. Theoretically, governance can be very well carried out just by a process of systematic decision making without involving responsibility or accountability. Responsibility is involved only if directing and controlling has a purpose other than serving the interest than those who are in charge of directing and controlling. Whereas accountability is involved when the function of how best to serve the interest is not left to the discretion of those directing and controlling, but when the directors and controllers themselves are in need of being directed and controlled.

From a stockholder's perspective, responsibility along with accountability become a corporate governance issue only if there is a separation of ownership and control. This is because there is a possibility for only those who are responsible for control not serving the interest of the owners. Even when the ownership and control are in the same hand, there is a need to ensure that those who control not only serve the interest of the owners and controllers but also serve the interest of other stakeholders, including the stockholders. The relationship between responsibility and accountability is shown in Figure 15.4.

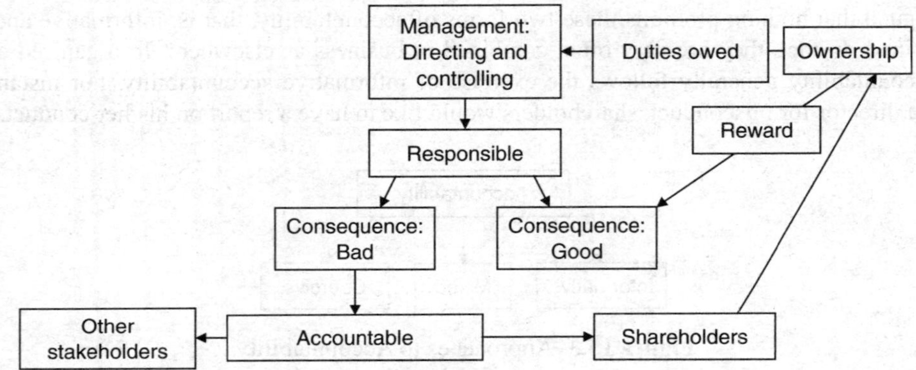

Figure 15.4 Relationship between responsibility and accountability.

In corporate governance, accountability is discharged through the informative approach, that is, reporting to the shareholders, as well as by way of being answerable to them without necessarily resorting to reporting. The latter kind of answerability or accountability is enforced by the shareholders by virtue of their being the authority to appoint and possibly dismiss those who are in charge of direction and control.

There is a tendency in modern corporate governance to take into account the interest of only the shareholders and not wider interest going beyond those of the shareholders. In this context, accountability is strictly of the informative variety, typically exercised through social, ethical and environmental reporting and auditing. Extra-organisational accountability that can be enforced through purely coercive action is generally not involved in corporate governance.

In corporate governance 'due recognition' is also an instrumentality to ensure the discharge of accountability. Giving credits and rewards (i.e., due recognition) is a spur to enhanced performance. However, performance is not ensured by due recognition alone. Accountability by itself also plays a role in ensuring performance. It is linked to performance in which any absence of effective accountability can result in a management that is lazy and complacent or foolishly reckless. Thus, performance is about both due recognition as well as accountability. Therefore, in corporate governance, 'due recognition' should take its place alongside accountability; and responsibility should have a place in the 'duties owed' sense of the term.

In order for responsibilities to be discharged, there has to be power to do so. If necessary powers are not possessed, then they have to be granted. Therefore, in corporate governance, powers necessary to fulfil responsibilities have to be granted. In governance in a public company with a separation of ownership and control, there is a triangular relationship between imposition of duties, granting of power or conferring rights and mechanisms for accountability and due recognition. First comes the imposition of duties with respect to directing and controlling mainly to serve the interest of shareholders. Related to it is the granting of necessary powers or conferring rights to carry out those duties. Next comes the causal responsibility to use mechanisms for accountability and due recognition. Accountability and due recognition generally operate in tandem.

15.3 CORPORATE RESPONSIBILITY

Corporate responsibility has been seen arises from business ethics and has three dimensions:

1. Good governance,
2. Corporate social responsibility and
3. Environmental accountability.

This is how business ethics becomes an all-pervading influence in the governance of business. The top management is not only responsible to envision such a change but also responsible to translate this vision into practices and to make sure that they adopt a balanced approach towards three dimensions. It should be evidenced from the conduct of business for it is not easy for them to get away from this by indulging only in lip service.

15.3.1 GOOD GOVERNANCE

The corporations are formed based on the division of ownership and control, in which the investor or owner relies on the manager, that is, CEO to manage the business on his/her behalf which implies that principal–agent relationship exists between investor and manager, which causes the room for asymmetric information. In other words, there is always a gap between the information possessed by the manager vis-àis the investors. This situation calls for a good and transparent governance, that is, corporate governance. The shareholders must have full and authentic information. There should be transparency in processes, so that the agent (manager) cannot mismanage or take the advantage of the asymmetric information. The objective of good governance is to have such system of controlling and managing so that the interest of owner may be protected. For this to be successful, first of all, whatever hurdles are there in the processes are to be removed. The processes are necessary to prohibit the manager to push their own agenda or self-interest, that is, the managers, as working in the capacity of agent, might have their own individual goals to pursue which are not in line with organisational goals. Such processes are to be institutionalised which protect the interest of the owner, that is, profit maximisation and wealth maximisation. Therefore, ethical structure has the implication for good governance, which means better profits. It is important to make profits within ethical framework. There is a shift in the psychology of investors that they are curious not only to know how much profit the company has booked, but also to know how this profit has been earned, that is, ethically or unethically. Therefore, business has to be done ethically, the profits are to be taken seriously, if not, it would be interpreted as if the business is not indulging into good governance.

15.3.2 CORPORATE SOCIAL RESPONSIBILITY (CSR)

Second ethical dimension of CSR includes the social practices where the company is discharging its responsibility towards community at large, that is, stakeholders. Stakeholders are the ones who can influence or can be influenced by the actions, decisions, policies, practices and goals of the company. Apart from shareholders, it includes employees, consumers, suppliers, government competitors and community at large. Traditionally, so far business was treated purely from the viewpoint of private–personal pecuniary motive. Now, a company has acknowledged its responsibilities to society that goes beyond the production of goods and services at a profit. It involves the idea that the corporate governance has a broader constituency to serve than that of shareholder alone. In more recent years, the term stakeholder has been widely used to express this broader set of responsibilities. By now, it has been accepted that corporations are more than economic institutions and they have responsibility to help society solve pressing social problems. CSR is about how companies manage the business processes to produce an overall positive impact on society. According to Richard Walls, 'Corporate Social Responsibility is the continuing commitment by business to behave ethically and contribute to economic development while improving the quality of life of the workforce and their families as well as of the local communities and society at large'. CSR is about business giving back to the society. The concept of social responsibility is fundamentally an ethical concept, as it involves changing notions of human welfare and emphasises a concern with the social dimensions of business activity that have to do with improving quality of life. The concept provided a way for business to concern itself with these social dimensions and pay some attention to its social impacts. As a result, many of them put a step forward for discharging their responsibility either by indulging into philanthropy or by bringing CSR into business strategy.

15.3.3 ENVIRONMENTAL ACCOUNTABILITY

Corporate responsibility has third dimension in the form of accountability of business towards environment. As business interacts with its natural environment, it draws its resources from the environment. It also influences the environment by its actions. Therefore, it is also accountable for any impact that it makes. Earlier corporates dumped their wastes with impunity in the environment. With the growing awareness and concerns about environmental degradation, depletion of natural resources such as water and fossil fuels and the phenomenon of global warming, there is moral and legal pressure on corporates to realise that the earth needs to be preserved, and looked after so that the upcoming generations are not adversely affected.

Corporate responsibility is closely linked with the principles of sustainable development, in proposing that the enterprises should be obliged to make decisions based not only on financial or economic factors but also on the social and environmental consequences of their activities. Therefore, corporate responsibility is about how businesses align their values and behaviour with the expectations and needs of different stakeholders. It also describes a company's commitment to be accountable to its environment (i.e., planet) to be responsible to its society at large (i.e., people) and to be transparent in his/her business practices (i.e., good governance which determines the profit for the investors).

15.4 INTEGRATED APPROACH

In most recent years, many of the corporates have adopted Triple Bottom Line Reporting, which is an integrated approach to public reporting of environmental, social and economic outcomes against benchmarks. This major step is taken by the companies to integrate all the three dimensions of business ethics with the business strategies. This line of thinking comes from the top management. A series of internal and external pressures influence the corporate leaders to address ethics such as increasing influence of non-governmental organisations (NGOs), a pervasive media in search of stories, knock-on effect of corporate accounting scandals such as Enron and WorldCom, increasing legislation, increasing growth of socially responsible investments (SRI), changing consumers' and employees' expectation and never-ending social activists' campaigns. Top management is responsible to integrate ethical consideration with company's decision making and manage on the basis of personal integrity and widely held organisational value. It is their prerogative to translate their vision, mission statements and ideas into practices.

Suggested Questions

1. Discuss the implications of primary and secondary aspects of responsibility.
2. Distinguish between the informative and coercive dimensions of accountability.

3. Explain hard and soft accountabilities.
4. 'Governance, as a system for "directing and controlling" does not by itself involve responsibility and accountability.' Discuss.
5. How is performance about both due recognition as well as accountability?
6. Discuss, in detail, the new concept of corporate responsibility (CR).

Bibliography

Kaler, J. (2002). Responsibility, accountability and governance, *Business Ethics — A European Review* 11(4), October 327–334.

Murthy, K. V. B. (2007). Business ethics and corporate responsibility — A new perspective, *International Standards Organization — International Seminar*, 15–16 April, New Delhi.

Murthy, K. V. B. and R. Jha (2000). Sustainability — Property rights, behaviour and economic growth, *Papers and Proceedings*, *World Congress on Managing and Measuring Sustainability, Ontario*.

Murthy, K. V. B. and R. Jha (2003). The non-global nature of WEO. In Hans Singer *et al.* (eds.), *Trade and Environment: Recent Controversies* (New Delhi: Vedam Books).

Chapter 16

Environment

Prof. K.V. Bhanu Murthy and Dr Usha Krishna

'We cannot command Nature except by obeying her.'

Francis Bacon

LEARNING OUTCOMES

This is a crucial chapter about a burning topic – the *environment*. After reading through this chapter, you would gain in the following respects.

- You would know about the basic issues in the environment.
- There emerges an understanding about the various responsibilities that businesses have towards the environment.
- You would develop a critical appreciation of the term 'sustainable'.
- You shall know about various aspects of environmental accounting.

16.1 INTRODUCTION

Let us understand the difference between 'business environment' and 'natural environment'. While the former refers to the environment that is external to the company, firm or business and to the pervasive influence of the economy, legal framework and policies, the latter refers to natural resources such as land, forests, air, water and energy sources (non-renewable).

16.2 BUSINESS AND ENVIRONMENTAL PROBLEMS

Various environmental problems now affect the entire world. As globalisation persists and the earth's natural processes transform domestic problems into global issues, few societies are being left untouched by major environmental problems.

Some of the major problems existing worldwide are acid rain, air pollution, global warming, hazardous waste, ozone depletion, smog, water pollution and rainforest destruction.

Any environmental problem has definite causes and brings about numerous effects. The primary factors that affect the natural environment are industrial activities, indiscriminate consumption promoted by companies, toxic wastes and effluents and emissions by factories and automobile industries. Therefore, it is the primary responsibility of businesses, in particular, to find solutions. Corporations have certain responsibilities towards society in this regard. However, if they fail to do so they should be made accountable towards the environment. Therefore, this is a part of 'corporate responsibility' and is one of the three pillars – corporate social responsibility, environmental accountability and corporate governance.

16.3 ENVIRONMENTAL DEGRADATION

When the environment becomes less valuable or damaged, environmental degradation is said to occur. There are many forms of environmental degradation. When habitats are destroyed, biodiversity is lost, natural resources are depleted and finally the environment is hurt. It has been established that environmental degradation occurs through human processes, intervention and consumption of goods and resources. Globally speaking, the largest areas of concern at present are the loss of rainforests, air pollution, smog, ozone depletion and hazardous wastes.

16.3.1 POLLUTION

In the recent years, the problem of pollution has become widespread and is seen polluting the oceans of the planet at large. Pollution may be in the form of air, water or soil. In some areas, the natural environment has been exposed to hazardous waste. In other places, major disasters such as oil spills have ruined the local environment. There are many well-known environmental disasters such as Love Canal, Bhopal Gas Tragedy and Exxon Valdez case, which point towards environmental accountability of business.

Chlorofluorocarbons (CFCs) are gases that are generated from air conditioners, refrigerators and industrial processes, and are the causal agents of ozone layer depletion. When these chemicals are released, they go up into the stratosphere and degrade the ozone. The ozone layer is an envelope in the earth's atmosphere which protects living beings from ultraviolet radiations.

16.3.2 ACID RAIN

Acid rain, smog and unpleasant air are the results of air pollution. Both industrial operations and automobiles have released enormous amount of emissions which have intensified these problems. Acid rain, one of the most important environmental problems of all, cannot be seen. The invisible gases that are responsible for acid rain usually come from automobiles or fossil fuel power plants. Acid rain moves easily, affecting locations far beyond those that let out the pollution. As a result, this global pollution issue causes great debates between countries that fight over polluting each other's environments.

16.3.3 GLOBAL WARMING

Global warming is otherwise known as the greenhouse effect because the gases that are gathering above the earth's atmosphere make the planet comparable to a greenhouse. By trapping heat near the surface of the earth, the greenhouse gases are warming the planet and threatening the environment. Current fears stem largely from the fact that global warming is occurring at such a rapid pace. Models are predicting that over the next few centuries, the global temperature will rise by several degrees. This is also referred to as climate change which has the effect of alternation of flood and drought on the planet.

16.3.4 RAINFOREST DEPLETION

Despite the opposition to the cutting down of rainforests, the problem continues. Every year, Brazil chops down an area of forest equal to the size of the state of Nebraska. Deforestation and the logging industry have destroyed many tropical rainforests around the world. This has destroyed many natural habitats, plants and animals that are native to the areas.

In addition to Amazon's rainforests, many other forests are being cut down as well. In Indonesia, Zaire, Papua New Guinea, Malaysia, Myanmar, the Philippines, Peru, Colombia, Bolivia and Venezuela, rainforests that were once great have been lost. According to certain estimate, 50 million acres of rainforests are cut down every year. The United Nations says that the figure is closer to 17 million acres. The World Wildlife Fund states that every minute 25 to 50 acres of rainforests are cut or burned to the ground.

16.3.5 HAZARDOUS WASTE

Apart from releasing gases and harmful substances into the atmosphere, human beings are also polluting the environment by either disposing the waste materials or burying them. Often, these wastes are hazardous and dangerous to both nature and human life. Corporations usually want to avoid the costs associated with having to limit creation of hazardous waste. Consequently, they build landfills on site and fill them with wastes, or sometimes pay garbage collectors to have their wastes removed. Often, hazardous materials are transported to the areas that accept money to take the wastes. The levels of toxic wastes continue to grow. Industries and individuals are largely unaware of these major environmental hazards.

16.3.6 OZONE LAYER DEPLETION

The fact that the ozone layer was being depleted was discovered in the mid-1980s. The main reason for this is the release of CFCs. Antarctica was an early victim of ozone destruction. A massive hole in the ozone layer right above Antarctica now threatens not only that continent but many others that could be the victims of Antarctica's melting icecaps. In the future, the ozone problem will have to be solved to conserve the protective layer.

16.4 RESPONSIBILITY OF HUMANS TOWARDS ENVIRONMENTAL HARMS

Even under the most laissez-faire system of the economy, businesses owe a responsibility and have to be made accountable to the natural environment. There is a need to examine environmental responsibilities of business along three dimensions: responsibility of humans towards environmental harms caused by the business atmosphere; responsibility to the non-human natural world and business ethics in the age of sustainable economics. The business must be made liable to environmental degradation such as air pollution, water pollution and toxic-waste disposal.

Every business should have some ethics concerning human rights and environment. Indeed, business should be set in such a way that it does not affect any particular individual or environment. When such harms do occur, business has a responsibility to compensate for the affected individuals. In this way, both law and ethics have always recognised the environmental responsibility of the business. Thus, by the early 1970s, business was required to meet a wide range of regulatory standards aimed at preventing environmental harms through the use of pesticides, fertilizers and other chemicals. Pollution control norms to air, water and the earth were laid down in order to respect the rights of individuals for clean environment. However, these developments are restricted to provable harms (e.g. physical injuries or financial loss) to identifiable individuals. This omitted a wide range of potential victims and potential harms, including aesthetic, ecological and health harms to present and future generations of humans, animals, plants and the ecosystem.

16.5 RESPONSIBILITIES TO THE NATURAL WORLD

Many ethicists have criticised the application, if not the appropriateness, of the right approach to environmental concerns. Peter Singer and Tom Regan argue that humans do have some moral responsibilities towards animals. Responsibility to the natural world is based on a wide range of values, including aesthetic, symbolic, spiritual, historical and moral values. If these arguments are sound, the compensatory and regulatory frameworks described above should be extended to include harms done or potential to other living creatures. Businesses involved in farming, agriculture, food service, recreation, logging, medical and commercial research would have to radically alter their practices to avoid causing harm to animals and plants.

However, extending moral standards of individual animals and other living things fails to address other environmental issues, and also conflicts with economic issues such as land development, resource use and wilderness preservation. The ecological science emphasizes ecological system rather than the well-being of individual animals that are part of the ecosystem. Thus, it has been argued that the business has responsibility towards preserving ecosystems because of their aesthetic, spiritual, historic or symbolic value.

16.6 BUSINESS ETHICS IN THE AGE OF SUSTAINABLE ECONOMICS

In recent times, the emphasis has been on economic growth rather than on ethics. The core problem concerning this approach is that growth creates all kinds of environmental and ecological imbalances and outright harm. The problem is that the harm is being done to people at far-off places in the globe. It is being done to living things – animals and plants – which cannot defend themselves. Harm is being done to future generations who are not present. Harm is being done to non-living things such as the atmosphere – the ozone layer – which does not have any representative to defend itself. The general laws of the environment are not enough. There is therefore a shift towards intrinsic value and new business ethics that recognises the social responsibility of a business towards the environment.

In many ways, this shift to discussion of intrinsic value can be seen as a return to a more traditional understanding of ethics. Greek ethics focused ethical responsibilities on the pursuit of the good, in all its forms. It was only in the modern period that 'ethics' took on a more narrow scope in which responsibilities extend only to other individual human beings or 'right bearers'. To sum up, environmental ethics has expanded to include aesthetic, religious, social and even metaphysical issues.

A final overlap between business ethics and environmental issues involves neoclassical economics and the value of economic growth. There are good reasons, however, for thinking that economic growth is ecologically and ethically deficient. This is because growth may be 'unsustainable'.

> *Sustainability* is a characteristic of a process or state that could be *afforded* to be maintained at a certain level indefinitely.

Often it is confused with 'sustained' which means ensuring a growth rate. Sustainability, in its environmental usage, refers to the potential longevity of vital human–ecological support systems, such as the planet's climatic system, systems of agriculture, industry, forestry and fisheries on the one hand; and the increasing pressures by human communities, their economic activities, consumption patterns in general and their impacts and various systems on which they depend, on the other hand.

> Thus the applicability of the notion of sustainability has ultimately got to be universal and refer to the indefinite future.
>
> (Jha and Murthy, 2000)

If this is so, then most theories of corporate social responsibility must be significantly revised. They can no longer be restricted to the immediate realm of the business. Thus, sustainable development ought to be the goal of the world economy and a primary ethical standard for business activity is as to whether the activity is 'sustainable', in the sense stated above.

Two fundamental norms of neoclassical economics are efficient allocation and equitous (or just) distribution. However, an economy should operate at a scale that can meet the needs of the present generation, without jeopardising the ability of future generations to meet their needs. One country should grow at a level that may be less than efficient but does not jeopardise any other country's existence. One business must not grow at such a pace that it endangers the existence of the entire society.

One important test focuses on the rate at which resources are being taken from the ecosystem and wastes are being disposed back into the ecosystem. Business should not use renewable resources at rates that exceed the ecosystem's ability to replenish it. Business should and cannot use non-renewable resources at rates that exceed the development of alternatives. Business should not and cannot generate wastes at rates that exceed the ecosystem's capacity to assimilate them.

These general conditions can be understood as side-constraints upon how business operates in meeting consumer demand. Business ought to respond to the market only in ways that are ecologically sustainable. However, we should recognise that business does not merely respond to markets, but business activity influences markets as well. Business should stop promoting products that are unsustainable, and help educate consumers to the need for ecologically benign, if not beneficial, choices.

16.7 OPERATIONALISING ENVIRONMENTAL ACCOUNTABILITY

For controlling environmental degradation, reversing climate change, preserving natural resources for the next generation, leading health lives, avoiding conflicts, containing poverty and hunger and, in short, saving the planet from disaster, the environmental accountability of business has to be concretised and operationalised.

As discussed earlier, businesses have responsibility towards the environment in many ways. The natural outcome is that businesses are to be made accountable towards the environment. However, this needs a more concrete approach. Accordingly, it shall be seen that environmental accountability hinges upon environmental accounting (EA), which estimates environmental costs and benefits. As shown in Figure 16.1, EA in turn, consists of three dimensions:

1. Identification and measurement of environmental costs, which is done through environmental management accounting (EMA).
2. Evaluation of environmental performance through environmental audit and standards.
3. Environmental reporting – environmental financial accounting (statements).

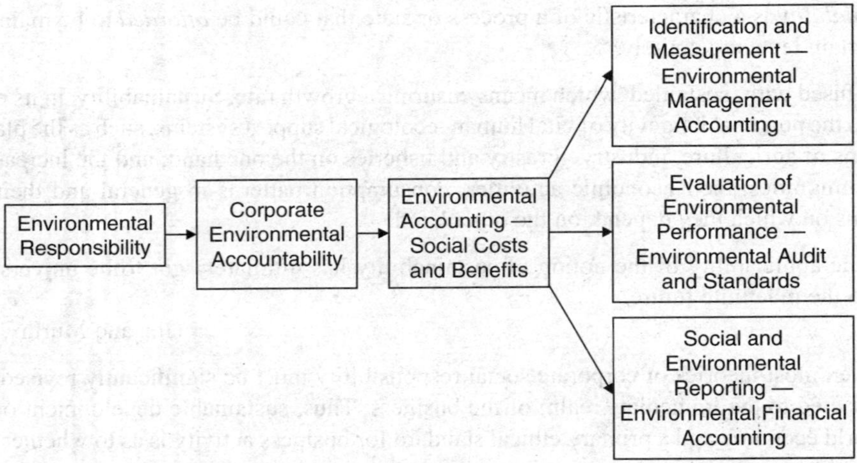

Figure 16.1 Environmental Accountability.

16.8 CORPORATE ENVIRONMENTAL ACCOUNTING

At its simplest, corporate EA is about making environment-related costs more transparent within corporate accounting systems and reports. One of the major distinctions within the field is whether the primary focus is to report environment-related costs within *internal* management accounts or *external* financial accounts or other public reports.

The focus on the corporate or business entity makes corporate EA different to the EA undertaken by organisations which attempt to develop monetised and physical statistics on the state of environmental and natural resource assets at the regional or national level, as well.

16.9 RATIONALE FOR ENVIRONMENTAL ACCOUNTING

There are several reasons why businesses may consider adopting EA as part of their accounting system:

- possible significant reduction or elimination of environmental costs;
- environmental costs and benefits may be overlooked or hidden in overhead accounts;
- possible revenue generation may offset environmental costs (e.g. transfer of pollution allowances);
- improved environmental performance which may have a positive impact on human health and success of the business;
- may result in more accurate costing or pricing of products and more environmentally desired processes;
- possible competitive advantages as customers may prefer eco-friendly products and services and
- can support the development and operation of an overall environmental management system, which may be required by regulation for some types of businesses.

16.10 DIFFERENT ENVIRONMENTAL ACCOUNTING DISCIPLINES

EA can be classified into three disciplines:

1. global EA;
2. national EA and
3. corporate EA.

Corporate EA can be further divided into three categories:

1. Environmental Management Accounting;
2. Environmental Financial Accounting and
3. Environmental Audit.

16.11 GLOBAL ENVIRONMENTAL ACCOUNTING

Global EA is an accounting methodology that deals with energetics, ecology and economics at a global scale. The earth is the system of interest with the input, sequestration and dissipation of solar energy – which constitute its energy budget (Odum, 1996; Tennenbaum, 1988).

16.12 EMA

EMA has a focus on providing the management of an organisation with better information on the actual private environmental costs already being incurred by the entity. Other directions being taken with corporate EA placing greater emphasis on the external reporting of environmental expenditures, and estimating the external environmental costs not recognised by the entity (external cost accounting). With external cost accounting, the estimation of external costs can be used to determine the profit that would remain if a provision or expenditure had been made to restore or avoid the external environmental impacts.

EMA is used by companies to make internal business strategy decisions. It can be defined as:

> … the identification, collection, analysis, and use of two types of information for internal decision making: 1) Physical information on the use, flows and fates of energy, water and materials (including wastes) and 2) Monetary information on environmentally related costs, earnings and savings.

16.13 ENVIRONMENTAL FINANCIAL ACCOUNTING

Environmental financial accounting is used to provide information needed by external stakeholders about a company's financial status. This type of accounting allows companies to prepare financial reports for investors, lenders and other interested parties.

16.14 ENVIRONMENTAL AUDIT

The financial benefits and improved efficiencies from adopting cleaner production and eco-efficiency encourage firms to undertake audits. However, environmental audit can also be an effective risk management tool.

By compliance with environmental legislation, companies avoid the risk of prosecution and fines arising from potential environmental breaches.

A good audit will include a number of components, some of which are listed below.

16.14.1 DATA COLLECTION

Data collection is used to identify and measure all inputs and outputs from the production process and to provide a baseline for comparison against targets and a background for improvement.

16.14.2 COMPLIANCE

Compliance is used to review and compare a company's activities and business targets against all relevant regulations, codes of conduct and government policies to assess compliance.

16.14.3 DOCUMENTATION

Documentation is used to document all aspects of audit to assess progress at a further date and to verify environmental performance of staff, regulators and the general community.

16.14.4 PERIODIC AUDITS

Periodic audits are used to assess the impacts of new or changed legislation on operations and to assess whether internal targets for environmental efficiency are being met.

16.15 INTERNATIONAL ENVIRONMENTAL STANDARDS – ISO 14000

The ISO 14000 series, currently being developed by the International Organisation for Standardization (ISO), is a collection of voluntary standards that assists organisations to achieve environmental and financial gains through the implementation of effective environmental management. The standards provide both a model for streamlining environmental management and guidelines to ensure environmental issues that are considered within decision-making practices.

ISO 14001 is the standard for Environment Management Systems. Many large businesses, particularly overseas businesses, have obtained certification under this standard.

16.15.1 BENEFITS OF INTERNATIONAL CERTIFICATION

The benefits of having ISO 14001 certification are mainly realised by large organisations, as small- and medium enterprises (SMEs) have a smaller turnover and thus a correspondingly small return on the costs of certification.

Although a fully certified ISO EMS may not be suitable for smaller organisations, it does provide guidelines that assist organisations to consider all the relevant issues, and thus gain most benefit from their EMS, even without certification. SMEs can therefore use ISO 14001 as a model for designing their own EMS.

However, larger organisations may find certification more valuable when considering the potential trade and market advantages of an internationally recognised and certified EMS. This was a significant factor for companies seeking certification under the ISO 9000 quality assurance standards, and is likely to be a factor in decisions regarding ISO 14001 certification.

16.16 CORPORATE SUSTAINABILITY REPORTING

Corporate reporting is the voluntary public presentation of information about an organisation's non-financial performance – environmental, social and economic – over a specified period, usually a financial year.

A report may be published as a stand-alone document, on a company web site or incorporated into an annual report. The release of a corporate sustainability, environmental or health, and safety report is seen as increasing transparency and therefore accountability.

16.16.1 FRAMEWORKS AND GUIDANCE

Internationally, the Global Reporting Initiative (GRI) *2002 Sustainability Reporting Guidelines* is rapidly becoming the accepted voluntary framework for corporate sustainability or triple bottom line (environmental, social and economic) reporting. The World Business Council for Sustainable Development (WBCSD) has developed outlines of the measurements, or metrics, which are useful for reports and provide background information about how organisations can move towards sustainability.

16.16.2 TRENDS AND DRIVERS

Corporate reporting is used by organisations to voluntarily communicate information on environmental and other non-financial performance (social and economic) with their stakeholders. It is recognised as an important mechanism for improving corporate sustainability performance. This is based on generating business value through measurement and management of environmental risks and opportunities, and reporting this information in a fashion that responds to the growing expectations of customers, business partners, investors and the wider community. Although corporate reporting is a relatively new approach to informing stakeholders about environmental performance, its uptake has been strong and is increasing steadily. Corporate reporting exemplifies the growing trend, globally and in Australia, towards taking sustainability seriously and towards open and transparent communication about the corporate impacts. The growth in the uptake of corporate reporting (45% of the world's top 250 companies now publish stand-alone reports with environmental information, up from 35% in 1999) is consistent with the current drive for good corporate governance, heightened transparency and sound risk management.

Suggested Questions

1. Explain the various dimensions of environmental degradation.
2. Write a note on International Environmental Standards.
3. Describe the three aspects of corporate EA.
4. What is sustainable consumption?
5. Write a note on corporate sustainability reporting.
6. Write a note on international environmental standards.

Bibliography

Jha, R. and K. V. B. Murthy (2000). Sustainability – property rights, behaviour and economic growth, *World Congress on Managing and Measuring Sustainability*, Ontario.

Murthy, K. V. B. (2007). *Environmental Accounting: An Overview*. Retrieved on http://www.authorstream.com/Presentation/bhanumurthykv-33057-environmental-accounting-accountability-management-green-revised-entertainment-ppt-powerpoint/.

Murthy, K. V. B. and R. Jha (2003). The non-global nature of WEO". In Hans Singer *et al.* (ed.), *Trade and Environment: Recent Controversies* (New Delhi: Vedam Books).

Odum, H. T. (1996). *Environmental Accounting and Environmental Decision Making* (USA: Wiley).

Tennenbaum, S. E. (1988). Network energy expenditures for subsystem production, MS Thesis. Gainesville, FL: University of FL, 131 pp. (CFW-88-08).

Chapter 17

Leadership

Sheila Dubey

'A leader is a dealer in hope.'

Napoleon 1, Maxims (1804–1815)

LEARNING OBJECTIVES

- Gain an understanding of the concept of leadership.
- Evaluate and analyse traits of successful leaders.
- Identify the relationship between responsibility, accountability and leadership.
- Become familiar with challenges faced by leaders today and tomorrow.

17.1 MEANING

Leadership is the process through which one member of a group influences other members towards the attainment of shared goals. Most, if not all definitions of leadership bring out the above in some form. Yet, the reader must bear in mind that the term leadership is hard to define, and it is because of this ambiguity that it is often misused today. Perhaps it is easier to draw a list of what leadership is not than to formulate a comprehensive definition. Leadership has long been studied, through the prisms of various fields including psychology, management and other social sciences. In the following discussion, we will restrict ourselves to relevant issues concerning the attributes of a leader, and challenges faced by leaders in the 21st century.

'A good leader inspires people to have confidence in the leader; a great leader inspires people to have confidence in themselves.'

Lao Tzu

17.2 QUALITIES AND ATTRIBUTES OF LEADERS

'The ear of the leader must ring with the voices of the people.'

Woodrow Wilson

Are great leaders born with truly innate qualities that set them apart from others? And if this is so, can these attributes be isolated and emulated? The common sense appeal of this idea led early researchers in the field to coin the 'great person theory of leadership', that all leaders possess traits which set them apart from most human beings. In recent years with advances in the understanding of human personality and improved research methods, some researchers contend that leaders *do* differ in several important ways. Broadly, traits that set leaders apart are motivation, knowledge, virtue and self-confidence. Leaders possess *drive* – a desire for achievement along with high energy and resolution, and a desire to be in charge, to exercise authority; *self-confidence* and *creativity* – unconventional approach to problem solving; and *integrity* – at least in the exhibition of honesty. In addition, successful leaders also must be able to conceive and communicate a clear vision, thus translating their passion to their followers. To the extent that they are successful in doing so often determines the intensity of commitment of those who choose to follow them. An important aspect of such communication is that it goes beyond a statement of goals and indicates a clear path of achieving them. Other qualities attributed to leaders are the willingness to lead by example and self-sacrifice. Both these emphasise sincerity on part of the leader and go a long way in inspiring others to follow them. An indicative list of attributes of a leader is given below:

- Honesty – A leader should appear credible and honest. Even the hint of deviation from such behaviour may seriously erode his authority.
- Forward looking – Visionary leadership believes the critical ingredient is vision and the ability to mobilise people towards a meaningful future. Leaders show the way to a brighter tomorrow with a need to seek and accept responsibility for the organisations future.
- Inspirational – To the able to inspire others with their enthusiasm and sense of optimums. The inspiration to rely met on quantity met in incremental improvements but in paradigm shifts.
- Competent – Leaders know their own strengths and weaknesses and are perpetual learners. People will follow leaders who show self-confidence and take the initiative. Trying always to shape events and not merely react to them.
- Leadership has a generic component – Leadership competence is fundamentally about whom they are character. 'Strong' character is not enough to be a leader one must have an unusual and paradoxical combination of self-worth and self-doubt, awareness of self and of others and the simultaneous ability to belong and to be detached.
- A leader must have the capacity to listen to other and hear the subtext as well as the text.

Ideally, leaders must be able to articulate vision and direction in an inspirational way and live what they are talking about.

> 'Where leaders do not practice what they preach; there are terrible disabling consequences.'
>
> Margaret J. Wheatly

Before a leader can lead, he/she must first belong, more than anyone else, must live up to the ideals and standards the group has already previously accepted. If he/she cannot do this he/she cannot lead; no matter what his/her ability or what his/her power is. A leader leads only with respect to a group that might accept him/her first as a member and then as first among them. Leaders do not arise in a social vacuum, and as such different situations call for different leaders, or leaders differing in personal style. It is misleading to claim that all successful leaders share all traits and qualities mentioned above. These form only a part of the picture.

17.3 LEADERSHIP AND MORALITY

How do we judge the ethics of a leader? No leader can be expected to be perfect in every decision and action made. The quality and worth of leadership can only be measured in terms of what a leader intends, believes in or stands for. In other words, character is one of the more crucial and elusive element of leadership. Character is the enduring mark or etched-in-factor in our personality, which includes inborn talent as well as learned and acquired traits realised through life experiences. These define a person. Set him/her apart and underlie the motives for his/her behaviour. Character establishes both, day-to-day demeanour and destiny. It is therefore essential to define character of those who desire to lead us. It has to be a careful choice.

The character, goals and aspirations of a leader are not developed in a vacuum. Leadership even in the hand of a strong confident charismatic leader remains at its core, relational. Leaders – good or bad, great or small – arise out of the needs and opportunities of a specific time and place. Leaders acquire causes, issues and more importantly a hungry and willing workforce. Leaders devise plans, establish agendas and often bring new and radical ideas to the table, but all of them are a response to the milieu and membership of which they are a part. Leadership is an active and ongoing relationship between the leaders and their workforce and a basic requirement for this process to work is for leaders to elicit a consensus. Conversely, the workforce should inform and influence their leaders. This process may be enabled through the use of power and education.

'Power' comes from the Latin word *passé*, which means to do, to be able to change, to influence or effect change. To have power is to possess the capacity to control or direct change. All forms of leadership must use power wisely and well. According to James Macgregor Burns, leadership is not just about directed results; it is about offering followers a choice among real alternatives. Hence, leadership assumes competition, conflict and debate whereas brute power denies it. Leadership mobilises whereas brute power coerces. Power need not be dictatorial or punitive to be effective. Power can be used in a non-coercive manner to orchestrate, direct and guide members of an organisation in the pursuit of a goal or series of objectives. Leaders must engage followers, not merely direct them. Leaders must serve as models and mentors 'power without morality is no longer power'.

The 'task' of leader as a teacher is to empower people with information, offers insight, new knowledge and alternative perspectives on reality. He/she should foster learning, offering choices and building consensus. Effective leadership recognises that in order to built and achieve consensus, followers must become reciprocally co-consensus. Leaders must try to make their follow constituents aware that they are all stakeholder in a conjoint activity that cannot succeed without their involvement and commitment. 'The achievement of an organisation is the result of combined effort of each individual.' Leadership is based on a compact that binds those who lead with those who follow into the same moral intellectual and emotional commitment. Responsive and responsible leadership requires as a minimum that democratic mechanism be put in place which recognises the right of the workforce to have adequate knowledge of alternative options, goals and programmes, as well as the capacity to choose between them.

The vision and values of the leadership must have their origin and resolutions in the community workforce of which they are a part. Leaders can drive, lead, orchestrate and cajole, but they cannot force, demand or dictate. Leaders can be the catalyst for morally sound behaviour but they are not by themselves a sufficient condition for it. Leaders by means of their demeanour and message must be able to convince, not just tell others, that collaboration serves the conjoint interest and wellbeing of all involved. Leaders must offer a vision that can be bought. Leaders must organise a plan that can be taken. Leaders must demonstrate conviction and will power in the new paradigm of leadership. With the number of option available, the ethics of decision making between alternatives is a challenge. Ethics is an evaluative enterprise. Judgement must be made in regard to competing viewpoints. Even in the absence of a belief in the existence of a single, universal, absolute set of ethical rules, basic question can be asked. How does it impact on self and other? What are the consequences involved?

Scientific method for evaluating ethical decisions:

- Observation – the recognition of problem or conflict.
- Inquiry – a critical consideration of fact and issues involved.
- Hypothesis – the formulation of a decision or action, consistent with the known facts.
- Experimentation and evaluation – the implementation of the decision or plan to see if it leads to the resolution of the problem.

There are of course no perfect answers to essentially ethical questions. The quality of our ethical choices cannot be measured solely in term of achievement. Ultimately, intention, commitment and concerted effort are important outcomes.

Ethics in business and organisational life will not occur or be sustained without the witness of 'moral' leadership. Leadership, even when defined as a collaborative experience, is still about the influence of individual character and the impact of personal mentoring. Behaviour does not always beget like behaviour on a one-on-one basis, but it does establish its tone, set the stage and offer options. Although it is mandatory that organisations as a whole from top to bottom make a commitment to ethical behaviour, for its achievement the commitment has to originate from the top. Creation of an environment with strong set of core values with ethical principal is the foundation of success. Honesty and integrity, respect for other, fairness and straight dealings are the ethical values that operate all over the world. Leaders can make values visible with a priority that gets measured and rewarded. Leaders should have good judgement to know how to preserve important values and hold fast to them, while at the same time knowing when and how to change in order to meet the challenges of a new world.

17.4 LEADERSHIP AND RESPONSIBILITY

> 'We must not promise what we ought not, lest we be called on to perform what we cannot.'
>
> Abraham Lincoln

Leadership requires ownership of the meaning of personal responsibility and accountability. It means recognising the truth that nothing happens unless one makes it happen. For every important responsibility, there is accountability. Accountability is the obligation to answer for the discharge of responsibilities that affect others in important ways. The answering is for intentions as well as results. It is a realisation and recognition that one is responsible for the result and outcomes. If this becomes a response to a particular situation then there exists the possibility to solve the problem or problems that caused the situation effectively. Leaders who manage by accountability know that there is a responsibility to do something, to make things better and achieve results. Possessing the attribute and ability to take decisions makes the esteem of that leader rise in the eyes of those around him/her. Accountability involves a clearly define set of periodical reviews leaders are ultimately accountability for everything that happens, both good and bad. Accountability should be linked to:

- What is to be done?
- Keeping organisational vision clear.
- Identifying the missing link between reward and reorganisation.
- Understand now about leadership link that balance style with results.
- Discover ways to keep everyone accountable.
- Witness new it all comes together as facilitative leadership.

Core values are the greatest point of leverage to get things done and achieve all that can be achieved. A leader's responsibility is to instil values throughout the organisation. Leadership responsibility is to put the organisation into a position where the highest level of performance is necessary to succeed. There is no escape from commitment. Accountability demands a promise and an obligation to fulfil an acceptance of the consequence and outcome. In today's increasingly borderless environment, accountability principles are paramount to everybody's interest. Managing by accountability is the greatest challenge any leader will ever undertake. To hold themselves up for others to see, to take responsibility when it is needed, and to accept change and the conflict that often accompanies it. The rewards are clear; credibility, effectiveness and an inner satisfaction that is priceless.

17.5 CONCLUSION – LEADERSHIP CHALLENGES

Twenty-first century leaders face challenges that are different from the prevalent ones as the world around have changed dramatically – incredibly. The fulcrum of leadership skills have changed from thrusting the dominantly analytical and logical, towards the inclusive intuitive and humane. This has had implication for leaders all over the world. There has been a shift from the analytical and directive style to the interactive humane and inclusive participative style. Good leader's overlay the humane facts with their gut feel and instinct, which they consciously develop through been listening reflection contemplation and mentoring.

In the fast-changing world around us, 'big ideas' have a limited shelf life and the premium today is on adapting and accepting change. A key challenge for leaders remains knowing when to discard a concept or an idea. No matter how long they have been in charge, no matter where the advice to change comes from, leaders must be ready to implement change, if not conceive of it.

Future leadership will be out to accomplish more than the science of management says is possible. Future leaders need to comprehend changes and what it means to their leadership. The trend towards globalisation makes the future a critical one for improving leadership throughout the organisation. The need of the hour is to create one's own brand of leadership, and put it into practice. Leaders will need to create an environment where others express their values and feel encouraged to do the right things. A strong foundation will need to be built on values and a heritage-based on ethical principles. Leaders must remain learners, they must remain curious. As technology evolves and paradigms change, the effective leader must be open to them, looking for new opportunities.

Suggested Questions

1. 'Leadership leading requires ownership of the meaning of personal responsibility and accountability.' Explain.
2. What are the qualities and attributes of a good leader?
3. How do we judge the ethics of a leader?
4. Explain the challenges that managers face in a fast-changing and increasingly globalised world.
5. Write a note on leadership and responsibility.
6. Write a note on leadership and morality.

Bibliography

Bennis, W. (1989). *On Becoming a Leader* (New York: Addison Wesley).

Burns, J. M. (1978). *Leadership* (New York, NY: Harper Torchbooks).

Chatterjee, A. and Hartman, L. (2007). *Perspectives in Business Ethic* (New Delhi: Tata McGraw Hill).

Dealy, M. D. (2007). *Managing by Accountability* (Westport, London: Praeger).

Edward, G. R. (1994). Is moral leadership possible? *Philosophy of Education 1993, The Proceedings of the Forty-Ninth Annual Meeting of the Philosophy of Education Society*, pp. 266–274.

Kirkpatrick, S. A. and Locke, E. A. (1991). "Leadership: Do traits really matter?" *Academy of Management Executive,* Vol.5, pp. 48–60.

Kouzes, J. M. and Posner, B. Z. (2002). *The Leadership Challenge* (San Francisco: Jossey-Bass).

Chapter 18

Workforce Diversity

Dr Usha Krishna

'True diversity is exemplified by companies that hire people who are different – knowing and valuing that they will change the way you do business.'

Dr Santiago Rodriguez, Director of Diversity for Microsoft

LEARNING OUTCOMES

This chapter is about a new concept in management that derives from the pluralistic nature of society. In as much as a company is a microcosm of society, it has to mould itself along similar lines as society. Through this chapter:

- you will gather the concept of workforce diversity.
- you will know of the forms of diversity.
- you would be able to evaluate the advantages and disadvantages of the practice.
- lastly, you will understand the role of training in this respect.

18.1 WORKFORCE DIVERSITY

Dr. Santiago Rodriguez, Director of Diversity for Microsoft said, 'True diversity is exemplified by companies that hire people who are different — knowing and valuing that they will change the way you do business.' If companies hire people without discrimination about their gender, class and colour, it will reflect true diversity in the workforce. If not, there is exclusion of a particular set of people from the workforce, calling for affirmative action by the lawmakers in the form of affirmative action. However, true diversity is not the same as affirmative action. Affirmative action is an outcome of ethical and legal interventions. It enforces legally and does not leave any choice with companies. It has been proved that diversity benefits workgroups. Despite these benefits, prejudice towards women and minority is universally reported in matters of recruitment, promotions etc. Though most countries have enacted laws that prevent such discrimination, yet it has not been rooted out and remains a hot topic of debate as 'social exclusion'.

18.2 FORMS OF DIVERSITY

Workforce diversity attempts to include different ethnic groups belonging to varied nationalities, gender and culture. Although anti-discrimination laws have helped in bringing down the discriminatory practices in organisations, yet most researches show discrimination laws have not been able to root out discriminatory practice in recruitment and other employment practices against women and ethnic groups. One in five employees has reported to have witnessed discrimination in employment practices.

The manifestation of discrimination exists at two levels: (i) at 'superficial level' in the form of differences in gender, ethnicity and nationality and (ii) at 'deep level' in the form of differences in knowledge, culture and values. By increasing amounts of interaction among individuals, the superficial discrimination does get reduced, but it is not the same as deep-level discrimination. Both forms of discrimination have resultant consequences for the organisation as well as the employees. It may be easier for the company to reduce superficial diversity by training than the deep-level discrimination. As far as the superficial discrimination is concerned, its negative effects are more perceivable in the sense that a fault line develops separating a group into distinct subgroups. This occurs when observable characteristics of individuals in a group correlate, for example, if all marketers in a group are young and female, whereas the engineers are old and male. With regard to deep-level discrimination, informational diversity (differences in knowledge base) has been found to have positive impact on performance, but value diversity (differences in what individuals find important) has been found to have negative impact on performance. Training is the only way through which sensitivity about discrimination can be imparted to reap the benefits of diversity.

18.3 DIVERSITY AND COMPETITIVE ADVANTAGES

Today's labour pool is dramatically different from the stereotype dominated by a homogeneous group of people. The available talent is now represented by people from a vast array of backgrounds and life experiences. The availability of highly skilled and employable workforce in many countries has been reducing. Multinational companies look towards developing countries for highly skilled workforce. It makes business sense to have diverse workforce due to demographic reasons also. Competitive companies cannot allow discriminatory preferences and practices to impede them from attracting the best available talent within that pool. Adapting diversity as a strategy ensures the social commitment as well as its legal responsibility of providing employment to local communities. Many companies are under legislative mandates to be non-discriminatory in their employment practices. Workforce diversity as a strategy enables a company has competitive advantage over others. Some of the benefits include:

- Non-compliance with equal employment opportunity or affirmative action legislation can result in fines and/or loss of contracts with government agencies. In the context of such legislation, it makes good business sense to utilise a diverse workforce. Appearance diversity that embraces ethnic representation and gender composition mirrors the demographics of the marketplace. Companies embracing ethnic/appearance diversity are better equipped to thrive in that marketplace than a company whose appearance is out of step with its market's appearance.
- Because many of the beneficiaries of good diversity practices are from groups of people who are 'disadvantaged' in our communities, there is certainly good reason to consider workforce diversity as an exercise in 'social inclusion'. By diversifying workforce, companies give individuals the 'break' they need to earn a living and achieve their dreams. In turn, ethnic variety offers cultural intelligence to understand the markets better; offers local expertise and increases credibility and strategic innovation in products, services and delivery mechanisms in regional markets.
- Employees from multicultural groups learn a great deal from each other, if they accept to live with each other. A study showed that medical scientists performed especially well when they maintained relationships with colleagues having a wide assortment of values, experiences and disciplines. On the other hand, constant close association with colleagues similar to themselves decreased the performance of these groups.
- In another study, it was reported that mixed-gender groups consistently produced better quality solutions to problems than the same did. It was proved that the greater the differences in perceptions among group, the higher the quality of their problem solving.

- It has also been observed that ill-defined or novel problems are best handled by a heterogeneous group in which diversity of knowledge and background allow a thorough airing of alternatives.
- There are arguments that attribute diversity to reduced turnover and absenteeism and enhance reputation as fair employer.

18.4 DIVERSITY AND COMPETITIVE DISADVANTAGES

When companies move from one place to other, cultural dissimilarity throws some operational problems:

- Diversity has inherent disadvantages in terms of conflict among genders, ethnicities and age groups. Conflicts arise because of distrust, prejudice and lack of confidence among group members.
- Another disadvantage relates to problems of communication or transmission of instructions.
- There are differences in the way people carry out instructions. In some cases, it may be an exasperating experience to get the work done from people with different cultural background. It takes time to adjust on both sides. The superior needs good amount of training before starting to deal with different workgroups. He/she should be familiar with his/her language, customs, behavioural patterns and expectations.
- Employee expectations differ in different countries, managing human expectations takes a lot of time and energy.
- Finally, the success of the enterprise depends on the sale of products, which in turn depends upon the choice of customers, who are attracted by advertisement campaign. While the same advertisement cannot be effective in all countries, the promotional strategy for each product has to be designed keeping in view the preferences of the people in terms of language, message, messenger and media.

18.5 MANAGING DIVERSITY THROUGH TRAINING

In the context of multinational organisations, workforce diversity is no longer a choice but a need that has to be fulfilled. As a corporation grows and starts business outside the boundaries of its own states, it has to induct people from different regions into its workforce. Thus, the composition of the workers changes from single community to diverse groups. These diverse groups bring their own culture, values, beliefs and styles into organisation that may result in interpersonal problems. The organisations need to deal with diversity through training. The answer to the question, could a company afford to ignore its workforce diversity is definitely negative. Therefore, the question remains how the organisation should put it to work. The following guidelines could be kept in mind.

18.5.1 NEED ASSESSMENT FOR DIVERSITY TRAINING

Every organisation should have a separate department dealing with this issue and appoint diversity manager. The job of diversity manager would be to 'assess' basic cultural differences that have a bearing on their performance. For doing so, he/she has to look into the attitude towards work and authority and expression of disagreements and aspirations of people.

18.5.2 ADAPTATION OF DIVERSITY

'Adaptation' to local culture concerns many aspects. The first adaptation may be in product policies and marketing strategies. The second adaptation relates to individual adjustment that managers should learn the local language, mannerism and behaviour. Finally, the third type of adaptation is known as institutional adaptation. It incorporates changes in the structure and policies to recreate the local culture in the host country while keeping the basic tenets of home country culture.

18.5.3 TRAINING IN DIVERSITY

Management of diversity is a very complex issue. Various inputs such as sensitising people with cross-cultural values, tolerance for others' beliefs and acceptance of each others' culture are required in training employees.

Attitudinal training to people is required to make them aware of their own biases and prejudices towards others. They can learn how to adapt themselves to the local culture, while working with them. Cultural sensitivity can be enhanced through forced interaction among people while they attend formal training sessions in intercultural and interpersonal skills. Training provides the most desired opportunity to break the barriers among genders and groups. However, training cannot solve challenges emerging from diversity overnight. In any case, ignoring diversity does not make a good business sense; the loser will be the home country and not the host country. The company can never harvest the fruits of even the best of training programmes, if the organisational climate does not support diversity with appropriate policies. However, training goes a long way in improving the process of adaptation. Thus, companies can make use of the diversity to their advantage and face the challenges.

18.6 CHALLENGES

'Mismanagement of diversity' – for example, in the form of denied access or unfavourable treatment to minority groups – can have negative workplace consequences such as inhibiting workers' abilities and motivation, thereby leading to diminished job performance. It can also happen that the executives of a majority ethnic group treat themselves as valued members of their organisation and work more conscientiously, making the minority group feel less valued due to stereotyping, ethnocentrism and prejudice. If the organisational climate does not support diversity with appropriate structures, norms and processes, the company can never succeed in the best of training programmes.

18.7 CONCLUSIONS

It has been recognised by multinational companies that diversity is not a legal compulsion but serves as a tool for competitive advantage. However, management of diversity remains to be the critical factor in reaping the benefits from diversity. The management of diversity is full of challenges, as it requires adaptation of the individuals and organisation to different cultures. Companies must give importance to attitudinal and behavioural training for employees, without that 'mismanaged diversity' can prove detrimental to the interests of the employees as well as have negative consequences for the organisation.

Suggested Questions

1. Explain the meaning and concept of workforce diversity and state its benefits to organisations?
2. What are the major forms of cultural diversity?
3. How is it different from affirmative action?
4. Discuss the advantages and disadvantages of workforce diversity to organisations.
5. What are the challenges faced by managers to manage the diverse workforce? Explain.
6. What is the role of training in managing diversity?

Bibliography

Bohlander, G., Snell, S. and Sherman, A. (2001). *Managing Human Resources*, 12th edition (USA: Thomson South-Western), p. 47.

Brady, T. (1996). The downside of diversity. *HR Focus*, 73(8), p. 22.

Iverson, K. (2000). Managing for effective workforce diversity. *Cornell Hotel and Restaurant Administration Quarterly*, 41(2), 31–38.

Malott, T. J. (1998). Crating your own workforce: When you need skilled workers, will you be able to find them? *Plan Engineering*, 52(7), pp. 30–38.

Sharan, V. (2007). *International Business*, Ch. 11, p. 229.

Unit V

Corporate Social Responsibility: An Overview

Dr Usha Krishna and Dr Ameeta Motwani

We live in an age in which companies, that are equivalent in wealth to countries, control much of the earth's resources. There is a growing realisation that since the financial capital markets and business corporations are created by society, they must serve it and not merely profit from it. The earlier mantra of 'maximising the medium-term earnings per share has come under pressure from a wide range of stakeholders: employees, customers and public affected in any way by the company's functioning. This unit deals with the various issues related with the idea of social responsibility of business, popularly known as *corporate social responsibility* (CSR).

What constitutes the 'social responsibility' of enterprises and other organisations is difficult to define. There are various conceptions of CSR. Just as the notion of CSR is different in different countries so are the reasons driving the CSR agenda.

Chapter 19 deals with the theme of 'corporate philanthropy' and its relation with CSR. The idea of social responsibility of business is closely related to the notions of charity or philanthropy by business but differs vitally.

Chapter 20 discusses the 'corporate social responsibility'. The meaning of CSR is argued. The history of CSR is highlighted as phases in the development of the CSR agenda. The chapter throws light on the concept of the responsible company. It also discusses definitions, tools, principles and standards of CSR.

Chapter 21 tells us that there are various 'CSR models' that have attempted to formalise our understanding of CSR. The three main models that are more debated are:

1. the ethical model,
2. the statist model and
3. the stakeholder model.

The main emphasis in this chapter is on the stakeholder model, which in any case is the most popular one too.

Chapter 22 is on 'Corporate Social Responsibility Agenda – Issues and Concerns'. There is discussion on:

- global CSR policies and practices,
- the role of CII and various other industries in CSR,
- unresolved issues in CSR and
- some recent developments.

Chapter 23 is 'Case for and against CSR'. The idea that business be made responsible to society though has been widely accepted now, has supporters as well as critics. The chapter presents the debate of case for and against CSR fought by these groups.

Chapter 24 is about 'Strategic Planning and CSR'. Strategic planning is an important factor for success in any endeavour. This chapter examines the role of strategic planning and its relationship with CSR.

Chapter 19

Corporate Philanthropy

Dr Ameeta Motwani

'I resolved to stop accumulating and begin the infinitely more serious and difficult task of wise distribution.'

Andrew Carnegie

LEARNING OUTCOMES

Through this chapter, you would be able gain in respect of certain outcomes such as:

- You will understand the meaning of the concept of philanthropy.
- You would be made aware of certain developments that relate to it.
- You would be able to evaluate the differences between philanthropy and other related concepts.
- The historical trends in philanthropy would be made known to you.

19.1 INTRODUCTION

Though the concept of corporate social responsibility (CSR) has only recently been formulated, there is a long history in both the East and the West of a commitment to social philanthropy, in the belief that the creation of wealth is primarily for social good. In order to understand the concept of social responsibility, it is important to understand how it is similar to and different from corporate philanthropy. This chapter describes the meaning of philanthropy and its history as well as the recent developments.

19.2 MEANING AND BACKGROUND

Derived from the Greek words *Philein* (to love) and *anthropos* (man), philanthropy means love for mankind and refers to charity. It is, thus, a love of humankind, expressed in charitable giving for promoting the welfare and progress of society as a whole. Corporate philanthropy refers to the practice of companies or corporations making charitable contributions.

Traditional corporate philanthropy dates back to the 19th century and emerged out of a variety of factors such as:

1. Concern for the welfare of the immediate members of the corporate body: the staff and employees, and their families.
2. Innovative contributions by visionary business leaders in quest of personal satisfaction, who built up philanthropic institutions out of their individual shares.

3. The desire to establish a strategic relationship with the state or society led some corporate bodies to invest in the establishment of institutions that fulfil the specific requirements of the community.
4. The establishment of trusts and foundations for tax benefits, which also supports socially beneficial activities.

Philanthropy is to some extent depends on whimsical attitude of the donor agent/agency. It simply depends on the whims of the company directors at a particular time. Many NGOs receive their funds from corporations to carry out work in such areas that are neglected by the government, but the continuation of their work depends upon the donations they receive from philanthropists/corporations. Nietzsche opposed philanthropy on the philosophical basis of 'weak as a parasite' on the strong. Many thinkers are opposed to welfare programmes of this type and have criticised the welfare programmes of governments too.

19.3 KEY DEVELOPMENTS

19.3.1 GLOBAL PHILANTHROPY

Today, most of the big corporations are operating on an international scale, employing a global workforce and depending on a global customer base. As a result, corporate philanthropy is expanding beyond its traditional geographical areas. Companies are finding that global philanthropy helps them enter new markets, develop effective relationships with business partners and earn more customers and reputation. Examples of global philanthropic efforts include: Coca-Cola Corporation and Ford Motors are spending large amounts towards AIDS control programmes in Africa and Microsoft Corporations donates funds for the containment of AIDS and tuberculosis in India.

19.3.2 STRATEGIC PHILANTHROPY

When it comes to philanthropy, executives increasingly see themselves as caught between critics demanding ever-higher levels of 'CSR' and investors applying pressure to maximise short-term profits. Increasingly, philanthropy is used as a form of public relations or advertising, promoting a company's image through high-profile sponsorships. However, there is truer strategic way to think about philanthropy. Corporations can use their charitable efforts to improve their competitive context — the quality of the business environment in the locations where they operate. Using philanthropy to enhance competitive context aligns social and economic goals and improves a company's long-term business prospects. Addressing context enables a company not only to give money, but also to leverage its capabilities and relationships in support of charitable causes. Taking this new direction requires fundamental changes in the way companies approach their contribution programmes. Adopting a context-focused approach requires a far more disciplined approach than is prevalent today. However, it can make a company's philanthropic activities far more effective.

Forced to explain why businesses should continue to give money away while laying off workers, contributions of managers in hundreds of companies have come up with an approach that ties corporate giving directly to strategy. In those companies, philanthropic and business units have joined forces to develop philanthropic strategies that give their companies a powerful competitive edge. The new corporate philanthropy encourages companies to play a leadership role in social problem solving by funding initiatives that incorporate the best thinking of governments and non-profit institutions while advancing the company's business goals at the same time.

19.4 PHILANTHROPY AND OTHERS

19.4.1 PHILANTHROPY AND CSR

Both concepts appear to be similar because in both cases the company indulges in social expenditure. The expenditure is not on the ordinary business of the company. The common thing is that there is some activity which is not related to the business of the company. However, corporate social responsibility is qualitatively different from the traditional concept of corporate philanthropy. Components of CSR include respect for people and communities, ethical values, compliance with legal requirements, environmental concern, consumer protection etc. CSR is concerned with treating the stakeholders of a company or institution ethically or in a responsible manner. 'Ethically responsible' means treating key stakeholders in a manner deemed acceptable to civilised societies. Social includes economic and environmental responsibility. Stakeholders exist both within a firm and outside. The wider aim of social responsibility is to create higher and higher standards of living, while preserving the profitability of the corporation or the integrity of the institution, for peoples both within and outside these entities.

Traditional corporate philanthropy is only one of the ways in which business can and should discharge their social responsibility. CSR is, thus wider in scope than philanthropy. Many companies voluntarily contribute towards various charities and causes. This does not, however, make them socially responsible. The emerging perspective on CSR acknowledges the debt that the corporation owes to the society and therefore focuses on responsibility towards multiple stakeholders such as shareholders, employees, management, consumers and community. If a company favours philanthropy but simultaneously eschews policies that are directed towards the people, planet and profits, it may not qualify as a socially responsible company.

19.4.2 PHILANTHROPY AND SPONSORSHIP

It is important to differentiate philanthropy from corporate sponsorship. It is different from corporate sponsorship. Corporate sponsorship is a business tool used by companies for advertising and is meant for their customers' consumption. Sponsorship usually requires a service, or action, in return for financial support that has clear marketing benefits. Sometimes, this may indeed be for good causes such as supporting UNICEF to associate the company's products with reducing child labour around the world. On other occasions, it may just be sponsoring a cricket match.

Philanthropy does not necessarily ask for a definite service or action in return and it is certainly not usually based on a business relationship or partnership. Philanthropy has no *quid pro quo*. At a personal level, this is like responding favourably to the postal requests made by the major charities. Moreover, often philanthropic donations are tax deductible, partially or wholly, whereas sponsorships are not. Philanthropy is generally a quiet affair. It is without fanfare or publicity. Sponsorship uses every opportunity to advertise and publicise the name of the sponsor.

19.5 CORPORATE PHILANTHROPY

19.5.1 PHILANTHROPY AS FOUNDATION OF CSR IN INDIA

Though most of the traditional business houses in India have contributed towards philanthropic activities which could be interpreted as CSR in today's context. Some of the prominent business houses that have historically made contribution towards philanthropy and are responsible for the present transition towards CSR are TATA, Birla, Bajaj, Godrej, Modis, Dalmias, Shri Rams, Hero group and TT Krishnamachari. Some of these groups have carried forward this tradition by moving towards CSR related to their core business, while others have either died out or stuck to philanthropy.

19.5.2 CORPORATE PHILANTHROPY IN INDIA

Corporate philanthropy in India can be traced back to the pre-independence days when Indian companies supported Mahatma Gandhi's call for the development of the nation by funding and providing education, health and other social services. Even after independence, companies such as TISCO and other public-sector enterprises voluntarily contributed to community development.

The story of Indian business philanthropy is largely a story of Indian business families and business dynasties. Prominent among them are the Tatas, the Birlas, the Goenkas, the Bajajs, the Dalmias, the Modis etc. The JN Tata Endowment scheme was launched in 1992, much before the first major foundation in the United States. Its biggest contribution was the establishment of Indian Institute of Science. Likewise, the Wadia family set up a full-fledged foundation on the lines of those in the West. Particularly significant examples are those of Ardeshir Godrej who gave Rs.300,000 to the Tilak Swaraj Fund, for the upliftment of Harijans, GD Birla who gifted away many of the palatial Birla homes to be used as temples and Jamanalal Bajaj who put himself and his wealth at the disposal of Gandhiji. In recent times, examples of corporate philanthropy are numerous: from disaster relief efforts by all big business houses to scholarships for deserving and needy students and education and health facilities for employees' families as well as neighbouring communities.

Religion has played an important role in Indian business philanthropy. However, it is disappointing to note that at present, fewer Indian companies follow the practice of corporate philanthropy as compared to the MNCs operating in India. According to a study [1] published in *IIMB Review*, only 12.4% of Indian companies pursue strategic philanthropy compared to 48% of the MNCs. Charity is pursued by 35% of the Indian companies and 62% of the MNCs. This may be because of the fact that while companies in North America and Europe are pressured by stakeholders to adopt CR practices, the Indian companies so far have not faced any such pressures. In addition, while companies in developed countries report their social activities as required by the global reporting initiative in Indian companies are still not legally bound formally to report CSR activities. However, it must be understood that mere charity or contribution to social welfare activities does not make a company socially responsible.

19.5.2.1 Tata Group

Tata Group has been in the forefront of the philanthropic activities even during the British rule. The company's philanthropic activities can be dated to as early as 1892, when Jamshedji Tata established the JN Tata Endowment Scheme to provide higher education for deserving Indians. Since then, 3,500 Tata scholarships have been awarded, recipients included KR Narayanan (former president of India) and Dr. Raja Ramanna (renowned scientist). JRD Tata believed that social responsibility of his companies should be institutionalised. Thus, in the 1970s, the group amended its Articles of Association according to which the group shall be mindful of its social and moral responsibilities to the consumers, employees, shareholders, society and the local community for all its major companies.

In 1979, the Tata Steel Rural Development Society (TSRDS) was established for rural development. Today, it covers 700 villages in and around Tata Steel's diverse, business operations in the states of Jharkhand and Orissa. TSRDS helps communities improve their quality of life by implementing a number of relevant programmes that are managed by trained members of the community in education, health care and sanitation services; family planning, drinking water, irrigation, agriculture, animal husbandry, adult literacy, afforestation, vocational training and the encouragement of rural industry, entrepreneurship and handicrafts.

[1] The study titled 'Corporate Philanthropy as Business Strategy: An Indian Perspective' has been authored by Laxman Mohanty and Neharike Vohra.

19.5.2.2 Birla Group

Krishna Kumar Birla, son of the founding father of the Birla Group, Ghanshyam Das Birla, was among the founder members of the Indian sugar industry which he joined in 1940. Birla had established one of the India's biggest business conglomerates and his industrial empire spans key industries such as sugar, fertilisers, chemicals, heavy engineering, textiles, shipping and newspaper. He was a respected parliamentarian, socialite, philanthropist and scholar apart from being an industrialist.

He established the K.K. Birla Foundation, which has instituted annual awards for excellence in Indian literature, scientific research and Indian philosophy. K.K. Birla, popularly known as K.K. Babu, was a builder of modern institutions, ranging from industry to education, one of the famous symbols of which is the Birla Institute of Technology and Science at Pilani, Rajasthan, his birthplace.

He built Radha-Krishna Temple (popularly known as Birla Temple) here and many other institutions all over the country that enriched the fabric of Indian society.

The A.V. Birla Group has been contributing to the poor and marginalised people in and around its plants across India for the past 50 years. In the earlier days, the group used to dole out money as charity. However, the late Aditya Birla felt that giving money to the poor is not the long-term solution and felt that social projects should be self-sustainable in the long run.

19.5.2.3 Infosys

Infosys, formed in 1981 by NR Narayana Murthy, follows a socially responsible and sustainable path in conducting business. Even during the booming time of the 1990s when the stock prices of IT companies were skyrocketing, the company believed in sharing the wealth with the society and its employees. This practice of the company stems from the personal belief of Narayana Murthy to give back to the society more than what it gave him. It also substantiates the role and motivation of the CEO and the top management in making the company a responsible corporation.

Murthy is of the belief that corporations have to show fairness in dealing with employees to retain them; corporations should ensure transparent disclosures to investors to attract global capital; ensure customer satisfaction to win confidence and must ensure fair dealings with their supply chains; and should be ethical to government by paying all taxes. Infosys has won many awards such as Best Employers to Work for in India, Golden Peacock Award for Excellence in Corporate Governance in the Global Category by the World Council for Corporate Governance, London and Corporate ship Award by *The Economic Times*.

A strong sense of social responsibility is foremost among the core values of Infosys that translates into a commitment to help people and communities, enhance living conditions and improve education. The social consciousness is included in the strategic plan of the company and serves as a guideline for the management to help in decision making. The Infosys Foundation was formed to focus on health care, primary education, social rehabilitation and rural upliftment and promote art and culture. Sudha Murthy (wife of Narayana Murthy), chairperson of the foundation, is taking a leadership role in influencing corporate India to discharge their social responsibilities besides focusing on profit generation. The Foundation began its activities in Karnataka in 1996. Today the activities have extended to Tamil Nadu, Andhra Pradesh, Maharashtra, Orissa and Punjab. According to a recent report, Infosys spends about Rs. 50 million on social activities.

19.6 CONCLUSION

The above efforts by the corporates, towards philanthropy, are only a part of a loose concept of 'corporate social responsibility' as has been practised in the past. A company would be truly a responsible when it has developed a framework for being responsible towards the people, planet and profit. A responsible corporation must cater proactively to majority stakeholders if not all. Any attempt to further philanthropy should ultimately be directed towards CSR. In this era, pure philanthropy cannot be justified when companies face such an overburden of corporate responsibility.

Suggested Questions

1. Discuss the meaning of corporate philanthropy. Describe some of the initiatives of Indian corporates in this context.
2. How is CSR different from corporate philanthropy?
3. Outline some of the key developments in corporate philanthropy.
4. Write a short note on strategic philanthropy.
5. Write a short note on philanthropy and sponsorship.
6. Write a note on the past and future of CSR in India.

Bibliography

Anu, A. (2003). Corporate social responsibility. *37th Annual A.D. Shroff Memorial Lecture*, 5 November, Mumbai.

Michael Hopkins (MHCi) (1998). *A Planetary Bargain: Corporate Social Responsibility Comes of Age* (UK: Macmillan). Updated by author January 2008.

Nayak, S. K. (2003). Corporate social responsibility: An Indian perspective. *Effective Executive* (May).

Porter, M. E. and Kramer, M. R. (2002). The competitive advantage of corporate philanthropy. *Harvard Business Review* (December), 56–68, Pt. II.

Smith, C. (1994). The competitive advantage of corporate philanthropy. *Harvard Business Review* (May).

Chapter 20

Corporate Social Responsibility

Dr Usha Krishna

'If they [companies] believe they are in business to serve people, to help solve problems, to use and employ the ingenuity of their workers to improve the lives of people around them by learning from the nature that gives us life, we have a chance.'

Paul Hawken

LEARNING OUTCOMES

This is one of the essential core chapters. By the end of this chapter, you would be in a position to:

- gain knowledge of the basics of CSR.
- know the meaning and nature of CSR.
- understand the concept of a responsible company.
- know the principles of CSR.
- know the various phases in the development of CSR.
- acquaint with the basic principles of CSR.

20.1 INTRODUCTION

As CSR has been an evolving concept, ambiguity about its meaning is inevitable. Since the concept of responsibility being the core of CSR, the terms 'social responsibility' and 'responsible company' have been used interchangeably while explaining its meaning. At times when unethical business practices were rampant, it highlighted the concept of responsible company, whereas the term corporate social responsibility was used when the domain of CSR functions was limited to community or employee relations and it used as a 'human resource function'. Over a period, the domain of CSR has expanded and it is supposed to address worldwide challenges such as global warming, hunger, health and poverty. Any discussion of CSR would be incomplete without a global focus. Global corporate responsibility demands cooperation among governments, corporations and civil society to achieve CSR objectives that outline the expectations of corporations.

20.2 MEANING

There is much confusion with regard to meaning of CSR across companies, countries and regions. Some equate CSR to philanthropy based on the similarity in their purpose. Philanthropy is based on the principle of charity; it has nothing to do with the philosophy of business and CSR. It requires setting aside a sum of money for activities that may or may not have anything to do with the primary business activity of the stakeholders. In addition, charity is dependent on many factors such as profits of the company and the intentions of the board of directors. It may or may not play a direct role in impacting the lives of employees and other stakeholders. CSR relates to core business values of the company. The philosophy behind CSR is to engage with stakeholders with an object of making a positive impact on all of them.

Often executives confuse CSR with obedience to laws, and think that if they obey the law on pollution control, or child labour, they are abiding by the charter of CSR. Laws however are meant to be abided by and companies that do so may deem themselves 'good corporate citizens'. This however does not describe the CSR commitments of a company.

Another source of confusion occurs when community development and PR are equated with CSR. Companies involved in projects related to community development may help their employees and the community indirectly and directly through community projects in areas such as education or health, respectively. The need for such interventions may arise for two reasons — in response to the 'philosophy of business' that is aimed at fulfilling the expectations of stakeholders or to fulfil a necessary requirement to provide basic facilities for education and health, where there are none. Though in both cases such services have a positive impact on society, the intention behind the two differs. For the former, the need may arise due to a company's obligations towards its stakeholders, whereas for the latter it could be a strategic attempt to retain its workforce by providing bare minimum welfare amenities. A point to be understood here is that the philanthropic activities arise out of the 'business philosophy' and lie outside the ambit of 'core business values' of a company, while CSR arises out of the 'philosophy of business' that is central to the core business values that take care of the workforce, marketplace, financiers and the environmental accountability.

There has been little attention paid to the creation of a CSR department in companies; therefore, all activities related to CSR are mostly handled by the HR departments (HRD). In other instances, CSR reporting is entrusted to the PR department. The overlapping responsibilities for CSR between HRD and PR create problems as far as CSR is concerned. Thereby it gets lower priority over HR and PR. Normally, HR and PR functions could be categorised as staff functions, whereas CSR is closer to line functions. CSR has a broader connotation because it touches every other function in an organisation as its essence and strength lie in business ethics and values. This lack of clarity with respect to functions of CSR, HR and PR can only be sorted by creating a designated CSR department with full authority and responsibility to discharge functions which encompass the role of CSR towards society in general and stakeholders in particular.

'Corporate responsibility' therefore emerges from philosophy of business and remains rooted in strategic planning process of business. It is a very basic differentiator among all these conceptions and related to the objectives with which CSR or other functional activities are carried out.

20.3 BASIC CONCEPTS

CSR is viewed with different outlook across the world. Following are some of its definitions:

> CSR is about capacity building for sustainable livelihoods. It respects cultural differences and finds the business opportunities in building the skills of employees, the community and the government.
>
> Ghana

> CSR is about business giving back to society.
>
> Phillipines

> CSR is defined as 'achieving commercial success in ways that honour ethical values and respect people, communities and the natural environment.'
>
> Anu Agha (India)

In the European Union white paper on CSR, there is no single definition for it. It is an umbrella term wherein concepts such as responsible trading, responsible consumerism, responsible investing, responsible reporting, environmental management and auditing system have been included. To some extent, these are reflected in the definition given by the World Business Council for Sustainable Development. It states that:

> Corporate social responsibility is the continuing commitment by business to *behave ethically* and contribute to economic development while improving the quality of life of the workforce and their families as well as of the local community and society at large.
>
> 'Making Good Business Sense' by Lord Holmes and Richard Watts

A broader definition of CSR, which encompasses different viewpoints, is that CSR is about how companies manage the business processes to produce an overall positive impact on society (Mallen Baker). Figure 20.1 clarifies this definition.

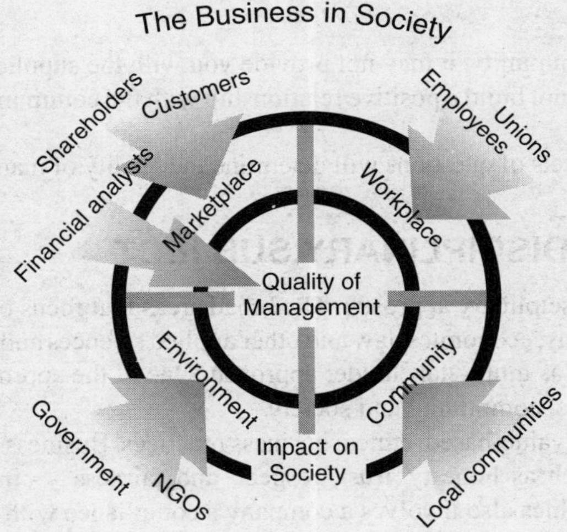

Figure 20.1 The Business in Society (Mallen Baker).

As explained earlier, business exists for society and therefore the quality of management is important in fulfilling society's expectations of business. The quality of management has a direct impact on the society through its role in community, markets, environment and workplace. A business that fulfils the role of doing 'good' to the society at large is labelled a responsible/respected company. One that is not has to pay a price eventually for the unethical behaviour. These days there is considerable pressure on management to behave ethically from various quarters such as shareholders, financial analysts, government, non-government organizations (NGOs), local communities and employee groups. A company cannot operate for a long time unless it responds to the expectations of the society. The responsibility for fulfilling them falls on (as per Figure 20.1) the management. Thus, management gets the licence to operate on the behest of society.

20.3.1 MARKETPLACE

For example, answers questions such as — What are the risk factors connected with the products made? Which stakeholders are about to boycott for the services you provide? What is the impact of your business on society, and how do you future-proof? What strategy do you implement to go well with the emerging trends? What plans do you have to getaway from the risks?

20.3.2 ENVIRONMENT

The crux of the environmental problem lies in the following questions:

- Do you use excessive resource use — especially of non-renewable nature?
- Do we produce excessive effluents in air, water and earth?
- Do we indulge in excessive consumption and waste?

20.3.3 WORKPLACE

Do you really treat employees like your greatest asset? Do you erect barriers to their development based on prejudice? Do you nurture their pride in the company — or simply burn their energy in every waking moment as they plan to migrate to your more family-friendly competitor?

20.3.4 COMMUNITY

If you do not invest in the community, it may not provide you with the suppliers, or the educated employees you need to operate. If you do not build a positive relationship with the community, it may not be so supportive when you need to expand.

The answer to the above sets of questions will determine the quality of management and its responsibility.

20.4 CSR—INTERDISCIPLINARY SUBJECT

CSR emerges from an interdisciplinary approach. The broad areas that focus on this subject include political economy, sociology, philosophy, economics, law and other applied sciences and technology. Another approach to the study of CSR is termed as multi-stakeholder approach. One of the approaches to deal with this subject is relationship among business, community and society.

Business ethics: relates to value-based, ethical business practices. Business ethics defines 'how a company integrates core values — such as honesty, trust, respect, and fairness — into its policies, practices, and decision making'. Business ethics also involves a company's compliance with legal standards and adherence to internal rules.

Workplace and labour relations: HR is most important and critical to a company. Good CSR practices relating to workplace and labour relations can help in improving the workplace in terms of health and safety, employee relations as well as result in a healthy balance between work and non-work aspects of employees' life. It can also make it easier to recruit employees and make them stay longer, thereby reducing the costs and disruption of recruitment and retraining. Equal opportunity employer, diversity of workforce that includes disabled people, people from the local communities etc., gender policy, code of conduct/guidelines on prevention of sexual harassment at workplace.

Public policy: Political economy is another subject that deals with the decisions related to efficient utilisation of resources in the context of public policy and relationship between the society and government. It includes environment, that is, environmental accountability and laws. Merely meeting legal requirements in itself does not comprise CSR, but it requires company to engage in such a way that goes beyond mandatory requirements and delivers environmental benefits. It should include, but not limited to, finding sustainable solutions for natural resources, reducing adverse impacts on environment, reducing environment-risky pollutants/emissions and producing environment-friendly goods.

Management: The quality movement and industrial management, to some extent, focused on the quality of management that structures the norms for application of business processes related to CSR. None of the subjects really deals with the concept of CSR directly; however, each subject will be indirectly related to CSR in some ways.

Supply chain: The business process of the company is not only limited to the operations internal to the company but also to the entire supply chain involved in goods and services. If anyone from the supply chain neglects social, environmental, human rights or other aspects, it may reflect badly on the company and may ultimately affect business heavily.

Philosophy: The business concerns that talk about the philosophy of an enterprise also throws light on the CSR values, vision and mission of management, which is not included in any one of the subject disciplines stated earlier.

The question is what are the fundamentals on which the CSR rests? The expectations of society are what CSR may be resting upon when it comes to service to the society through action projects in CSR is concerned.

Approaches to CSR differ as per the importance attached to CSR by organisations. Some consider charity is good enough, while others regard it as strategic importance. Out of all these approaches, we find one approach that explains the concept most effectively — 'triple bottom line approach' to CSR as it is the most accepted, complete and recent approach developed so far.

20.4.1 Responsible Company — Triple Bottom Line Concept

George Goyder (1960) in his book titled *Responsible Company* introduced the concept of 'social audit' for the first time. The idea of social auditing came about in 1970s in the form of an audit performed by an independent group such as NGOs. It was not until the mid-1990s that the term became used in terms of the impact of a company's footprints on triple bottom line. A holistic approach to responsible behaviour of a company can only be determined by how ethical its behaviour is, in terms of fulfilling the expectations of society. For doing so, the company should integrate CSR into core business philosophy of the company. Therefore, the case for CSR and the role of business in CSR revolve around the stakeholders and the environment.[1] We have maintained that the CR can be well understood through the 'triple bottom line approach'. It refers to concern for *people, profits and planet.* It implies that these three concerns are important and must be kept in mind by all those who want to claim the title of 'ethical businesses'. The integration of these three concerns with the core business model is essential for companies. However, how does one judge whether companies are actually following the triple bottom line approach? Companies claiming to be following triple bottom line, must be able to prove that. It becomes imperative for the companies to report their performance on three parameters namely financial, environmental and social.

In achieving those objectives, companies need to educate employees and engage stakeholders towards CSR mission, vision and objectives. By doing so, the society will reward 'responsible companies' with better grading, when it comes to the buying behaviour. Therefore, CSR very clearly relates to the concept of 'responsibility towards triple bottom line' and this differentiates this concept from CSR, PR or HR function. To understand the meaning of the term CSR, 'responsibility' is the key term. Responsibility towards triple bottom line has two parts, one that is demonstrated voluntarily by companies, and if that does not happen through punitive actions which is the accountability part.

Each one of these concerns remains equally important as far as the strategic planning for CSR is concerned. The key to be effective in achieving CSR outcomes lies in the fact that these three dimensions must be reflected while planning for CSR. The companies must ensure that the business processes are aligned in a manner that takes into consideration all these concerns that show results in the areas of 'least degradation' of environment, empowerment of people and communities. Just as the survival of business is important so is the survival of planet. The underlying message of triple bottom line approach is based on the integrated approach. It is the responsibility of business to nurture its people, communities and thereby society as a whole without overlooking the environmental accountability and responsibility.

---

[1] By now, the distinction between the concepts of corporate responsibility and corporate social responsibility must have been clear to the students (for distinction, see Unit III).

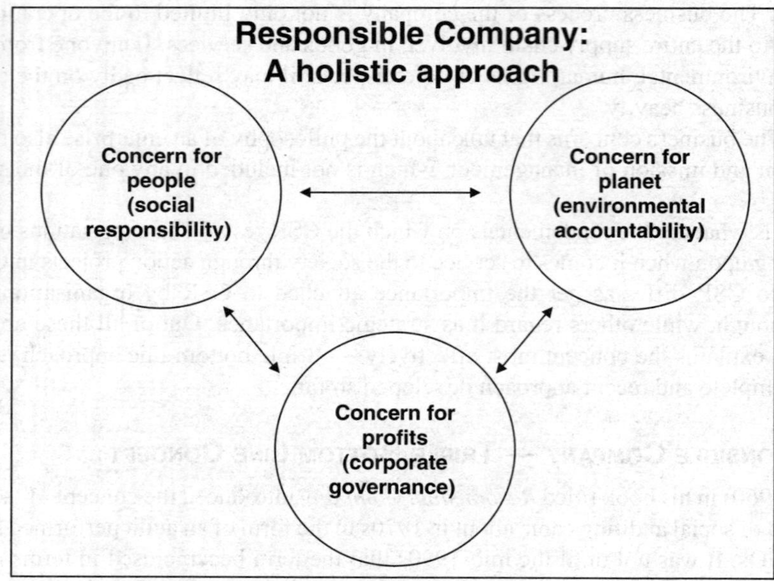

Figure 20.2 Responsible company a holistic approach.

20.5 HISTORY

The history of CSR is almost as long as that of companies. There has been a tradition of benevolent capitalism in the United Kingdom for over 150 years. However, the modern expression of CSR is very recent and has at least three streams involved in the process which are philanthropy and community involvement, socially responsible investment and social auditing. It is a fact that in terms of concrete CSR activities, companies have little to showcase their agenda. Let us take this opportunity to briefly state the various phases of the CSR agenda.

The results of unethical practices of the English East India Company followed by the Dutch, and other Europeans instigated the search for ethical business practices and principles. CSR is a journey from 'unethical behaviour of companies with purely monetary profit motives' to 'responsible behaviour for good global concerns'.

20.5.1 PHASES IN THE DEVELOPMENT OF SOCIAL RESPONSIBILITY AGENDA

If we explore 10–15-year-old published literature on this subject, we can observe the approaches to CSR had a fragmented view. We have combined the bits and pieces of literature to form a holistic view. There are five phases that can be identified with social responsibility agenda. They are

1. pre-phase,
2. first phase: people phase,
3. second phase: responsible profit phase,
4. third phase: environmental concern phase and
5. the future phase.

In the pre-phase 'social responsibility' was narrowly defined and had found acceptance among the leading thinkers of management. There are two notions about social responsibility. The first decried anything done in the name of social responsibility. Milton Friedman said that 'The business of business is business'. It was believed that businesses were meant only to profit. The second equated social responsibility with charity.

The first phase of CSR was mainly concerned with the 'social' dimension of social responsibility which dominated the agenda of CSR. During this period, labour and community development were the focus of all CSR actions. In fact, the term corporate *social* responsibility is derived from there. In this phase, the primary focus of companies was 'profit'. It was realized that this could not be achieved without the wholehearted participation of employees in tasks including management. Thus, companies focused on training and promoting employees and introducing welfare measures for employees and their families.

The second phase was a reaction to the tendency of companies to become irresponsible towards its main stakeholders — the investors or owners. There were many cases of corporate scandals, accounting frauds, unethical nexuses and the lack of transparency and accountability towards investors. This led to the movement towards good corporate governance. This meant better financial reporting, greater transparency, responsibility and accountability in matters of profit.

In the third phase, consumerism reached its peak. During this period, it was very well realised that the pace at which the resources of the world are being consumed may not be sustainable for long. Thereafter, the focus of social responsibility was shifted to the environment. Today, it is one of the most vibrant topics of concern as it is linked to serious environmental threats such as global warming and melting of arctic icecaps. This was the phase of environmental accountability.

We are on the threshold of the phase where transnational boundaries are getting blurred throwing new challenges. These challenges will require solutions through alternate modes of governance, responsibility and accountability. There is renewed search for the meaning of political, sociological and economic concepts such as liberty, equality, justice, rights, recognition, diversity, culture, growth and poverty. It is well recognised today that the role of state has diminished as far as tackling worldwide problems goes. Corporate responsibility is being looked upon as the new panacea for achieving sustainable growth in the world. With this background, the concept of 'corporate responsibility', by combining environmental accountability, corporate governance and social responsibility within its ambit, is slowly replacing the concept of 'corporate social responsibility'

This concept cannot be better exemplified than by this saying of the visionary industrialist JRD Tata:

In free enterprise, the community is not just another stake holder. But it's in fact the very purpose of its existence.

CSR is meaningless unless business meets the expectations of society. This is the fundamental basis for social responsibility. It lays out the ethical basis of a business and is laid down in the three inter-related aspects of the philosophy of business:

1. the nature of business,
2. its role in society and
3. its moral obligations towards society.

In this globalised world, society's expectations from the corporate world have been rising, reflecting the needs and aspirations of society that determine the CSR agenda. Society expects corporations to produce goods and services that could help the masses in a manner that removes social ills, helps sustainable growth and is eco-friendly.

20.6 CSR TOOLS

Companies interested in improving their social and environmental performances as part of their business have a wide range of tools available for application. Businesses have options in how they can use the tools.

For example, companies can use the tools that have been developed by others or they can develop their own tools — either independently or in partnership with other stakeholders. In some cases, the tools may be focused on one element of CSR such as environmental protection and in others may be more comprehensive such as the global reporting initiative. Initiative for the design of these tools has come from mainly three sources. First, one relates to the initiative of responsible companies along with the initiatives of international alliances or institutions and the joint initiatives of group of governments and civil society. The classification of these tools is shown in Figure 20.3.

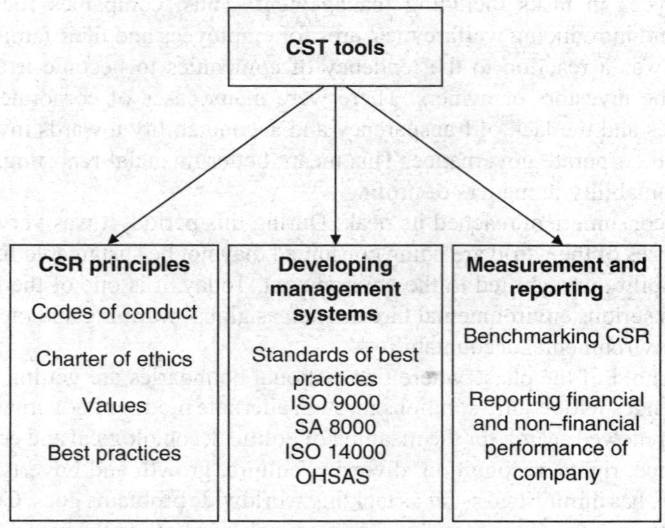

Figure 20.3 CST tools.

20.6.1 CSR Principles

A company institutionalises ethical climate by internalising values based on ethical charter of the company. It demonstrates the same by introducing and adopting the best practices in each of its functional areas of management process. The ethical charter of the company is based on CSR principles. CSR principles are acceptable norms of behaviour globally. These norms have been evolved over centuries, and therefore, assume importance from the viewpoint of the internal management of companies and its relationship with the outside world, for example, its relationship with stakeholders — internal as well as external. Continuous improvement in the best practices is sought through stakeholders' dialogue and transparency. How CSR principles evolved and their relevance to ethical climate is discussed below. We have discussed these under two heads namely (i) general principles (international conventions) and (ii) specific principles.

20.6.1.1 General Principles

These principles have been evolved through international treaties. Thus, each nation as a signatory to such principles is bound to accept them. The key themes that encapsulate these principles relate to fair business practices, pollutant to pay for environmental degradation, respect for human rights, recognition for democratic rights of ethnic minorities, respect for accepted labour conventions, protection of consumer rights, safeguarding the interests of diverse cultures and respect for rule of law of each nation to safeguard rights of local communities.

The prevailing CSR principles include Sullivan Principles, OECD Principles, Caux Round Table Principles and UN Global Compact.

20.6.1.2 Sullivan Principles

Sullivan principles were the first set of principles developed by a company.

20.6.1.3 OECD Principles

OECD conducted survey on prevalent practices of CSR in 247 companies with a view to provide a common framework for CSR, and later on were known as OECD principles.

20.6.1.4 Caux Round Table Principles

The Caux Round Table, an organisation of senior business leaders from Europe, Japan and the United States has its own benchmarks for ethical functioning.

20.6.1.5 UN Global Compact

The UN efforts to get agreement on certain basic principles from the corporate world, international chambers of commerce and NGOs issued the ten principles of Global Agenda. The Global Compact's ten principles in the area of human rights, labour, environment and anti-corruption enjoy universal consensus and are derived from the Universal Declaration of Human Rights, the International Labor Organization's Declaration on Fundamental Principles and Rights at Work, the Rio Declaration on Environment and Development and the United Nations Convention against Corruption.

The Ten Principles

Human Rights

Principle 1 Businesses should support and respect the protection of internationally proclaimed human rights.

Principle 2 Make sure that they are not complicit in human rights abuses.

Labour Standards

Principle 3 The elimination of all forms of forced and compulsory labour.

Principle 4 The abolition of child labour.

Principle 5 The elimination of discrimination in respect of employment and occupation.

Principle 6 Businesses should uphold the freedom of association and the effective recognition of the right to collective bargaining.

Environment

Principle 7 Businesses should support a precautionary approach to environmental challenges

Principle 8 Undertake initiatives to promote greater environmental responsibility.

Principle 9 Encourage the development and diffusion of environmentally friendly technologies.

Anti-Corruption

Principle 10 Businesses should work against all forms of corruption, including extortion and bribery.

20.7 TEN PRINCIPLES OF UN GLOBAL COMPACT

20.7.1 Specific Principles

Keeping in mind the general principles, companies evolve their charter, for example, Ethical Trading Initiative, a multi-stakeholder group of retailers, NGOs, and trade unions, and is supported by the international development wing of British government (DFID) to evolve and implement practical way of ensuring international norms in their supply chain across the globe. India as one of the key players in this sourcing chain is also one of the countries of operation. Europe joined to implement OECD guidelines and UN Global Compact in order to boost their responsibility towards CSR. CII-UNDP Social Code of Ethics in another such example that is accepted principles of CSR in India. Ethical behaviour of companies can be measured in terms of standards.

20.7.1.1 Codes of Conduct

Detailed analysis of codes of conduct is given in Chapter 14 of Unit IV.

20.7.1.2 Values

There are two sets of values — individual and organisational. Individuals act according to organisational values or the absence of it. The examples of individual values may be many, for example, honesty, integrity, empathy, love for mankind and so on. The same may not be true as far as organisational values are concerned. There is always a difference in the two sets of values. However, such differences do not dither individuals with high moral values from practising those in the context of their organisation too. Whether values can be taught or not remains an unanswered question forever.

20.7.2 Management Systems and Standards

There are number of standards developed in the areas of labour relations, environment, safety and governance. There has been a continuous effort to upgrade CSR standards with the active participation of NGOs, professional and accounting institutions from governments and bilateral/multilateral agreements between governments.

20.7.2.1 NGOs Initiatives

These NGOs were responsible for raising awareness and advocacy for standards. For example, many types of campaigns were launched by NGOs for issues related to labour, employees, supply chain, environment and waste management, ethical trading, social accountability, sustainability and human rights. Forestry Stewardship Council and Marine Stewardship Council are working in specific areas of their concern. Some world famous NGOs are Transparency International, Ethical Trading Initiative, Amnesty International etc. In addition, in India Partners in Change, Business and Community Foundation, Centre for Science and Environment and many more are voluntarily and actively involved in these initiatives.

It will not be possible to look all international standards related to specific industries; therefore, we have selected what is important from the Indian perspective.

20.7.2.2 SA 8000

Social Accountability International was responsible for developing this standard. It proposes an international workplace performance standard dealing with issues such as child labour, forced labour, health and safety, compensation, working hours, discrimination, discipline, free association and collective bargaining and management systems. Management systems relate to institutionalising CSR. Indian and Chinese businesses have also received SA 8000 certification under this programme. SA 8000 is particularly important for export-oriented small- and medium-sized enterprises and the government is aware of its importance. Government is helping business units to get them accredited, yet, there is a long way for India to go, as it covers only 10% of the total number of facilities so far.

20.7.2.3 AA 10000

AA 10000 has been discussed in Unit IV. ISO 9000, ISO 14000 and OSHAS are accepted by Indian business and remain to be significant from Indian perspective. Development of standards has been a continuous process and so is the adoption by business.

20.7.3 MEASUREMENT, REPORTING AND BENCHMARKING

20.7.3.1 Measurement

Action projects related to CSR should result in quantifiable results. The quantification is necessary for two reasons: firstly, for the measurement of the results as against the set standards and secondly, to improve upon the benchmarks. There is benchmark against which we try to measure the success of CSR in different companies belonging to the same sector or industry. With each passing year, the bar of benchmarking has to be raised further and further. Nike, Gap and Levi Strauss have been developing benchmarks for their own companies. Business leaders from the United States, European Union, Japan, Canadian Business for Social Responsibility and Asia-Pacific Economic Corporation (APEC), the European Business Network, the International Chambers of Commerce were responsible for benchmarking their own principles of trade in the form of Caux Round Table. OECD principles of corporate governance, FTSE4 good index for responsible investing, UNDP CII code of ethics for managers are some examples of business-led initiatives in developing standards.

Though there is nothing mandatory as far as reporting for CSR is concerned, yet many companies are publishing sustainability reports. However, the number of such companies is very few. Thus, major transnational companies have been including reporting on environmental accountability and social audit. The standardised reporting mechanism for reporting has been developed by an independent agency called Global Reporting Initiative (GRI). GRI is an initiative based on 'triple bottom line'. The GRI guidelines formalise the system of tracking company performance not only on financial matters but also on non-financial matters and provide a framework for disclosure and reporting and benchmarking. As has been stated earlier, it is not enough for companies to initiate some CSR programmes but also set the benchmark of their performance in terms of its impact on environment and society.

20.8 CONCLUSION – THE WAY AHEAD

Management guru, C.K. Prahlad, in his book *Fortune at the Bottom of the Pyramid* has said that the way forward for companies is to engage with the poorer sections of the world population, not because they are poor, but because economic growth has not touched their lives so far. According to him, markets at the higher end of the population are going to shrink and expand through the lower end. The same is echoed by Dr. Madhav Mehra, president of World Council for Corporate Governance in his article 'CSR for bridging the gap'. According to him, the two critical challenges facing humankind today are widening socio-economic disparities and global warming. The strategy to deal with both the problems is summed up in POISED (Poor-Oriented Innovation for Sustainable and Eco-friendly Development). This will not only provide the products and services needed for four billion poor but also include them in the process of growth through eco-friendly means. CSR in future will move towards more inclusive policies and strategies for growth.

Suggested Questions

1. 'CSR is not just about giving?' Explain.
2. 'CSR is about how companies manage the business processes to produce an overall positive impact on society', Mallenbaker. Explain.
3. How has CSR evolved over the times?
4. 'CSR is about business giving back to society.' Comment.
5. Why are CSR tools necessary?
6. Explain principles of CSR.
7. What is the role of CSR standards? Explain with some examples.

Bibliography

Adawal, S. 'Corporate social responsibility'. Retrieved on www.manavadhikar.net.

Anu, A. (2004). Corporate social responsibility. Annual Lecture, 9th December, *The Business & Community Foundation.*

Mehra, M. 'Corporate social responsibility for bridging the gap'. Retrieved on http://www.wcfcg.net/CSR%20for%20bridging%20the%20gap.pdf.

Mitra, M. (2007). *Its only Business!* (USA: Oxford University Press).

http://www.insiderreports.com/storypage.asp.

http://www.mallenbaker.net/csr/CSRfiles/definition.html.

http://www.insiderreports.com/storypage.asp.

Chapter 21

Corporate Social Responsibility—Models

Dr Usha Krishna

'This ideology functions on the idea that businesses, like people, have moral obligations and responsibilities that extend beyond the financial world.'

Elizabeth Redman

LEARNING OUTCOMES

In continuation to the previous chapter, the focus of this chapter is to acquaint you of various models of CSR.

- You shall come to know about the four contending models of CSR.
- You will be able to understand what different stakeholders expect of the company.
- You would be informed about certain practices followed by some leading companies.

21.1 INTRODUCTION

There are various models that have attempted to formalise our understanding of CSR. The four main models that are more debated are:

1. the ethical model,
2. the statist model,
3. the liberal model and
4. the stakeholder model.

The main emphasis of this chapter is on the stakeholder model, which in any case is the most popular one too.

21.2 ETHICAL MODEL

The origin of the first ethical model of corporate responsibility lies in the pioneering efforts of 19th century corporate philanthropists such as the Cadbury brothers in England and the Tata family in India. The pressure on Indian industrialists to demonstrate their commitment to social development increased during the independence movement, when Mahatma Gandhi developed the notion of 'trusteeship'. The principle of trusteeship according to him provides a means of transforming the present capitalist order of society into an egalitarian one. It gives no quarter to capitalism but gives the present owning class a chance of reforming itself. It does not recognise any right of private ownership of property except so far as it may be permitted by the society. Under the state-regulated trusteeship, an individual will not be free to hold or use his wealth for selfish satisfaction or in disregard of the interests of the society. The owner will be duty-conscious to manage his property for the service of society. As a trustee, he will be entitled only to statutory commission for his labour. This cannot be exorbitant. Gandhi's influence prompted various Indian companies to play active roles in nation-building and promoting socio-economic development during the 20th century. The history of Indian corporate philanthropy has encompassed cash or kind donations, community investment in trusts and provision of essential services such as schools, libraries and hospitals. Many firms, particularly 'family-run businesses', continue to support such philanthropic initiatives.

21.3 STATIST MODEL

A second model of CSR emerged in India after independence in 1947, when India adopted the socialist and mixed economy framework, with a large public sector and state-owned companies. The boundaries between the state and society were clearly defined for the state enterprises. Elements of corporate responsibility, especially those relating to community and worker relationships were enshrined in labour laws and management principles. This state-sponsored corporate philosophy still operates in the numerous public-sector companies that have survived the wave of privatisation of the early 1990s.

21.4 LIBERAL MODEL

Indeed, the worldwide trend towards privatisation and deregulation can be said to be underpinned by a third model of corporate responsibility which believes that companies are solely responsible for their owners. This approach was encapsulated by the American economist Milton Friedman, who wrote a famous article over three and a half decades ago in the *New York Times* whose title sums up its main points: 'The Social Responsibility of Business Is to Increase Its Profits.' Many in the corporate world and elsewhere agree with this concept, arguing that it is sufficient for business to obey the law and generate wealth, which through taxation and private charitable choices can be directed to social ends.

21.5 STAKEHOLDER MODEL

Citizen campaigns against irresponsible corporate behaviour along with consumer action and increasing shareholder pressures have given rise to the stakeholder model of corporate responsibility. This view is often associated with R. Edward Freeman, whose seminal analysis of the stakeholder approach to strategic management in 1984 brought stakeholding into the mainstream of management literature (Freeman, 1984). According to Freeman, 'a stakeholder in an organization is any group or individual who can affect or is affected by the achievement of the organization's objectives'. If we can visualise a company operating in a bounded space, which looks like a hexagon, which exerts competing pressures. The six sides are represented by:

1. customers,
2. employees,
3. shareholders and investors,
4. environment and community,
5. suppliers and
6. government.

At the centre of the hexagon is the Board of Trustees that holds accountability for all the stakeholders occupying the hexagon. The responsibility of the board is to perform a stewardship role, which balances the short-term interest of the present-day shareholders with the need to safeguard the interest of all the stakeholders now and in the future.

Let us now look at each of the stakeholders and what they expect from corporates.

21.5.1 Customers

The first obligation a business has is towards its customers. CSR starts with producing quality products on time at fair prices and ploughing back a substantial part of profits so that the products can be further improved, delivered faster at much lower costs.

Merely making a good product does not reflect quality. Quality means 'We Care'. Quality is not just a product, nor is it just a package of services and attributes. It is a way of life.

Though customers are located in multiple locations, they have very critical stakes and their interest is represented by their choice to buy or not to buy somebody's products or services in the marketplace. In India when we had a closed economy, many companies got used to producing shoddy goods and services at exorbitant prices. Liberalisation has brought in competition and the customer has the choice to keep you in business or to cast a 'no confidence' vote against the company.

As Azim Premji had said 'People and organisations live for the future, and it is the customer who really has the choice to grant us that future.'

Box 21.1 Relations with customers.

Relations with customers

Canon has established a global quality assurance standard based on canon quality standard. Canon aims for product quality that gives customers a sense of trust and satisfaction while working with customers to achieve sustainable prosperity. It works towards safest standards for product development. Canon products achieved a high satisfaction rating overall, with particular commendations for low rate of incidence for repairs, and cost of ink relative to other manufacturers. Canon established a Call Analysis Tracking System (CATS) for answering consumer problems and used this information to improve the quality of service to all customers.

21.5.2 Employees

Employees are the internal stakeholders of the company. They are the brand ambassadors of the company. If the employees are treated as the greatest assets, they will never prove as liability. With the advent of information technology and service industry, corporates have suddenly realised that employees today represent the most valuable 'intellectual property' which is their most precious asset. What is more, they have become aware that this asset has legs and could walk out! As of now, there is a great shortage of skilled workforce particularly in the highly technical and technology areas. In this environment, retaining skill is a challenge before the companies. There is no prescribed formula for creating a caring and energising work culture. Today's young new entrants are not willing to accept a hierarchical and dictatorial workplace where authority demands obedience. Fancy titles, huge salaries and perks may attract people but cannot retain them.

Box 21.2 Cathay Pacific policies towards its employees.

The company's employment practices provide equal opportunities to all individuals irrespective of gender, race, ethnic origin, family status, religion, disability, sexual orientation and physical features. Getting feedback from our staff is very important. Staff surveys are conducted on an ongoing basis with the cabin crew community and other staff groups. In addition, we have undertaken staff surveys every two years in most of our overseas locations. In 2006, we began a process of moving towards a more systematic approach to monitoring and understanding employee sentiment and work satisfaction. We will be undertaking comprehensive staff surveys worldwide.

Diversity

We are proud of our multicultural environment, which creates a rich diversity not seen in many companies. In 2006, we employed pilots from 36 different countries and cabin crew representing 33 nationalities. We are pleased to promote diversity in our workforce because we believe this promotes an outward looking international perspective fitting with the visions of the company. Any type of discrimination based on background, culture or preference is viewed as a serious misconduct and is not tolerated by the company.

People development and education

As part of our commitment to continuing education, we hold regular guest lectures at Cathay Pacific City. In 2006, seminars and lunchtime forums brought in external speakers to talk about a range of topics including stress management, cancer prevention, effective communication, personal empowerment at work and in the family, effective parenting and the importance of protecting the environment. As part of our regular staff development programmes, we run workshops and individual coaching and counselling sessions on career development to help staff become better informed and equipped to maximize their opportunities and employability with Cathay Pacific. The company operates a Learning Zone, which offers access to books, videos, online e-learning modules and other course materials for education and personal development purposes. Our online Learners World offers over 10,000 catalogue items covering topics ranging from specialist courses on technical matters pertaining to our business, to personal development, coping with change, career management, language development and intercultural communications skills.

The Cadet Pilot Programme

To demonstrate our commitment to Hong Kong, and with an eye towards our future, we introduced our Cadet Pilot Programme in 1988. This meticulously designed programme has already put many valuable, dynamic individuals into the cockpits of our aircraft. Our selection process and training programme are rigorous. Cadets need not have previous flying experience, but have to demonstrate that they are ambitious, enthusiastic and capable. This is a career path programme with an ultimate goal of becoming a captain, and the chance to be the leading member of our onboard team. In total, we currently have 244 cockpit crew who have graduated from the Cadet Pilot Programme since 1988 and are still working for Cathay Pacific. In 2006, 22 new cadets entered the programme and 15 who completed the programme have started working as pilots. Another five of these graduates will join the company in 2007.

21.5.3 SHAREHOLDERS AND INVESTORS

21.5.3.1 Disclosure to Shareholders

These include, of course, the general meeting of shareholders, presentations on the financial statements for analysts, presentations on business operations for the media, seminars for analysts with top management, visits to domestic and overseas institutional investors and various special annual report events for analysts and institutional investors.

21.5.3.2 Shareholder Returns

Continuously increasing shareholder returns through the development of the technology that increases the shareholder returns and efficient use of resources. Judicious use of resources is indispensable to environmental protection too.

Box 21.3 Box showing relations with shareholders and investors.

> **Relations with shareholders and investors**
> The company has been carrying out dialogue with shareholders and investors through various meetings as well as rresponds to institutional investor and analyst enquiries by conducting interviews (more than 400 a year). The company encourages surveys and research requests regarding socially responsible investment (SRI). It has been giving consistent return to them on their investment with the company.

Socially responsible investing (SRI) is becoming an important practice for fund managers to include in ethical investment and financial governance of a company. UN Global Compact has introduced 10 principles of responsible investing (PRI). These are aimed at helping investors integrate consideration of environmental, social and governance (ESG) issues into investment decision making and ownership practices, and thereby improving long-term returns to beneficiaries. These principles are based on the premise that ESG issues can affect investment performance and that the appropriate consideration of these issues is part of delivering superior risk-adjusted returns and is therefore firmly within the bounds of investors' fiduciary duties. These principles apply across the whole investment business and are not designed to be relevant only to SRI products.

21.5.4 ENVIRONMENT

Climatic change is the biggest threat faced by humanity. It has been well recognised that electricity and transport leading to burning of fuel are responsible for carbon emissions and climate change. From 1992 onwards, the Inter-government Panel on Climate Change is focusing its energies on reduction of greenhouse gases and carbon emissions. Each country is given targets to reduce carbon emissions. With this growing awareness about environmental degradation, depletion of natural resources such as water and fossil fuels and the phenomenon of global warming, there is moral and legal pressure on corporates to realise that the earth needs to be preserved and looked after so that our children and future generations are not adversely affected. In 1992, the World Bank conducted a study and gave it a very apt name The Cost of Inaction. In a study conducted in 1992, it was estimated that at the all India level, the environmental damage cost India Rs. 34,000 crores every year, which is 4.5% of the national GDP. Rising health costs due to growing air and water pollutions, depletion of natural resources, such as deforestation, and loss of revenue due to reduced international tourism are the fallouts of climate change.

21.5.4.1 Reducing Carbon Emissions

Cathay Pacific is committed to being a sustainable and responsible business, while at the same time meeting the growing needs and expectations of our customers. Sometimes, when an environmental performance improvement in one area results in a different impact in another, we carefully consider all options and the overall environmental costs and impacts as part of our decision-making process.

Box 21.4 Environmental responsibility of Cathay Pacific.

> **Reducing carbon emissions**
>
> - The major contribution that Cathay Pacific can make in mitigating its impact on climate change, as well as local air quality, is to maximise fuel efficiency. At Cathay Pacific, the company has improved the fuel efficiency of the Boeing 747 by helping the Boeing company bring about technological innovations in the aircraft.

Improving fuel efficiency

- IPCC noted that improved traffic management could reduce aircraft fuel consumption by up to 18%. IATA is currently estimating these inefficiency losses as 12% of total fuel consumption. Take fuel efficiency and emissions as a key consideration in the renewal process of ground vehicles.
- Continue to improve fuel efficiency against 1998 baseline begin operational trial to introduce flexible routes.

21.5.5 SUPPLIERS

21.5.5.1 Waste Disposal

Dell and most of computer manufacturers are taking back the used computers for disposal of waste. Kodak is managing its film and battery disposal on behalf of its customers. The hazardous materials such as nuclear waste disposal are getting the highest priority through the citizen campaigns all around the world. No country is willing to pollute its surroundings with such hazardous material.

21.5.5.2 Supply-Chain Management

Risk Management

There are a number of stages in the product supply chain, from the procurement of raw material to sale/ service to the end consumer. Each stage of exchange of goods is subject to its own risks. In order to operate safely and deliver high-quality services, several audit and control measures need to be institutionalised within the organisation as well as the point of supply chain through quality system management. Companies ensure the customers that the quality of their products right from the source of the raw material to finished good is free from any risk. Customer complaints are analysed for reasons thereof and used for improving the standard of goods and services. These complaints lay the foundation for research and product development.

Nike is an appropriate example of how the reputation of the company can be at risk due to supply-chain issues. Nike invests heavily in independent third-party audits of its suppliers, the findings of which it agrees to publish even though they may be unfavourable.

Box 21.5 Developing ethical supply chain – Canon Inc.

Relations with suppliers

Green procurement policy

Procurement division began conducting internal audits at manufacturing sites outside Japan. The company introduced electronic ordering system and electronic estimate system with green procurement policy for its supply chain. Green procurement favours procurement of materials and products that have a lower burden on environment by establishing management systems that are compliant with ethical code of conduct. The company educates all employees through a written set of codes and charter of behaviour.

Supplier standards

To develop a set of supplier qualifications that will include principles relating to labour standards, health, safety and the environment.

To implement a supply chain code of conduct, and initiate audits of key suppliers.

21.5.6 Government

The government through its various regulatory bodies tries to protect the interests of various stakeholders. The corporate sector in India very often blames the government for poor governance and lack of far-sightedness, similarly civil society criticises the corporate sector. The time has come when public–private and government should co-operate to look into policy imperatives for each in the sphere of their influence. Government must initiate the process of dialogue and set the agenda rolling for the corporate sector. There is no point in the blame game. Society expects better governance; better governance will lead to meeting the expectations of society and a step towards nation-building. Business and government should not be viewed as adversaries in different camps. We need to move away from this mindset; industry and government together need to find solutions that will meaningfully address problems of the community. If government throws entire responsibility on business, which does not fall in the domain of business then business will not accept that and without the co-operation of business also the government cannot fulfil the expectations of the society. Therefore, both sides must co-operate as mature adults discuss debate and arrive at actionable agenda for complementary responsibility for each.

21.6 CONCLUSION

There is pressure placed on companies by various stakeholder groups. There are various groups trying to define socially responsible behaviour. This makes the debate continue over the existence of 'true CSR'. The models presented here simplify the discussion in a way that makes it possible to identify the interactions among social, environmental and financial goals across a variety of situations: a necessary first step in paving the way for a discussion about how to proceed. Plans are necessary to promote CSR and must be tailored to fit the prevailing business models for CSR. For encouraging CSR without first understanding, the motivation is a lot like designing a ship without testing the waters. The four models above make us better understanding of the architecture of the ship we wish to build in the light of the waters that it has to face.

Suggested Questions

1. Enumerate the four models of CSR.
2. Compare and contrast the statist and liberal models of CSR.
3. 'Stakeholder model gained maximum acceptability in explaining CSR.' Enumerate the components of this model.
4. Who are the internal stakeholders of the company? Discuss their importance.
5. 'Shareholders are the only stakeholders of company in true sense.' Discuss.
6. Is government's role important as a stakeholder in CSR? Explain.
7. Explain the ethical model of CSR.
8. Ethical concerns of CSR are best taken care of by the ethical model. Do you agree?

Bibliography

Adawal, Shanker. Corporate Social Responsibility (www.manavadhikar.net).

Agha, A. (2003). Corporate social responsibility. *37th Annual A.D. Shroff Memorial Lecture*, 5th November, Mumbai.

Freeman, R. Edward (1984). *Strategic Management: A Stakeholder Approach*. Boston: Pitman.

Mehra, M. (2004). *National Conference on CSR: Corporate Social Responsibility for Bridging the Gap*, 9th November, New Delhi.

Mitra, M. (2007). *It's only Business!* (USA: Oxford).

Redman, E. *Three Models of Corporate Social Responsibility: Implications for Public Policy*. Retrieved on http://rooseveltinstitution.org/news-files/review/redman.pdf.

http://www.insiderreports.com/storypage.asp.

Chapter 22

Corporate Social Responsibility Agenda—Concerns and Issues

Dr Usha Krishna

'People are going to want, and be able, to find out about the citizenship of a brand, whether it is doing the right things socially, economically and environmentally.'

Mike Clasper, President of Business Development, Proctor & Gamble (Europe)

LEARNING OUTCOMES

This chapter is about Corporate Social Responsibility Agenda – Concerns and Issues. Through this chapter, you would gain a number of things.

- You will be acquainted with the CSR agenda – policies and practices followed globally.
- You would also learn about CSR agenda followed by companies in India.
- Finally, you will be able to understand that this debate is continuing and has left many unresolved issues.

22.1 INTRODUCTION

This discussion considers the issues that have pushed CSR to centre stage. It examines the key ones which form the basis for the social responsibility (SR) agenda. The CSR agenda differs according to national, social and economic priorities of a nation or corporation which themselves are influenced by historic and cultural factors. Apart from CSR practices in India, the role of various organisations in promoting the CSR in India is also discussed. India as a fast-growing economy is attracting foreign investors and multinational firms to participate in this growing economy. Therefore, it is all the more imperative for the Indian companies to be sensitised to the multi-cultural environment and principles of CSR for equitable partnership between the civil society and business.

22.2 GLOBAL CSR POLICIES AND PRACTICES

The concept of a responsible organisation is universal, but its workings differ according to national, social and economic priorities. These in turn are influenced by historic and cultural factors.

The SR agenda in India has its roots in philanthropy, but is now increasingly influenced by market liberalisation and increased exposure to international competition. Likewise, in South Africa, it was common for businesses to make charitable donations and to seek patronage from traditional chiefs during the apartheid era. However, in the run-up to and following the 1994 elections, the business community started to develop a more holistic SR strategy, and this was reinforced by a legislative drive. The agenda in South Africa is now strongly shaped by the need to respond to the legacy of apartheid, which means that certain issues (among them affirmative action and skills development) are given priority. There is little agreement on the SR agenda not only between nations, but also within each nation. However, there is no 'one size fits all'. In different countries, there will be different priorities and values that will shape the CSR agenda. Multinational companies operating in different countries are expected to play a supportive role to the state in development planning. Companies operating in remote parts of the world or where host country government capacity is lacking, often find that they are expected to provide public goods such as health care, education or infrastructure.

As business strategy, CSR is recognised as an important agenda item for today's CEOs worldwide. A study conducted by Price Waterhouse & Coopers states that according to nearly 70% of CEOs, CSR is vital to profitability. Even in the current economic climate, it will remain a high priority for 60% of CEOs globally.

Africa, for example, perceives a strong connection between corporate profitability and societal improvements, including infrastructure and education, and addressing the ravages of AIDS and its CSR programmes are driven by this perception.

In North America, CEOs recognise that corporate social reputation has less to do with earnings and more to do with reputation across a broad array of stakeholders. In Europe, the foremost issue is provision of a sound-working environment, followed closely by responsibility to all stakeholders and ensuring shareholder value.

For Asia-Pacific CEOs, external endorsements are relatively unimportant in their societies, in which public opinion is unlikely to be as consistently focussed on issues of corporate reputation as elsewhere in the world.

China represented by red flag is turning green. In 2006, the government set compulsory targets requiring the country to reduce GDP energy intensity by 20% by 2010, as part of the eleventh Five Year Economic Program. This may be a long shot for a country with an overheating economy, where energy resources are increasingly used causing pollution and global warming.

Central and South American CEOs agree on first things first: a safe and healthy working environment is their dominant concern, followed by responsibility to their stakeholders.

In India, companies realise that their success depends on what happens in the marketplace. It also depends on the morale, commitment and loyalty of the workforce; the loyalty of the customer base and the company's reputation. All these factors contribute to the long-term success of the company. They also believe that if environmental awareness and social responsibility are growing, these things will be reflected in the attitude of the workforce. Companies cannot command respect among the employees if they do not have a reputation for being environmentally and socially responsible. A recent survey by Price Waterhouse & Coopers of 140 chief executives of US-based multinational companies found that 85% of them believe that sustainable development will be even more important to their business model in five years than it is today.

There is a global awareness that CSR is vital to the industry. In common with other large-scale businesses that are being exhorted to respond positively to the challenge of CSR, the pharmaceutical industry, in particular, has been criticised by various stakeholders for a variety of reasons including their allegedly high profit levels, use of patents, marketing expenditures, political lobbying, considerable investment requirement for new drug development, 'creative accounting', high price levels and price fixing, excessive executive salary levels, limited patient access to life-saving/-extending drugs, animal testing, research ethos and patient clinical trials, as well as environmental concerns. The industries that make high profits, relative to other industries, the stakeholders and regulators continue to place more demands on financial performance compared to social and environmental concerns. Those industries who will not prepare themselves to face the social and environmental challenges will represent a small minority and could put themselves at risk.

As per the Survey of European companies in 2007, most of the companies are aware of the importance of CSR and the global relevance. When asked how the companies have been reporting and embedding CSR practices, the results show the following.

Companies were asked to indicate the perceived impact of CSR on doing business. Respondents indicated this on a scale from 1 to 5.

- corruption prevention 4.6,
- poverty 3.0,
- education 3.5,
- ecological diversity 3.7,
- fair trade and fair procurement 3.9,
- income equality and fair wages 3.9,
- climate change 4.3,
- labour rights 4.3,
- health and safety 4.5 and
- transparency of business practice.

As per the Canadian Center of Philanthropy, CSR is 'a set of management practices that ensure the company minimized the negative impacts of its operations on society while maximizing its positive impact'. In most cases, either the CEO (33%) or another board member (34%) is ultimately responsible for CSR within the company. In 8% of the companies, no particular person has final responsibility. Companies were asked whether they have official policies in place to address the 10 CSR issues. In addition, they were also asked whether quantitative targets have been defined to measure and improve corporate performance in CSR. 60% of the companies were found to have policies on at least 7 of the 10 CSR issues, while 34% of the companies had set quantitative targets for at least 5 CSR issues (see Table 22.1).

Table 22.1 CSR Policy and Targets.

CSR ISSUES	POLICY(%)	QUANTITATIVE TARGETS(%)
Health and safety	96	69
Corruption prevention	96	39
Labour rights	90	35
Climate change	63	55
Fair trade and fair procurement	71	28
Income equality and fair compensation practices	71	28
Transparency of business practice	86	41
Ecological diversity	53	31
Education	41	37
Poverty	18	4

Source: (Canadian center of Philanthrophy)

22.2.1 DISSEMINATION OF INFORMATION ON CSR AND REPORTING

Companies involve employees as internal stakeholders in disseminating their CSR philosophy, principles and practices. Some companies do it through employee training; others make it obligatory for executives to conform to codes of ethics in their day-to-day activities. Stakeholder engagement is the key that helps companies to embed CSR in the core business.

- Information on corporate website 98%
- CSR/sustainability report 90%
- Whistle-blowing procedure to address CSR issues 84%
- ISO 14001 82%
- Section in financial annual report 80%
- CSR in marketing campaigns 75%
- Information brochures 47%

22.2.2 COOPERATION AMONG COMPANIES, GOVERNMENT AND COMPETITORS ON CORE CSR ISSUES

The stakeholders who cooperated with most to improve performance on 10 CSR issues are governments and NGOs as can be seen from Table 22.2. Cooperation on climate change is most widespread. Companies were asked to indicate whether or not they cooperate with stakeholders. As can be expected, cooperation with labour unions and suppliers concerns those issues that are in their direct interest. With customers, climate change is the issue that is discussed most.

Table 22.2 Cooperation Among Government, Competitors and NGOs on Key Issues.

CSR ISSUES	GOVERNMENT	COMPETITORS	NGOs
Climate change	65	47	61
Fair trade practices	26	18	26
Poverty	18	6	35
Income equality and fair wages	20	10	18
Education	28	8	28
Labour rights	29	16	28
Corruption prevention	37	20	29
Ecological diversity	31	16	47
Health and safety	41	26	33
Transparency of business	39	29	33
Average issue coverage	33	19	34

Source: (Canadian center of Philanthrophy)

Climate change also receives most attention in collaborations with governments, competitors, NGOs and customers. Climate change, health and safety were the only issues for which more than 50% of the companies have defined quantitative targets. The companies surveyed perceive transparency of business practice, corruption prevention and health and safety as most important. Most have adopted policies on these and labour rights issues. Codes of conduct and employee training are the most widely used parameters to assess the effectiveness of CSR. The hottest issue requiring most attention and urgency happens to be climate change. It is also the only issue on which more than 50% of the companies have engaged in stakeholder dialogue.

Charity seems to have disappeared from the SR agenda and more urgent issues have taken their place in CSR. These issues are global in nature and demand cooperation among governments, industries, civil society and rest of the stakeholders. There is very little data available to talk about the CSR issues in a more comprehensive way because it is novel subject and at the same time, all organizations are grappling with the definitional framework of CSR.

22.3 CSR CONCERNS AND ISSUES IN INDIA

22.3.1 Background

Corporate philanthropy in India can be traced back to the pre-independence days when Indian companies supported Mahatma Gandhi's call for the development of the nation by funding and providing education, health and other social services. Even after independence, companies such as TISCO and other public-sector enterprises voluntarily contributed to community development. Mahatma Gandhi's model of trusteeship motivated the businesspersons of India. His view of the ownership of capital was one of trusteeships. The trusteeship model was an inspirational model, strengthening the belief that essentially society was providing capitalists with an opportunity to manage resources that should really be seen as a form of trusteeship on behalf of society in general. 'Today, we are perhaps coming round full circle in emphasizing this concept through an articulation of the principle of social responsibility of business and industry' said R.K. Pachauri. Indian business leaders themselves knew that business cannot succeed in a society that fails.

Historically speaking, Indian companies by virtue of the cultural ethos have been conscious of their responsibility towards environment and society. SR of business in India is well understood as far as the public-sector enterprises are concerned. At the same time, large private enterprises have been engaged in philanthropic activities through the involvement of community-based programmes. Though most of the traditional business houses in India have contributed towards philanthropic activities which could be interpreted as CSR in today's context.

The debate about CSR has heated in the year 2003/04. During this period, hundreds of articles appeared in journals and newspapers that shaped the meaning of CSR and the expectations of business from society.

It resulted in number of perspectives about CSR generated within different regions of the world. In India, the disenchantment of people with the government and its service delivery system of education and health was at its peak. Thereby, the expectations of business as provider of good education and health services accentuated. It was expected that the private sector will take up the role of the states in improving these by funding the existing education and health systems. Thus, these expectations were the topics of debate by corporate magnets, NGOs and media. Thus, the role of the states and central government was expected to be fulfilled by the corporations. Another kind of aberration in this respect was caused by coincidence of the phase of liberalisation with the arrival of the concept of CSR on the world scene. In India, we had barely peeped into the domain of ethics as most actors in business community has been following unethical corrupt practices of tax avoidance due to high incidence of taxes (generating black money 'known as number two'). The expectations of business from society included business to change these practices. Governments and business were not in haste to change these because of nexus between business and political parties, whereby political parties would benefit through business, in funding the parties for elections.

22.3.2 Socially Responsible Companies in India

Some of the prominent business houses that have historically made contribution towards philanthropy and are responsible for the present transition towards CSR include the public-sector enterprises that operated on the twin objectives of social goals more than profit motive. The basic objective of public sector was to do business ethically. According to a study conducted by Centre for Social Markets, socially responsible companies in India from private sector include Infosys, Tata and Wipro as model CSR companies. Besides these, Birla Group of companies, BSES (Bombay Suburban Electric Supply), DSP Merril Lynch, Hindustan Lever, ITC (Indian Tobacco Corporation), Larsen & Toubro, Mahindra BT, Mitsui, NTTF, Price Waterhouse & Coopers, Reliance, Tata, Tata Consultancy Services, TISCO (Tata Steel), WBPDCL were also mentioned. Out of the multinationals, IBM, EDS, Goodyear, Conagra Inc., Siemens Training Institute, Germany, R&S, Germany, Cisco Systems, Motorola and Microsoft were also mentioned.

1. community development for livelihood,
2. disaster management,
3. education and literacy,
4. population and health,
5. HIV/AIDS,
6. physically challenged,
7. vocational training and skill development,
8. empowerment of women and
9. sustainable-livelihood programmes.

22.4 CSR AND THE ROLE OF CONFEDERATION OF INDIAN INDUSTRY (CII)

CII set up the Social Infrastructure Development Council (SIDC) in 1995, to ensure that the benefits of economic reform and industrial growth are available to unemployed people living in poverty. Facilitate industry CSR to achieve holistic community development, and build a strong partnership across the sectors for better governance, accountability and empowerment. The council, through its team of experts, offers specialised services to help companies plan and implement development initiatives. In its efforts to sensitise the corporate sector to social development, CII has been organising a social summit every year (since 1998) at different locations.

The role of the council is to initiate and implement projects and programmes under various schemes of the government of India and to provide necessary help, assistance, and guidance to strengthen CSR initiatives of industry/CII membership.

Changing mindsets and the growing demands of industry have driven the council to work towards strengthening CSR and help businesses ensure corporate participation in social development.

22.4.1 AREAS OF FOCUS

- Community development (for livelihood programmes),
- Disaster management,
- Education and literacy,
- Population and health, with a special focus on HIV/AIDS through the Indian Business Trust for HIV/AIDS,
- Physical challenges,
- Vocational training,
- Empowerment of women and
- Sustainable-livelihood programmes: It has taken up special projects and programmes in Jammu and Kashmir, Bihar and Gujarat.

22.4.2 SOLUTION DELIVERY CENTER (SDC) PARTNERS

SDC works closely and in partnership with the government of India, multilateral and bilateral agencies and other civil society organisations on various innovative projects and programmes. It has been receiving financial support and technical assistance for these projects. The SDC has signed several MoUs and contracts with state governments and multilateral agencies (UNDP, UNIFEM, UNESCO, WHO and World Bank) for specific sectors such as health, education and watershed. CII and UNDP have also set up the India Partnership Forum (IPF) to promote CSR. This programme has the following initiatives.

22.4.3 ADOPTION AND OPERATIONALISATION OF IPF SOCIAL CODE

To persuade more and more companies to sign up for the global compact (GC), CII and UNDP have brought out a social code for business, which facilitates the operationalisation of GC. About 125 companies across various sectors have volunteered to participate in the IPF Social Code (IPF is a joint programme of CII and UNDP). Several initiatives have been undertaken to facilitate effective implementation of the code.

22.4.4 MAINSTREAMING SOCIAL CONCERNS IN BUSINESS EDUCATION

CII, in collaboration with UNDP and in partnership with the All-India Council for Technical Education and the Management Development Institute has published a book entitled *Corporate Social Responsibility Concepts and Cases — The Indian Experience*. With this, CII is trying to approach management institutes and business schools to introduce CSR as a curriculum.

22.4.4.1 CSR Survey India 2002

To assess the key dimensions of CSR in India, including the drivers and barriers, a national survey on CSR was undertaken in mid-2002 in collaboration with CII, the British Council and Price Waterhouse & Coopers. This was one of the first such efforts in India. The survey offers pointers on possible ways to further the CSR agenda in the country[1].

There has to be some common principles and practices guiding CSR. The GRI is an independent institution to develop and disseminate sustainability reporting guidelines that are used by organisations for reporting on the economic, environmental and social dimensions of their activities, products and services.

22.4.5 THE ROLE OF FICCI IN PROMOTING CSR

FICCI-SEDF Corporate Social Responsibility Award was the first of its kind to recognise the best socially responsible business practices of Indian companies. Since 1999, when the award was instituted, a number of companies such as SAIL, Tata Chemicals, Tata Steel, Tata Motors, HINDALCO, Satyam Computers, Gujrat Ambuja Cements, Kinetic Engineering, Canara Bank and Titan Watches have been recognised for their innovative CSR initiatives.

22.5 THE ROLE OF VARIOUS INDUSTRIES IN PROMOTING CSR

22.5.1 IT AND ITES COMPANIES

One of the most significant contributions taking place in IT industry has been related to school education at primary level. School education is primarily a government responsibility in India. There are nearly 40% of children who do not access to this education. As a result, top technology companies namely Wipro, Infosys

[1] For more information, please visit www.indiapartnershipforum.org.

and NIIT have started the initiative to targeted improvements in the quality of school education through its outreach to neglected areas. They have made a foray into e-learning by using their old computers and having a team of developers.

22.5.2 ITC

Through the e-choupal initiative of the ITC Group, ITC has been able to reach remote villages through the traditional choupals (village meeting places), by installing V-SAT, computers, public address systems and solar power. It uses e-choupal (the name of its agriculture portals) to market its products as well as procure raw material. The system benefits the farmers, because they can sell directly to the company without intermediaries.

22.5.3 TATA GROUP

In July 2002, Tata Steel presented the first corporate sustainability report, which would serve as a benchmark and a confidence-builder for other Tata companies. It has also formed group resource under the TCGI (Tata Council for Community Initiatives) on corporate sustainability and a strategy to assist other Tata companies on CSR. The group resource on corporate sustainability would work on developing a Tata model using technical inputs from the UNDP.

The Tatas have spent 1.5 billion rupees on social services – the highest by any corporate house in the country during 2001/02. The thrust area was rural development, which included community health, basic education and vocational training. It also spends on basic infrastructure and disburses money through various charitable trusts and relief and reconstruction societies. Besides philanthropic interests, in 1970s, the group amended its Articles of Association according to which the group shall be mindful of its social and moral responsibilities to the consumers, employees, shareholders, society and the local community for all its major companies.

22.5.4 NANO CAR

The cheapest and most affordable one-lakh-rupees 'nano car' has grabbed the attention from around the world not only for the low price but also for the beautiful looks and striking features. Tiny Nano is not just a car but is revolution of innovation. The car gives best mileage for the price, thus an environment friendly car.

22.5.5 TATA ENERGY RESEARCH INSTITUTE (TERI)

Nobel Prize of the year 2007 was shared by R.K. Pachauri, founder CEO of TERI, for environment advocacy and conservation. As an NGO, it has influenced the Indian companies with respect to CSR. As per the website, several companies have joined the efforts of TERI through CSR, environmental and sustainable development. Its Core Business Council for Sustainable Development (CORE-BCSD) is a unique grouping of corporate organisations that are trying collectively and individually to build in sustainable development concepts in their operations. In addition, the most significant step in pursuing CSR is to proactively protect the environment.

22.5.6 AV BIRLA GROUP

The Group's welfare-driven initiatives are channelled through the Aditya Birla Center for Community Initiatives and Rural Development. All the Group companies are dedicated to social development. Hindalco, a group company has won the FICCI-SEDF Social Responsiveness Awards 2001, instituted by FICCI Socio Economic Development Found (a constructive partnership among Businessworld, ICICI Communities, Partners in Change and KPMG). Other activities of the group include innovative projects involving the development of rural youth and employment generation, education and training and health care projects, helping the disable people, social causes such as widow remarriages, dowryless marriages and women empowerment programmes. In addition, the group undertakes sponsorship of the arts and Indian culture, which are need based. The Birla Academy of Art and Culture set up in 1962 in Kolkata treasures artworks and exquisite exhibits and has evolved into one of India's premier institutions for art and culture.

22.5.7 INFOSYS

Formed in 1981 by N.R. Narayana Murthy, Infosys follows a socially responsible and sustainable path in conducting business. Even during the boom time of the 1990s when the stock prices of IT companies were skyrocketing, the company believed in sharing the wealth with the society and its employees. This practice of the company stems from the personal belief of Narayana Murthy to give back to the society more than what it gave him. It also substantiates the role and motivation of the CEO and the top management in making the company a responsible corporation.

Murthy is of the belief that corporations have to show fairness in dealing with employees to retain them; corporations should ensure transparent disclosures to investors to attract global capital; ensure customer satisfaction to win confidence and fair dealings with their supply chains; and should be ethical to government by paying all taxes. Infosys has won many awards such as Best Employers to Work for in India, Golden Peacock Award for Excellence in Corporate Governance in the Global Category by the World Council for Corporate Governance, London and Corporateship Award by the *Economic Times*.

A strong sense of social responsibility is foremost among the core values of Infosys that translates into a commitment to help people and communities, enhance living conditions and improve education. The social consciousness is included in the strategic plan of the company and serves as a guideline for the management to help in decision making. The Infosys Foundation was formed to focus on health care, primary education, social rehabilitation and rural upliftment and promote art and culture. The Foundation began its activities in Karnataka in 1996. Today, the activities have extended to Tamil Nadu, Andhra Pradesh, Maharashtra, Orissa and Punjab. According to a recent report, Infosys spends about 50 million rupees.

Coca-Cola's has achieved a goal of being a 'net-zero' water company, a term used to describe that at minimum, they are putting back into the ground as much water as they are taking out.

ACC Cement Ltd. partnered with both Christian Medical College and the National AIDS Control Organisation (NACO) to create the world's first Corporate Anti-Retroviral Treatment (ART) Centre in Vellore, Tamil Nadu, providing testing, counselling and treatment services. Further, more than 95% of the patients who use the centre are not ACC employees, but members of the surrounding community.

Ashoka has supported 2000 leading social entrepreneurs in 70 countries across the globe to work in the social arena to solve society's problems. They are now connecting corporations to social entrepreneurs/enterprises and have established a global network of business and social leaders to share best practices.

22.6 FEW UNRESOLVED ISSUES

22.6.1 HARMONIZATION OF DISTINCTIVE NATIONAL CSR AGENDA

In developing countries, in particular, CSR initiatives are often identified with long-term national development priorities and defined by current capacity gaps. In this context, it is usual for a national CSR agenda to include a focus on solutions for social problems that in developed countries would be the clear responsibility of government. Each national CSR agenda is likely to have certain themes specific to it, such as the South African focus on black economic empowerment and affirmative action, and the Indian concern for disaster-affected communities. Similarly, worker conditions, environmental aspects, community issues and social development are more firmly established in the Chilean CSR discourse than human rights, bribery, corruption and anti-competitive practices.

22.6.2 Standardisation of CSR Agenda

A European firm that observes Organization for Economic Cooperation and Development (OECD) guidelines on CSR may find it difficult to apply CSR guidelines in countries that do not mandate the same. This makes asymmetric framework of CSR in a country's policies regarding the practice of CSR at home and abroad. In countries where enforcement of laws and pressure from civil society and consumers to act responsibly is weak, it is difficult to relate with them for the reasons that common framework of CSR standards do not exist. A few countries are found as weak when it comes to consumer organisations, others are weak on labour standards and similarly, each country has its own weaknesses as far as CSR is concerned. It makes developing uniform CSR standards problematic from the viewpoint of implementation of the standards in different countries.

Clearly, developing a CSR standard will require a certain degree of definitional and perceptual clarification regarding each of these subject areas. However, standardisation should not stifle the development of distinctive national CSR agendas, and it should allow for specific local and national priorities. One way to ensure this flexibility is to intentionally develop an international standard with the expectation that it will be refined before being adopted at the national level. CSR is an issue that is working its way into many policy debates and corporate agendas. The other unresolved issues relate to the following questions.

22.6.2.1 *CSR as Philanthropy or Core Business*

By philanthropic model, we mean companies make profits, unhindered except by fulfilling their duty to pay taxes. Out of the profits, they donate a certain share of the profits to charitable causes. However, in more recent times, there are attempts to involve CSR agenda into core business and distance from philanthropy. In the United States, CSR had been accepted much more in terms of a philanthropic model. In Chile, it is common for industry leaders to talk of switching from traditional, paternalistic and philanthropic activities to more strategic CSR function. In India, there is a strong view that CSR activities can include not only a direct responsibility for core activities but also an engagement in social and/or community issues. However, the European model is much more focused on operating the core business in a socially responsible way. This means SR becomes an integral part of value addition and wealth creation process of the business. The literature reveals CSR being used as a tool to make companies more competitive. Though there is a growing awareness about the importance of CSR and its advantages over philanthropy, yet the latter remains more popular in most parts of the world today.

22.6.2.2 *CSR as Voluntary or Regulatory*

It is often assumed that CSR relates to voluntary commitments that go beyond compliance with legal obligations. On the other hand, many feel that business should be made 'accountable' to society through mandatory regulations. There is no need to debate on the issue because the two approaches are not really exclusive (either–or situations) as is often assumed. Both voluntary and regulatory approaches can be mixed to have a balanced approach towards eradicating bad (socially irresponsible) behaviour and encouraging responsible activities. For example, in India, ISO 14001 is applied by many firms voluntarily to meet buyers' expectations while it is also required by the Central Pollution Control Board's Standards (regulatory). From the viewpoint of the organisation, it is of little importance whether the demands for responsible behaviour come from the market forces or the regulatory bodies since they have to take these into account in either case. The debate about voluntary and regulatory appears to be of less concern in view of the fact that the regulatory mechanism of different governments lacks teeth of a regulator. In the absence of strong regulatory framework, the basic purpose of regulation is defeated.

22.6.2.3 *Social, Environmental and Economic Aspects*

Most conceptions of CSR refer to both social and environmental issues and sometimes these are integrated with the economic aspects too. In the current CSR discourse however, there seems to be a greater emphasis on social issues. This may be due to the general feeling that environmental responsibility has been enforced largely by the environmental legislation and regulation in the 1990s and also due to the requirements of the international markets. For example, compliance with ISO 14001 that deals with environmental management is considered important for gaining access to international markets while SA 8000 that deals with social standards is not given similar importance. In both India and South Africa, the current emphasis within the CSR agenda is more on social challenges and the compliance with environmental legislation may suffer because of this. In Chile, the main focus of the firms involved in CSR is on their relationship with workers and communities.

There is therefore a need to integrate the social, environmental and economic issues into the CSR agenda, especially, if we want to move towards developing global CSR standards.

The integration of differing aspects in different nations remains key problem while the same is coupled with other unresolved issues.

22.7 EVALUATION OF CSR

While companies in North America and Europe are pressured by stakeholder to adopt CSR practices. In the United Kingdom, some NGOs and commentators appear to be on the verge of withdrawing from the SR debate, arguing that it is being used as a fig leaf while companies continue 'business as usual'.[2] There is an emerging critique of SR practice from civil society organisations in many countries. For example, in Chile and South Africa, there is a widespread view (outside the private sector) that there is a large gap between the discourse and practice of SR, due to a response from enterprises that is often superficial and reactionary rather than strategic. Likewise, surveys in India indicate that senior managers commonly lead SR initiatives, without necessarily translating and internalising them across their organisations. CSR is generally acknowledged as weak in India. Partners in change in collaboration with IMRB, the market research organisation conducted a survey in 2003. The study related to institutionalising CSR in India. Only 17% of companies surveyed have a written CSR policy according to this survey. The CSR activity was driven from top management and did not relate to the core business of the company. Individual companies have taken the responsibility of institutionalising CSR in India mainly, Tata Council for Community Initiatives remains the guiding focal point of the institutionalisation process across Tata companies and others too. There is a need to develop a more coherent and ethically driven discourse on CSR. However, CSR is still sometimes seen as 'green wash' to clean the sins of pollution, or 'white wash' to provide a facelift to the company's image. It is often seen as old wine in a new bottle – just another trendy name for good old philanthropic initiatives by companies. There is need to move beyond such transitory illusions about CSR.

22.8 RECENT DEVELOPMENTS AND THE WAY FORWARD

In future, the global CSR concerns would get enmeshed with the local concerns. Though the trend is towards local concerns of CSR getting priority over the global concerns; however, the global concerns should get priority over the local concerns, particularly when it relates to environmental issues. For example, climate change and fair trade practices must get the first priority over education, health and labour rights. Similarly, corruption prevention and poverty reduction should get priority as a local concern in our country because the country's corruption index is quite high. Largely, the question of priority remains an unresolved issue. The priorities may keep on shifting as the expectations of the society from industry changes. The list of concerns given below shows the differences in terms of priority as far as CSR in India is concerned.

- Education,
- Climate change,
- Poverty,

[2] See for example Christian Aid's report *Behind the Mask*, at http://www.christian.aid.org.uk/indepth/0401csr/.

- Income equality and fair wages,
- Health and safety,
- Labour rights,
- Corruption prevention,
- Fair trade and fair procurement and
- Ecological diversity.

There is no conclusive research evidence of the CSR priority areas of Indian enterprises so far. However, education, climate change, corruption prevention and poverty reduction seem to be the key areas.

Because of the successful campaigns and ever-increasing solidarity between the media and international advocacy and campaign groups throughout the world, changes have been felt in corporate attitudes, allowing SR to be directed towards non-traditional stakeholders. Thus campaigning, the media and consumers formed a partnership that led to the introduction of environmental protection as part of the factors that determine company success. More recently, other corporate elements of SR, such as labour practices – and, more specifically, child labour – underwent similar processes.

The above efforts by the corporates are only a part to the broad concept of 'CSR'. A company would be truly responsible when it has developed a framework for being responsible and implements it as line function. A responsible corporation must cater proactively to majority stakeholders if not all. In addition, it is important for the organisation involved in social activities to allow the company to leverage existing skills and capabilities in discharging its social obligation. Thus, companies in India have a long way to go to become a socially responsible corporation by world standards.

Though a few big Indian companies (such as those described in the previous section) practice CSR, the degree to which it is done is very passive among the corporate India. Recognising the need to sensitise the future managers of this nation to the societal needs, the management institutions in India have started including CSR as a subject in their curriculum. This apart, the government and the association of industries must devise policies and regulations for companies to strictly comply with and report. There must be a fundamental change in the corporate culture to enable businesses take ethical, social and environmental considerations in decision making. As rightly said by Prof. Amartya Sen, intervention is required for the equitable distribution of wealth and improving the quality of life of the society and it must come voluntarily from the corporate houses and its top management.

22.9 CONCLUSION

The awareness about CSR is there but the prioritisation of issues and urgency towards implementing CSR in the core business will determine the quality of CSR practices. The global issues and concerns must receive the attention of the industry and civil society in Indian companies. A responsible corporation must engage proactively with majority stakeholders if not all. Thus, companies in India have a long way to go to become a socially responsible corporation by European standards.

Suggested Questions

1. Explain the global view of CSR.
2. 'The historical, political and cultural contexts of a nation drive its CSR agenda.' In the light of the above statement describe the differences in CSR agendas of the developed and the developing countries.
3. What are the challenges before companies as far as CSR is concerned?

4. What are the expectations of society from Indian corporate sector with respect to CSR?
5. CSR means different things in different countries. Explain.
6. What are the unresolved issues as far as CSR is concerned?
7. What is the future of CSR?
8. The way ahead for companies is to integrate CSR in the core business. Do you agree?

Bibliography

Agha, A. (2003). Corporate social responsibility. 37th Annual A.D. Shroff Memorial Lecture, 5th November, Mumbai.

Canon – Sustainability Report, 2006.

Cathay Pacific – Sustainability Report, 2006.

Nayak, S. K. Corporate Social Responsibility: An Indian Perspective, 'Effective Executive', May 2003.

Report on European CSR Survey, July 2007, RSM Erasmus University.

Samuel, J. and Saari, A. Corporate social responsibility: Background and perspective. Retrieved http://infochangeindia.org/index2.php?option=com_content&do_pdf=1&id=5934.

Chapter 23

Corporate Social Responsibility: Case For and Against

Dr Ameeta Motwani

'For either perspective, as well as from several in between them, corporate social responsibility has enough of a history of debate and discussion behind it to merit a wide-ranging and nuanced treatment.'

Steve Kent May

LEARNING OUTCOMES

This chapter raises the controversy about corporate social responsibility. Briefly, this is the argument over the business case for CSR. The things you will learn are listed below.

- You will understand why should companies be responsible socially and how being socially responsible is also in the interest of the corporate business.
- You will know the various arguments put forth by the critics against CSR.
- You will be able to judge whether or not the objections to CSR are reasonable.
- You will learn what the CSR expectations in India are.

23.1 INTRODUCTION

In the last few years, there has been much talk and hype about the subject of corporate social responsibility (CSR). Today, it is acknowledged that business not only has financial accountability but also has social and environmental responsibility, popularity known as the triple bottom line approach.[1] In fact, today the debate is not about whether corporates need to take on social responsibility, because that is taken as given. The only dilemma is how this responsibility is to be discharged.

However, there are some who still question the justification of CSR. We present here some of the arguments given for and against CSR by its supporters and critics, respectively.

23.2 CASE FOR

The fundamental idea embedded in CSR is that business corporations can no longer act as isolated economic entities in detachment from the broader issues of society. Although there is a clear difference between CSR

[1] The triple bottom line approach argues that the success of a business should not be judged in terms of a single bottom line, that is, profits but in terms of the net impact of business on **People** (social costs and benefits), **Planet** (environmental cost and benefits) and **Profits** (economic costs and benefits).

stemming from a desire to do good (the normative case) and CSR that reflects an enlightened self-interest (the business case) in many cases a firm's reasons for embracing CSR reflect a mixture of both these motivations.

23.2.1 BEING SOCIALLY RESPONSIBLE MAKES GOOD BUSINESS SENSE

CSR is good even from the viewpoint of business's own interest. This is due to the fact that socially responsible firms earn reputation and goodwill for themselves. It leads to higher sales and profits in the long run. For example, Merck, the pharmaceutical giant, developed a treatment for a tropical disease, which in layman's language is called 'river blindness'. This disease afflicts millions of people in some of the world's poorest regions. Despite having no commercial market for this drug in the West, Merck invested millions of dollars in developing this drug. In 1987, in collaboration with the World Health Organization, Merck organised free distribution of this drug. Around 25 million people a year are treated under this programme to eliminate the risk of premature blindness. Doing this has in no way diminished the profitability of the company. As a matter of fact, this humanitarian gesture has enhanced its reputation capital.

The major corporations have realised that cause marketing, development partnerships and environmental concerns make good business sense – particularly in terms of recycling materials, employee satisfaction and morale, building up reputable capital and as a distinctive brand marketing tool.

23.2.2 INCREASED CONSUMER AND SOCIETAL EXPECTATIONS FROM BUSINESS

A powerful set of external forces and changes have contributed to the recent rise in pre-eminence of CSR voiced by powerful NGOs such as Greenpeace and closer home, the Delhi-based Centre for Science and Environment which has exposed the cola and bottled water majors or the FDA's pursuit of the chocolate-worms controversy. Consumer boycotts, direct action, shareholder action, ethical shopping guides, ethical product labelling schemes, media campaigns and ethical competitors became increasingly effective in changing corporate perspective.

The mid-90s were the watershed years for the new consciousness in international corporate polity. This was the time when two prominent MNCs were compelled by public pressure to reorient their business attitudes. In 1995, Shell dumped its Brent Spar oil platform in the North Sea. Public agitation in Europe was so intense that in Germany, sales fell by 70% within a fortnight. Similarly, in 1999, the share price of Monsanto, the American biotechnology MNC, nose-dived due to public protests about its genetically modified products.

The heightened reach of media, assisted by advances in information technology has made these corporates run for cover, forcing them to orchestrate expensive and elaborate damage control exercises. The internet has rapidly become the tool of choice for spreading information about multinationals around the world. The thing every company fear most is becoming the target of a powerful single-issue campaign group. So rather than wait for it to happen, managers are taking pre-emptive action in the form of environmental product development and labelling, or engaging in such ideas as codes of conduct and social audits.

Today, consumers are demanding more than products from their favourite brands. A recent survey showed that 88% of about 4000 people aged 15 or older in Europe, expressed a preference for purchasing a product from a company 'engaged in activities to improve society'. Employees are choosing to work for companies with strong values. Shareholders are more inclined to invest in businesses with outstanding corporate reputations. Quite simply, being socially responsible is not only the right thing to do; it can distinguish a company from its industry peers.

The moral of the story? Put your house in order. Better still, be proactive. What is different today is that the demand is more specific, more urgent and more persistent. It is a call to action and not just paying lip service to the idea of being a good corporate citizen by donating a few park benches to a public garden or a few old computers to an old age home.

23.2.3 Part of Society

Corporates are part of the society in which they operate. Can corporates flourish if society is suffering? Is it not the moral responsibility of business to give back to society from which it gets all its resources? Corporates are not islands unto themselves, but exist in the community. In the long run, in their own enlightened self-interest, they need to invest in the community because it is from there that they get their talent pool, their customers and their shareholders. The more educated and prosperous the community, the more business will eventually benefit.

Not showing concerns for the environment and society can be very detrimental and can actually shake the foundations of a business that has been built over decades. This is best illustrated by the examples of Union Carbide in India and Asia Brown which has been fighting a long protracted asbestos liability suit in the United States.

It is myopic and ill advised for business to divorce itself from the rest of society. How companies behave affects many people, including the flora and fauna, and not just the shareholders. A company should be a responsible member of the society in which it operates. That means contributing to sustainable development by working to improve the quality of life of employees, their families, the local community and the stakeholders up and down the supply chain. It can mean a day-care facility for working mothers, a new clinic, health insurance, playgrounds; it can mean biodegradable packaging, cleaner fuel for buses and trucks, community tree plantation drives, reduced water and energy consumption. It can mean a lot of things. The list is endless.

Michael Porter in an excellent article called Green and Competitive has demonstrated that properly designed environmental standards can trigger innovations that lower the total cost of a product or improve its value. He gives the example of the Dutch flower industry that was polluting the soil due to intensive cultivation of flowers in small areas with pesticides, herbicides and fertilisers. With strict regulations on the use of chemicals, the Dutch flower industry started growing flowers in greenhouses, water and rock wool and not in the soil. This system has reduced the risk of infestation, cut down costs, would reduce or eliminate pollution and at the same time make them more competitive.

Many corporates that have embraced CSR and sustainable development models are extremely successful. For example, in the United Kingdom, more and more consumers are buying free-range eggs, now accounting for 35% of sales in the United Kingdom though they are 25% more expensive than eggs laid by battery hens. What is the difference? The free-range eggs are a result of more humane and ethical poultry practices. It shows that the consumer is far more receptive to environmental and social issues than we think.

23.3 CASE AGAINST

23.3.1 Increased Costs and Prices

The critics of CSR argue that meeting the expectations of a wide range of stakeholders and complying with new monitoring and accounting systems raise costs which will be passed on to the customers. They cite the case of body shop that became famous for its ethical and sustainable approach, but has ultimately not prospered as a business.

23.3.2 Lack of Skills to Deal with Social Issues

Some people put forward the excuse that corporate business houses are not equipped to deal with social issues. They feel that business model is best suited for running an enterprise to make profits while the NGOs and government should take care of the social problems.

23.3.3 NOT THE RESPONSIBILITY OF BUSINESS

Critics of CSR argue that it is not the responsibility of business to solve social problems. They cite the remark by Milton Friedman that the only social responsibility of business is to make profits. They argue that looking after the welfare of citizens is the responsibility of the state not that of the corporate sector.

This is simply not true in today's times. Gone are the times when business was only accountable to its owners/shareholders. Modern corporations are accountable to a multitude of stakeholders as explained in the first chapter of this unit.

23.4 CSR EXPECTATIONS IN INDIA

A survey was conducted by ORG-MARG for TERI-Europe in several cities of India in 2001. The basic purpose of the survey was to capture perceptions and expectations (related to corporate responsibility) of the following three sets of stakeholders: general public, workers (skilled, semi-skilled and unskilled) and corporate executives (head of corporate relation, labour relations, welfare department and manufacturing department in MNCs, large- and medium-sized Indian companies). The poll gathered that people believe that companies should be actively engaged in social matters. A majority of the general public feels that companies should be held fully responsible for roles over which they have direct control. These include providing good products and cheaper prices, ensuring that operations are environment friendly, treating employees fairly without any discrimination based on gender, race or religion and applying labour standards globally. More than 60% of the general public felt that the companies should also be held responsible for bridging the gap between the rich and the poor, reducing human rights abuses, solving social problems and increasing economic stability.

Suggested Questions

1. Being socially responsible makes good business sense.' Do you agree?
2. 'The business of business is business.' Comment.
3. What is the role of public opinion in CSR?
4. 'A business cannot be separated from society. It needs to do CSR, therefore.' Discuss.
5. How would you argue a case against CSR?

Bibliography

Aga. A. (2004). Corporate social responsibility. Annual Lecture, 9th December, *The Business & Community Foundation.*

Griffin, J. and J. Mahon (1997). The corporate social performance and corporate financial performance debate. *Business and Society*, 36: 5–31.

May, S., Cheney, G. and Roper, J. (2007). *The Debate over Corporate Social Responsibility* (USA: Oxford University Press).

Porter, M. and Kramer, M. The link between competitive advantage and corporate social responsibility. *Harvard Business Review*. Retrieved on http://harvardbusinessonline.hbsp.harvard.edu/email/pdfs/Porter_Dec_2006.pdf.

Reich, R. B. (2008). *The Case against Corporate Social Responsibility*. Goldman School of Public Policy Working Paper No. GSPP08-003.

Chapter 24

Strategic Planning and CSR

Dr Usha Krishna

'Companies intertwine with the societies in which they operate in mutually beneficial ways. In growing recognition of this interdependence, the overlap where economic benefit and social benefit meet, defines the essence of how corporate social responsibility is integrated with strategic planning.'

Bill Valentino

LEARNING OUTCOMES

In this chapter, we have the last topic of CSR. Here you will understand the following things.

- You will understand the philosophy and process of 'CSR strategic framework'.
- You will be able to grasp as to how CSR strategic planning is translated into actionable projects that impact stakeholders.
- As CSR strategy assumes lot of significance for all stakeholders, communication and reporting on CSR achievements would also be known.

24.1 CSR STRATEGY

CSR strategy is the plan of action aimed at sustained efforts on the part of organisations to achieve CSR goals. Usually, CSR goals relate to the core competence areas of the company. CSR strategy and business strategy being overlapping in nature, creates synergy for providing additional value to all the stakeholders. Companies need to move from philanthropic activities to inclusive approach of building competitiveness through stakeholder engagement in planning CSR strategy. CSR planning or strategic planning for CSR dwells on the plan of action for desired CSR outcomes that a company wants to achieve in specific areas of operation for a specified period.

There are two aspects of CSR strategy. The first relates to the definition of CSR outcomes that need to be achieved and the second relates to time framework. That means CSR planning refers to plans of action to be achieved within a specified period.

The need for CSR strategy arises for the following two reasons: (i) CSR strategy provides guidelines to build and operate the framework for the attainment of CSR goals and (ii) it helps in prioritising the CSR goals. CSR strategy may be classified into 'internal' and 'external'. While internal CSR strategy relates to concerns for employees and related internal processes, external CSR strategy relates to supply chain, customers and clean environment etc. While writing the CSR strategic goals, a company has to answer questions such as: How to integrate CSR with the core business processes in order to make it more competitive? Do CSR goals help the company in fulfilling its responsibility towards environment? How is it going to produce goods and services affordable to poorest sections of society? How is it going to generate employment for largest number of people and the like? While answering these questions, the company should be able to show the roadmap towards achieving the goals with assurance from top management in providing for financial and non-financial resources. Thereby, strategy for CSR is stated in the form of action programmes that are sustainable, tangible and achievable. The quality of CSR strategy and action programmes is ensured by a company by adapting to the best practices available in the form of CSR framework. The commitment of the company towards CSR strategy can be ensured through the process of communication and engagement with different stakeholders. The areas of concern for CSR may relate to one or more areas that include environment, governance, sustainability, community relations, employee relations, diversity, customer relations and poor-oriented product development.

If the companies earnestly attempt to utilise their core competence to bring value to all the stakeholders, they can be successful in achieving desired outcomes from CSR.

The following text box gives the examples of three companies for the better understanding of CSR strategies, they have successfully embarked upon.

HINDUSTAN LEVER LTD. (HLL)

Employment generation: HLL provides direct employment to more than 29,000 people. Apart from this, through suppliers, third parties, transporters etc., it indirectly provides a source of livelihood to more than 1.8 lakh people. HLL Network provides income-generating opportunities to about 2.75 lakh people. Through Project Shakti, the company has provided income-generating opportunities to over 13,000 rural women who had no prior experience of carrying out a business.

Health and hygiene education: Lifebuoy Swasthya Chetana started in 2002, now spread across 18,000 villages in eight states touched the life of 70 million people and has imparted hygiene education to over 25 million children.

Integrated Rural Development Programme (IRDP): The project has seen tribal families benefit from it. About 55 acres of land were used for wheat cultivation and around 148 bags of produce obtained.

Watershed development: HLL's initiative has resulted in an annual conservation of 8,000 cubic metres of water.

TATA STEEL

Anti-discrimination or Diversity Policy

While recruiting all its press advertisements always specify, 'We are an equal opportunity employer. Women candidate are encouraged to apply.' The company appoints fresh professionals from reputed campuses that have an all-India selection pattern. This ensures diversity among its employees.

Human Rights Policy

Tata Steel does not have an explicit Human Rights Policy; however, the Social Accountability Policy in keeping with the principles of SA 8000 (policy attached) standard includes commitment to conventions such as Universal Declaration of Human Rights, Rights of Child and ILO.

HERO HONDA

Corporate Governance Policy

The company has a formal shareholders'/investors' grievance redressal forum in its Shareholders' Grievance Committee. The company discloses remuneration paid to executive directors giving bifurcation of all components of salary, and remuneration paid to non-executive directors by way of sitting fees, are disclosed in annual reports. Hero Honda was awarded the National Award for Excellence in Corporate Governance 2004.

Environmental Management Policy

The company is certified for its environmental management system as per ISO: 14001:1996. State-of-the-art environmental laboratories have been set up in both the plants to monitor the performance of pollution control facilities in conformance with defined standards.

Products and Services

The company has bikes priced at around Rs. 30,000 for people living in rural and semi-urban areas.

24.2 CSR STRATEGIC FRAMEWORK

CSR being voluntary in nature, companies have to demonstrate that they are behaving ethically towards internal as well as external stakeholders. In order to do so they have to adhere to the strategic framework. CSR strategic framework in other words refers to policy framework pronouncement meant for guidance of companies for seeking the cooperation of stakeholders in achieving social and environmental objectives. The framework is evolved through the consultative mechanism by corporate responsibility clusters in action, which consists of professionals, academia, professionals and practitioners from different parts of the world for respective areas of concern, for example, governance of companies, employees rights, human rights, environment standards, and so on. It may be represented as shown in Figure 24.1. Some of the CSR frameworks are given in the following textbox:

AA 1000 Framework Launched in 1999 and is designed to improve accountability and performance by learning through stakeholder engagement.

ISO 9000 series for quality of goods and services.

ISO 14000 series developed by World Business Council for Sustainable Development relates to environmental standards.

SA 8000 deals with supply-chain requirements.

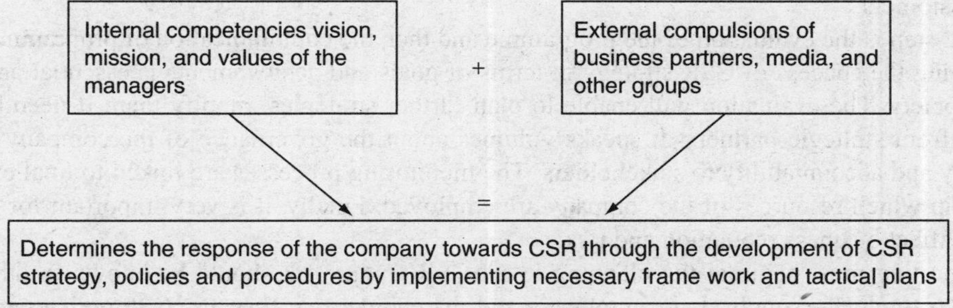

Figure 24.1 CSR Strategic Framework.

Determines the response of the company towards CSR through the development of CSR strategy, policies and procedures by implementing necessary framework and tactical plans. The procedure for the implementation of CSR strategic framework is complex. The procedure is determined by the quality of vision, mission and values of management of the company and its relationship with communities, employees and other stakeholders. There are various stages through which the procedural implementation of CSR strategic framework takes place.

24.3 CSR STRATEGIC FRAMEWORK – IMPLEMENTATION

There are three stages of implementation of CSR strategic framework, as shown in Figure 24.2. The first stage consists of planning stage. During this stage, the plan of action for CSR strategy is chalked out based on core business competencies. The object is to improve the competitiveness of the business.

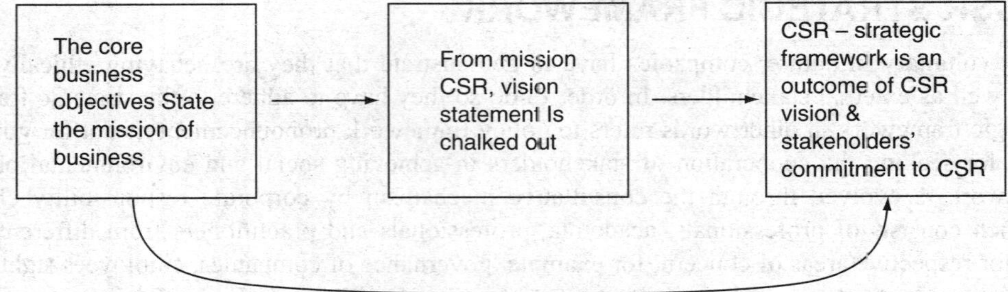

Figure 24.2 Relationship between core business objectives and CSR strategy.

CSR vision reflects the quality of business processes and their impact on employees, community, as well as environmental sustainability. CSR strategy is policy statement emerging from the vision statement. The other sources that may drive CSR strategy is the result of external factors such as competitors from industry, global competition and public campaigns.

The second stage consists of implementation of CSR strategy. Management's commitment to build a response in terms of CSR programme for the implementation of CSR is the highest priority. The same is communicated and shared with internal and external stakeholders. CSR policies related to business risk, stakeholder policies, labour practices, consumer relation policies and environment are enumerated. It demands evolving structures to execute plans and policies (internal as well as external) and implementing them through communication with stakeholders. Reporting structures to partners in business such as supply chain and customers.

The next step is the evaluation of the programme and then the communication of programme.

Monitoring the success of CSR strategy in terms of goals and achievements is essential and it is what matters to society. The evaluation will enable to plan further strategies, modify them if need be and seek cooperation from strategic partners. It speaks volumes about the governance of the company in terms of responsibility and accountability to stakeholders. The monitoring processes are linked to final evaluation of the projects in which resources of the company are employed. Finally, it is very important for competitive reasons that affect business reputation and risk.

CSR reporting must begin at the planning level. CSR framework should be known to other strategic partners, for example, the supply chain, employees and shareholders etc., because CSR policies and strategies cannot be implemented without their support. CSR strategy, vision and values should be circulated widely. Companies are realising the strength of CSR reporting. It improves their competitiveness.

24.3.1 JUBILANT ORGANOSYS: VISION AND STRATEGY FOR SUSTAINABILITY

Jubilant Organosys Limited, one of the largest custom research and manufacturing services companies in India and an integrated pharmaceutical industry player was conferred with 'the Golden Peacock Award' for CSR 2005.

This award is in recognition of Jubilant's sustained and result-oriented effort towards improving efficient utilisation of resources, limiting the impact of its operations on environment, implementing operational and transportation safety norms at facilities and contributing to better employee health and social welfare.

Nowadays, more and more companies are adopting CSR reporting for *reputation and risk management.* The leadership for evolving the CSR framework has been seen from the companies themselves, the civil society and several professional bodies. The following examples are given from the excerpts from **Dr Reddy's Laboratories Global Reporting Initiative, 2004:**

Vision of Jubulant Organosys

To be among the top ten admired companies to work for.

To sustain and acquire the first and second position in the chosen area of our business.

To continuously create new opportunities for growth in our strategic business.

To continuously achieve a return on invested capital of at least 10 points higher than the cost of capital.

Our values drive our vision

We will with utmost care for the environment continue to enhance value: for our customers by providing innovative products and economically efficient solutions; and for our shareholders through sales growth, cost-effective and wise investment of resources.

Our strategy

The sustainability report gives detailed economic, environmental, and social indicators that show that strategic objectives have been met. Those interested may visit the website www.jubilantorganosys.com.

24.4 CONCLUSION

More and more companies are realising the importance of CSR and are attempting to switch over from 'CSR as philanthropy' to 'building competitiveness through strategic CSR planning'. There are two aspects of CSR strategy. The first relates to the definition of CSR outcomes that need to be achieved and the second relates to time framework. The two parts of the strategic framework of CSR deal with how to do strategic planning (with examples of CSR goals) and how to implement it. Since the core competence areas of companies are different, so are their CSR goals. However, the path of realisation of those goals demands involvement and commitment of stakeholders and following CSR strategic framework. Since responsible companies are expected that they evolve CSR framework, there has been continuous attempt to do that with the help of professional bodies and clusters of civil society.

When supported by CSR, business strategy could become a source competitive advantage. A company can buttress its internal strengths and competencies with external opportunities. The revenue of a company comes from customers and stakeholders who are satisfied with the value a company delivers. Both CSR and strategy are primarily focussed on a company's relationship to the environment in which it operates and most importantly to its stakeholders. Strategy addresses how a company competes in the marketplace but CSR complements this by deliberating what the impact of that strategy is on stakeholders. Although the relationship is much more complex, to some extent the complexity of integrating CSR into the vision-mission-strategy-tactics linked process while meeting the ever-changing expectations of society is the answer. The results of effectively combining CSR and strategy enable businesses to operate from the perspective of multiple stakeholders and balance the means they use with the results they want to achieve.

Suggested Questions

1. What do you understand by the CSR strategy, its need and importance?
2. Explain how companies formulate CSR strategy.
3. What do you understand by CSR strategy response of companies stating some examples?
4. What do you mean by CSR strategic framework? Give examples.
5. What are the steps for implementation of CSR strategy?
6. 'CSR being voluntary in nature requires a framework for adherence.' Explain.
7. Explain the three stages of CSR implementation process.
8. How can strategy and CSR be combined?

Bibliography

Milliman, J., Sylvester, K. and Ferguson, J. (2008). Implementation of Michael – 'Porter's strategic corporate social responsibility. *Model Journal of Global Business Issues*.

Position Paper on *Corporate Social Responsibility, UNIDO*.

Understanding what matters: CSR and strategic focus. British Telecom. http://globalservices.bt.com/static/assets/pdf/white_papers/business_sustainability_understanding_what_matters_en.pdf.

Unit VI

Issues of Corruption and Unethical Practices

Dr Usha Krishna

If there is a challenge facing civil society today, it is the coalition of politics and business. If one analyses the role of politics and ethics in business, there would be universal agreement on the negative role of politics in business but necessary too. The Enron scandal is a classic case to cite. The following events describe the unholy nexus between business and politics.

Enron Chairman Kenneth Lay contributes more than $290,000 to George Bush's election campaign in September 2000.

In October 2000, Enron hires Linda Robertson, from Clinton administration, as vice president for federal government affairs to head its office at Washington, infuriating Republican leaders who oppose business groups hiring Democratic lobbyists.

In the year 2001, Enron backer Patrick H. Wood III appointed Bush's Chairman of the Federal Energy Regulatory Commission. Lay is one of the 474 people Bush names to advise his presidential transition team. Jeffery Skilling takes over from Lay as Chief Executive, Lay remains as Chairman. Skilling resigns for personal reasons and Lay takes over. Enron goes into problems during this year reporting huge losses. Lay tries to cover up the losses but fails miserably. The scandal is reported by media, and Enron, the world's largest electricity and natural gas traders, files for Chapter 11 bankruptcy protection.

Kenneth Lay, CEO of Enron, resigns his position in January 2002. Reports show Lay's relationship with George Bush was a mix between close friend and lobbyist. On 25 June 2002, Rabobank files a lawsuit claiming that three UK bankers colluded with former Enron executives in setting up off-balance sheet deals that ultimately led to US energy group's demise.

From the above facts what is clearly seen is the unethical behaviour of leadership, amoral behaviour of a large number of employees, governance through greed and deceiving shareholders, no accountability and no transparency in financial reporting and immoral behaviour of lies and more lies by the management.

The need for ethical business practices assumes importance when aforementioned unholy alliance between politics and business affects everyone in a society. Ethics is generally confused with traits of goodness or rightness of actions as a subject of debate. It is important to clarify here that the subject of ethics guides decision makers when they are in a dilemma emanating from ethical standpoint. It is needless to say that most managers face the ethical dilemma in their day-to-day decision making. It is more so in the realm of CSR when they have to involve and engage the stakeholders both internally and externally. Besides the conflict of interests in the apportionment of profits towards various stakeholders, ethical issues may relate to quality of product versus cost; ideal amount of profits a company should be earning without hurting the interest of shareholders on the one hand and consumers on the other and many more. Consumer campaigns have also played a decisive role in bringing unethical practices of business to light. Consequently, the legal framework of governance of companies as well as countries changed to stop the unethical practices and pin down responsibility.

CSR is generally understood to be the way a company achieves a balance or integration of economic, environmental and social imperatives while at the same time addressing shareholder and stakeholder expectations. The way businesses engage the shareholders, employees, customers, suppliers, governments, non-governmental organisations (NGOs), international organisations and other stakeholders is usually an important feature of the concept. While business compliance with laws and regulations on social, environmental and economic objectives set the official level of CSR performance, CSR is often understood as involving the private-sector commitments that extend beyond this foundation of compliance with laws. Laws act as the tools which determine the extent to which industry is responsible. Lesser the compliance with laws, more controls will follow. More the compliance with laws, lesser will be the political controls. The real ethical imperative calls for voluntary actions by businesses to demonstrate responsible behaviour and effective responses to social and environmental problems — both in the domestic and in the international contexts. Nexus between politics and business is very hard to crack. One wakes up to find a new scandal every day. The harm done by the scandals cannot be controlled after disasters take place. It is in the interest of society/industry to evolve self-regulatory mechanism to prevent the scandals taking place. The concepts related the governance of companies that were discussed in Unit IV remain to be crucial for all times to come. Unethical practices and socio-environmental concerns that affect the reputation of companies and are antithesis to good governance have been explained in the following chapters in this unit. To name these include corporate scandals and the role of whistle-blowers. Discrimination against ethnic minorities, insider trading and its impact on shareholders, laws related to consumer rights and unethical aspects of advertising have been dealt at length. This enables students get the overall view of unethical business practices to be able to understand and desist from such practices.

Chapter 25 relates to 'Corporate Scandals'. It explains the meaning, analysis, forms and the impact of corruption. It also highlights certain cases.

Chapter 26 is about 'Whistle Blowing'. It consists of meaning, types and theories of the phenomenon. Some cases have also been discussed.

Chapter 27 debates the phenomenon of 'Insider Trading'. Insider trading occurs when a trade has been influenced by the privileged possession of corporate information that has not yet been made public. The chapter argues the controversial position that IT may in fact be beneficial to the economy.

Chapter 28's aim is to analyse the nature and forms of 'Discrimination in Workplace' and focus on the other aspects of discrimination, i.e. affirmative action programmes. It discusses concepts, forma and practices of discrimination. It analyses the affirmative action taken by corporations.

Chapter 29 tells us about 'Ethical Issues in Advertising'. It is known that advertising is one of the major devices that business uses to promote sales. Unethical aspects of advertising have been discussed under the following headings: Advertising Message, Quantum of Advertising, Inappropriate Advertising and Undesirable Influences on the Society.

Chapter 30 clarifies 'Consumer Rights'. In the present scenario, though the consumer can exercise more choice in the satisfaction of his/her needs, yet he/she does not always have the necessary skills to make a rational choice or to understand the implications of the offerings made. It explains the Indian Consumer Protection Act, 1986.

Chapter 25

Corporate Scandals

Rana Sudhir Kumar

'Rather fail with honour than succeed by fraud.'
Sophocles

LEARNING OUTCOMES

After reading this chapter, you will be able to:

- know the genesis of corruption.
- understand the nature of corporate fraud.
- identify various forms of corruption.
- assess the impact corruption has on society, economy and the corporation.
- know about some of the major cases of corporate frauds the world has seen.
- understand what companies can do to combat fraud.

25.1 INTRODUCTION

In 2002, at a meeting of the ASSOCHAM 'Best Practices for Corporate Governance and Shareholder Alignment', the former Central Vigilance Commissioner, N. Vittal said that after the end of the Cold War, the prevailing conventional wisdom all over the world is that government should not intervene in the economy. This means that market dynamics is the decisive factor as far as all economic matters are concerned. Corruption is directly related to the market dynamics, politics, and unethical practices.

25.2 MEANING

The starting point in determining what constitutes corrupt practice, says Gerald E. Caiden, relates to specific form of behaviour that is considered wrong and offensive. By nature, these acts are deliberate, not accidental or incidental. Corruption is the antithesis of morality. Jim Wesberry captured the essence of corruption when he observed: 'Corruption thrives on darkness and invisibility. It is anonymous and immeasurable. It is rooted in the very human vices of greed and lust for power … it is colorless, shapeless, odorless, collusive, secret, stealthy, and shameless.'

Getz and Volkema have defined corruption as 'the abuse of public roles and resources for private benefit or the misuse of the office for non-official ends'. The most common forms of corruption in international business that affect strategic manoeuvring are bribery, extortion and embezzlement. The World Bank Institute estimates bribes alone drain the equivalent of more than $1 trillion annually from the legitimate global economy of $30 trillion (based on 2001–2002 economic data). That estimate does not include the embezzlement of public funds or the diversion of assets, which might double the total cost of corruption.

25.3 ANALYSIS

The first area to look for corporate frauds, therefore, is the operating system which may be weak and which can be exploited. According to Professor John C. Coffee Jr. of Columbia University Law School, different kinds of scandals characterise different systems of corporate governance. Corporate scandals, particularly when they occur in concentrated outbursts, raise two serious issues.

1. Why do different types of scandals occur in different economies?
2. Why does a wave of scandals occur in one economy, but not in another, even though both economies are closely interconnected in the same global economy and subject to the same macroeconomic conditions?

Conventional wisdom explains a sudden concentration of corporate financial scandals as the consequence of a stock-market bubble. When the bubble bursts, scandals follow and eventually new regulation. Europe had its share of financial scandals (e.g. the Parmalat Scandal) over the same period as the United States. However, most were characteristically different from the US style of earnings manipulation scandals (e.g. Enron and WorldCom). What explains this difference?

According to Professor Coffee Jr., it is the differences in the structure of share ownership that accounts for differences in corporate scandals, both in terms of the nature of the fraud, the identity of the perpetrators and the seeming disparity in the number of scandals at any given time.

25.4 FORMS OF CORRUPTION

25.4.1 INDIVIDUAL AND SYSTEMIC CORRUPTION

Inidividual corruption marifests in various economic and non-economic forms such as bribery, embezzelment, tax evasion, descrimination and nepotism. Individual corruption can be rooted out by organisational sanctions buttressed by the legal system. Individual wrongdoers are confronted with the evidence and disciplined for minor offences. Major offences warrant immediate exit – dismissal, possible professional discipline and possible prosecution that may result in life imprisonment or worse.

Systemic corruption occurs when the whole organisation, its culture, leadership, management and staff knowingly indulge in corrupt practices, turn a blind eye to wrongdoing, or even encourage such inappropriate behaviour. Systemic corruption requires major reforms in business law, professional practice, organisational and professional culture, ethics and education, public accountability and political economy.

25.5 IMPACT OF CORRUPTION

25.5.1 DIRECT IMPACT

Fraud can significantly impact the financial performance of a firm as it can cost a typical company between 1% and 6% of annual sales. As Karen Schnatterly of Carlson School of Management, Minnesota, explains, white-collar crime alone causes 30% of new business failures without regard to the quality of the firms' strategy or assets.

Fraud has brought down many apparently well-performing firms. Enron, Sunbeam, Cendant and Waste Management are some of the most spectacular examples. Even before Enron's Collapse, the US Securities and Exchange Commission was investigating more companies than ever for possible accounting fraud.

Corruption, acknowledges Caiden, is an obstacle to world development because it discourages investment, undermines stability, destroys effective governance and demoralises people. Aside from its out-of-pocket cost to bribers and its cost to non-bribers in lost business or delayed or non-performance by government, corruption, writes P. Richardson, has numerous indirect costs.

25.5.2 INDIRECT IMPACT

- Especially where it is pervasive, corruption can deter honest people from entering government service.
- Corruption reduces tax revenues thereby requiring higher tax rates.
- Corruption undercuts necessary regulations.
- Corruption facilitates crime.
- Corruption can erode political stability and respect.

The price society has to pay for corruption is, indeed, too high and needs to be curbed at all costs. Before we examine what governments and corporations have done or are doing to combat corporate fraud, let us have an overview of some of the scandals which highlight significant ethical issues.

25.6 CASES OF CORRUPTION

25.6.1 ENRON

Enron tops the list of America's biggest corporate collapses. Enron Corporation is an American energy company based in Houston, Texas, that employed around 21,000 people by mid-2001, and was one of the world's leading electricity, natural gas, pulp, paper and communications companies with claimed revenues of $101 billion in 2000. Fortune magazine named Enron as 'Americas Most Innovative Company' for six consecutive years. However, at the end of 2001, it collapsed when it was revealed that it is reported financial condition was sustained mostly by institutionalised, systematic and creatively planned accounting fraud.

Enron's bankruptcy in 2001 was the largest in the US corporate history at the time. The bankruptcy filing came after a series of revelations that the giant energy trader had been using partnerships, called 'special-purpose entities'(SPEs), to conceal losses. Enron had created offshore entities, units which may be used for planning and avoidance of taxes, raising the profitability of business. This provided ownership and management with full freedom of currency movement, and full anonymity, which would hide losses that the company was taking. These entities made Enron look more profitable than it actually was, and it created a dangerous spiral. Kenneth Lay and Jeffrey Skilling, former chief executive officers (CEO) of Enron, went on trial for their part in the Enron scandal in January 2006. Their indictment covered a broad range of financial crimes, including bank fraud, making false statements to banks and auditors, securities fraud, wire-fraud, money laundering and insider trading.

Enron's demise caused tens of billions of dollars of investor's losses, triggered a collapse of electricity-trading markets and ushered in an era of accounting scandals that precipitated a global loss of confidence in corporate integrity. Fallout from the scandal quickly extended beyond Enron. The trial of Arthur Andersen on charges of obstruction of justice related to Enron also helped to expose its accounting fraud at WorldCom.

Enron's collapse also led to the creation of the US Sarbanes-Oxley Act. It is considered the most significant change to federal securities laws since Roosevelt's New Deal in the 1930s. Other countries have also adopted new corporate governance legislations. This law provides stronger penalties for fraud and, among other things, requires public companies to avoid making loans to management to report more information to the public, to maintain stronger independence from their auditors and, most controversially, to report on and have audited their financial internal control procedures.

25.6.2 Arthur Andersen

In its role as Enron's auditor, Arthur Andersen was responsible for ensuring the accuracy of Enron's financial statements and internal bookkeeping. The accounting firm was a major business partner of Enron. It sold about $50 million a year in consulting services to Enron.

Andersen was found guilty of obstruction of justice in March 2002 for destroying Enron-related auditing documents during an SEC investigation of Enron. As a result, Andersen has been barred from performing audits. The ethical ramifications of the Andersen scandal became apparent, in that Andersen was more concerned about its own revenue growth compromising its independence as an auditor. This had its own implications for regulation and accounting ethics. For the accounting profession, the Sarbanes-Oxley Act of 2002 emphasised auditor independence and quality, restricting accounting firms' ability to provide both audit and non-audit services for the same clients, and requires periodic reviews of audit firms.

25.6.3 WorldCom

WorldCom, which owns the American long-distance MCI network, was at one time poised to become one of the largest telecommunications corporations in the world. Instead it had to file for bankruptcy, disgraced by accounting scandals.

Unfortunately, for thousands of employees and shareholders, WorldCom used questionable accounting practices and improperly recorded 3.8 billion dollars in capital expenditures, which boosted cash flows and profit over all the four quarters in 2001 as well as the first quarter of 2002. This disguised the firm's actual net losses for the five quarters because capital expenditure can be deducted over a longer period, whereas expenses must be immediately subtracted from revenue. Investors, unaware of the alleged fraud, continued to buy the company's stock, which accelerated the stock's price. Internal investigations uncovered questionable accounting practices stretching as far back as 1999. The SEC chairperson described tile company's statements 'wholly inadequate and incomplete', WorldCom's accounts did not comply with American accounting standards.

25.6.4 The Stamp Paper Scam

Across 72 towns and 18 states and over a period of 10 years, the counterfeit stamp paper scam has dealt the Indian economy a shattering Rs. 32,000 crore blow. The figure is official. Apprehensions are that it could be much higher.

It was an operation that respected no system and thrived on the brittle moral fabric of the bureaucracy and its political bosses, exposing the inadequacies of the system. Be it in Maharashtra, where it originated, or in Andhra Pradesh, where it spread its net, or in Karnataka and other states, where it flourished, the scam left a trail of stink that every party is trying to cover up. The scam also throws light on the culpability of officials and political leaders and is yet another piece of evidence of the criminalisation of politics.

Telgi's operation involved the sale of not only counterfeit stamp paper but also related items such as judicial court fee stamps, insurance policies, share transfer certificates and brokers' notes. It is evident that the scam would not have taken place without massive official collusion. The Telgi scam should serve as a wake-up call to modernise the process by which the country transacts its business, legal and related matters.

25.6.5 The Bhopal Gas Tragedy

In the early morning hours on 3 December 1984, a poisonous grey cloud (40 tons of toxic gases) from Union Carbide India Limited (UCIL's) pesticide plant at Bhopal spread throughout the city. Water carrying catalytic material had entered methyl isocyanate (MIC) storage tank.

What followed was a nightmare. The killer gas spread through the city, sending residents scurrying through the dark streets. No alarm ever sounded a warning and no evacuation plan was prepared. The magnitude of the devastation was unprecedented. Estimates suggested that as many as 10,000 may have died and nearly 50,000 fell seriously ill.

The catastrophe raised some serious ethical issues. It is a brazen example of evasion of corporate responsibility. The pesticide factory was built in the midst of densely populated settlements. UCIL chose to store and produce MIC, one of the most deadly chemicals in an area where nearly 120,000 people lived.

The MIC plant was not properly designed to handle a runaway reaction. When the uncontrolled reaction started, MIC was flowing through the scrubber at more than 200 times its designed capacity. MIC in the tank was filled to 87% of its capacity while the maximum permissible was 50%.

As part of the UCC's drive to cut costs, the workforce in the Bhopal factory as brought down by half from 1980 to 1984. This had serious consequences on safety and maintenance.

In addition to causing the Bhopal disaster, UCC was also guilty of prolonging the misery and suffering of the survivors. By withholding medical information on the chemicals, it deprived victims of proper medical care. By denying interim relief, as directed by two Indian courts, it caused a lot of hardship to the survivors.

25.7 COMBATING CORPORATE FRAUDS

There is now a widespread recognition by international governmental organisations, by national governments and civic and professional groups that major efforts to combat corruption are needed. Business organisations and corporations should work in support of such efforts. This requires a comprehensive anti-corruption strategy.

Corporate governance guidelines and the best practices have evolved over a period. The Cadbury Report on the financial aspects of corporate governance, published in the United Kingdom in 1992, was a landmark. The Sarbanes-Oxley Act 2002 has brought about sweeping changes in financial reporting and has laid down new accountability standards.

The OECD Principles of Corporate Governance have recommended good practices in corporate behaviour with a view to rebuilding and maintaining public trust in companies and stock markets. The revised principles call on governments to ensure effective regulatory frameworks and on companies to be more accountable. The principles include increased awareness among institutional investors, enhanced role for shareholders in executive compensation, greater transparency and effective disclosure to counter conflicts of interest.

The recommendations of the Kumar Mangalam Birla Committee on Corporate Governance set up by SEBI are now enshrined in clause 49 of the Listing Agreement of every Indian Stock Exchange.

25.8 CONCLUSION

Most countries are discovering that corrupt practices can be managed and brought under control, although constant vigil will be necessary to prevent deterioration. In Caiden's opinion, the following factors seem to be crucial.

Moral and trustworthy leaders: Able and virtuous people have to be attracted to public service and retained without great personal sacrifice. There has to be instant removal from office of anyone with dirty hands, and immediate disciplinary action against anyone who condones corruption.

Appropriate social regulation: A root cause of corruption is virtually no support for social controls.

Regular law revision: Repeal is needed of vague, anachronistic and internally contradictory laws and regulations that prevent the law-abiding from conducting their business in a lawful manner.

Reduction of monopolies: Inevitably and almost unconsciously, monopolies exploit their position. Where competition cannot be introduced, they have to be carefully monitored and subject to transparency and there must be full accountability to ensure that their actions are legal, moral, productive, sensitive and effective.

Open democratic governance: Autocracies have a higher propensity to corruption. Every effort has to be made to ensure government in the sunshine.

Professionalism: Democratic governance requires professionals who adhere to professional ethics and standards avoid harm and ensure competence, discipline and reliable self-policing.

Competence: Wherever there is incompetence, corruption creeps in. System, order and regularity are essential for detection of abuses.

Personal integrity: When all is said and done, there is no substitute for individual integrity and the unwillingness of people to compromise with corruption. People who know right from wrong rarely depart from norms. Ethics education is imperative.

Suggested Questions

1. Explain the meaning and forms of corruption.
2. Analyse the reasons for widespread corruption and explain its impact.
3. How corruption impacts organisations and what can organisations do to prevent corruption?
4. What are the various forms of corruption that have led to the downfall of giant organisations such as Enron and WorldCom?
5. What are the manifestations of corruption in society? Explain the measures to combat corrupt practices in society.
6. If you were the CEO of an organisation, what measures would you take to safeguard your organisation from becoming another Enron?
7. State one example of corporate fraud in India. What measures are taken by the Indian Government to prevent frauds taking place in India?

Bibliography

Alan, E. Singer (2007). *Business Ethics and Strategy*, Volume II (UK: Ashgate).

Frederickson, H. George and Richard, K. Ghere (2005). *Ethics in Public Management* (India: Prentice-Hall).

Mauro, P. (1995). Corruption and growth, *Quarterly Journal of Economics*, 110.

Richardson, P. (2001). The global assault on corruption, *Journal of Public Inquiry* (Fall/Winter).

Rose-Ackerman, S. (1999). *Corruption and Government: Causes Consequences and Reform* (Cambridge: Cambridge University Press).

William B. Werther, Jr. and David Chandler (2006). *Strategic Corporate Social Responsibility* (USA: Sage).

Chapter 26

Whistle-Blowing

Rana Sudhir Kumar

'Men occasionally stumble over the truth, but most of them pick themselves up and hurry off as if nothing ever happened.'

Sir Winston Churchill

LEARNING OUTCOMES

After reading this chapter, you will be able to:

- learn the meaning and significance of the concept of whistle-blowing.
- clearly distinguish between the internal and external dimensions of whistle-blowing.
- know about some important whistle-blowing cases.
- understand the theory of whistle-blowing.
- see what is being done to protect whistleblowers and judge whether that is adequate.

26.1 INTRODUCTION

The corporate world had been hit by a slew of scandals involving high-profile corporate frauds in companies around the world such as Enron, Tyco, WorldCom, Adelphia and Parmalat. As a result of these scandals, not only the financial sector was scarred beyond repair, stakeholder confidence too plummeted to an all-time low. Among those instrumental in the exposure of most of these scandals were 'whistle-blowers'such as Sherron Watkins of Enron, Cynthia Cooper of WorldCom and Coleen Rowley of the FBI, who were selected by the *Time* magazine as 'Persons of the Year' in 2002.

26.2 DEFINITION AND MEANING OF THE TERM 'WHISTLE-BLOWING'

According to Post, Frederick and Lawrence, 'Whistle-blowing means an employee's disclosure to the public of alleged organizational misconduct, often after futile attempt to convince organizational authorities to take action against the alleged abuse. The immoral behaviour or ethical misconduct may relate to an individual employee or the top management.' Rothschild and Miethe had defined whistle-blowing as 'the disclosure of illegal, unethical or harmful practices in the workplace to parties who might take action'. Tina Uys has stated that whistle-blowing is an important tool in fighting fraud and corruption and the ethical lassitude that accompanies it. Senator Joe Bidden termed 'whistle-blowers' as 'national assets'. Senator Tom Devine of the Government Accountability Project said that they were the 'lifeblood of anti-corruption campaigns'.

Blowing the whistle is something that can be done only by a member of an organisation. Whistle-blowing is not concerned with action that amounts to dissenting publicly with one or group of persons on certain issues; or reporting a crime or misconduct to the police. Whistle-blowing necessarily involves the release of non-public information to members within the organisation or outside the organisation that had been deliberately withheld from them. The intentions, with which the information is withheld from the members often is for private gains, while neglecting the interests of the stakeholders. The act of making the information public by a whistle-blower is termed as whistle-blowing. According to Sissela Bok, 'The whistleblower assumes that his message will alert listeners to something they do not know, or whose significance they have not grasped because it has been kept secret.' The information is generally evidence of some significant kind of misconduct on the part of an organisation or some of its members. The term whistle-blowing is usually reserved for matters of substantial importance. The information must be released outside normal channels of communication. In most organisations, employees are instructed to report instances of illegal or improper conduct to their immediate superiors. When a whistle-blower chooses to report the information within the organisation, it is termed as 'internal whistle-blowing' or else he/she may choose to blow the whistle externally by 'going public' to reveal information outside the organisation. In either case, it is important that the information must be revealed in ways that can reasonably be expected to bring about a desired change. Merely passing on information about wrongdoing to a third party does not necessarily constitute whistle-blowing.

Whistle-blowing may be undertaken as a moral protest, that is, the motive must be to correct some wrong and not to seek revenge or personal advancement. The release of information must be something that is done voluntarily, as opposed to a legal requirement. Taking into consideration all these points, Joan R. Boatright has defined whistle-blowing as 'Voluntary release of non-public information, as a moral protest, by a member or former member of an organization outside the normal channels of communication to an appropriate audience about illegal and/or immoral conduct in the organization or conduct in the organization that is opposed in some significant way to the public interest.'

26.3 TYPES OF WHISTLE-BLOWING

26.3.1 INTERNAL WHISTLE-BLOWING

Where the whistle-blower talks to people higher up in the organisation, it is called internal whistle-blowing. The purpose of internal whistle-blowing is to get the allegation investigated as per the procedures of the organisation, and includes cases such as disloyalty, disobedience, insubordination and improper conduct.

26.3.2 EXTERNAL WHISTLE-BLOWING

Where there is a disclosure about improper conduct or immoral conduct is reported to the media, enforcement agencies or public interest groups, it is called external whistle-blowing. It is sometimes argued that external whistle-blowing is always wrong because employees have a contractual duty to be loyal to their employer and to keep all aspects of the business confidential. When an employee accepts a job, he/she implicitly agrees to keep all aspects of the business confidential and to single-mindedly pursue the best interests of the employer. The whistle-blower violates this agreement and thereby violates the rights of his/her employer. According to Manuel Velasquez, 'External whistle-blowing can be justified only if other means — such as internal whistle-blowing — of preventing a wrong have been tried but failed.' External whistle-blowing is, says Velasquez, morally justified if there is clear, substantiated and reasonably comprehensive evidence that the organisation is engaged in some activity that is seriously wronging others; reasonably serious attempts to prevent the wrong through internal whistle-blowing have been tried and have failed. It is reasonably certain that external whistle-blowing will prevent the wrong; and the wrong is serious enough to justify the injuries that external whistle-blowing will probably inflict on oneself, one's family and other parties.

26.4 THE THEORY OF WHISTLE-BLOWING

In the opinion to Tina Uys, a whistle-blower's 'political' career typically begins with the reporting of some ethical malpractice in the organisation that he/she expects management to deal with constructively. Whistle-blowers generally believe that they are valued employees whose commitment to the organisation would be appreciated. Rather than addressing the issue of malpractice, management retaliates against the whistle-blower. This sets in motion the process through which the whistle-blower is transformed from loyal employee to agent of political change.

When an employer retaliates against a whistle-blower, a power struggle develops between the two. While the employer may try to discredit the whistle-blower by referring to a 'difficult personality' or by creating a labour dispute, the whistle-blower wants to focus on the evidence of organisational wrongdoing. The power struggle then escalates and whistle-blowers are left with no choice but to defend themselves by publicising the wrongdoing even more widely.

The irony of whistle-blowing is that the whistle-blower usually expects the organisation to respond positively to his/her report to ethical malpractice. However, reporting of this information is met by fierce retaliation from management. Rothschild and Miethe state that any challenge to management's judgement is usually immediately followed by the employee being fired or if this is not possible, processes would be set in motion which would justify the termination of employment. Glazer and Glazer discuss blacklisting, dismissal, transfer, personal harassment and sexual exploitation as ways used by organisations to discredit and destroy whistle-blowers.

According to Rothschild and Miethe whistle-blowers tend to be highly competent and respected employees and among the core professionals within an organisation. They tend to have a dedication to higher moral principles rather than to the organisational norms that management holds dear. They tend to be naïve in their initial beliefs that the organisation is really committed to its mission, and that it wants to be informed about misconduct in the workplace. They start with the belief that their actions would be appreciated and rewarded.

The act of whistle-blowing points out to the fact that there exist serious deficiencies in the processes of an organisation. Davis regrets that whistle-blowing is evidence of the inadequacy of the communication channels in the organisation. It is also evident of the failure of management to deal satisfactorily with the whistle-blower's complaint. Davis believes that organisations should attempt to avoid the 'tragedy' of whistle-blowing. This could be achieved by institutionalising a climate where the reporting of bad news is encouraged as part of the regular way of going about the organisation's business. Communication channels of the organisation should be opened up so that nobody is in a position to prevent bad news from filtering through to the highest structures.

26.5 CASES OF WHISTLE-BLOWING

26.5.1 Daniel Ellsberg and the Pentagon Papers

In 1971, Daniel Ellsberg — a former Marine and Vietnam War Veteran, who was working as an analyst at the Rand Corporation — blew the whistle on a top-secret Defense Department document on the Vietnam War, which came to be known as the Pentagon Papers. Claiming to be driven by his conscience, Ellsberg revealed to the *New York Times* and the *Washington Post* how successive US presidents had dragged the country into an immoral and unwinnable war, and had lied to Americans about its courses and outcomes. His disclosure played a major part in turning the tide of public opinion against the Vietnam War.

26.5.2 FRANK SERPICO

Frank Serpico is the legendary ex-cop of the New York Police Department (NYPD) whose story was the subject of best-selling book and a film starring Al Pacino — both titled 'Serpico'. When he became a cop in 1960, pay-offs, kickbacks and protection rackets were rampant in NYPD. Refusing to look the other way, Serpico complained to the Police Commissioner and the Mayor, but they ignored him. Frustrated, Serpico revealed NYPD's dirty laundry to the *New York Times* in 1971, after which the cops as well as the criminals started gunning for him. He was shot in the face and no one came to his help.

26.5.3 SHERRON WATKINS

In August 2001, Sherron Watkins, vice-president at Enron, blew the whistle in a letter she wrote to chairman Ken Lay where she clearly outlined her concerns about the company's accounting practices. Risking her job and her career in order to draw attention to corporate wrongdoing in her organisation, she said, 'I am incredibly nervous that we will implode in a wave of accounting scandals.' Her words could not have been more prophetic.

26.5.4 COLEEN ROWLEY

In May 2002, Coleen Rowley blew the whistle on her employer, the FBI, when she accused her bosses of ignoring clear warnings of the September 11, terrorist attacks.

26.5.5 W. MARK FELT

W. Mark Felt (Code-named Deep Throat) was a secret informant who in 1972 leaked information about the US President Richard Nixon's involvement in Watergate. The scandal would eventually lead to the resignation of the president, and prison terms for White House Chief of Staff H.R. Haldeman and presidential adviser John Ehrlichman.

26.5.6 SATYENDRA DUBEY

Satyendra Kumar Dubey was project director at the National Highways Authority of India (NHAI). He was shot dead in November 2003 in Gaya, Bihar, for fighting corruption in the Golden Quadrilateral Highway Construction Project. The CBI confirmed on 14 March 2005 the murdered engineer's allegations that some big firms had illegally subcontracted the multi-crore works awarded to them in the project.

26.5.7 SHANMUGHAM MANJUNATH

Shanmugham Manjunath was a graduate of the prestigious IIM Lucknow, 2003 batch. He was working as a sales manager with Indian Oil Corporation Ltd. (IOCL) refused bribes and ignored threats in his drive to check rampant adulteration of petrol in the pumps owned by the erstwhile monopoly Indian Oil. On 19 November 2005, he was shot dead in Lakhimpur Kheri, allegedly by a petrol pump owner and his gang.

26.6 PROTECTING WHISTLE-BLOWERS

The United States has a Whistleblowers Protection Act of 1989 (amended in 1994). It has been strengthened by new laws such as the Sarbanes-Oxley Act of 2002, which contains new protections for corporate whistle-blowers, and the False Claims Act that was first proposed by Abraham Lincoln way back in 1862 to combat fraud by defence contractors and strengthened in 1986. It is the application of both the Whistleblowers Protection Act and the False Claims Act that confer protection to US whistle-blowers.

The UK's Public Interest Disclosure Act of 1998 provides protection to employees in the public, private and non-profit sectors. All the five states in Australia have whistle-blowers legislation. New Zealand too has the Protected Disclosures Act 2000 that came into force in 2001. South Africa has followed the UK example in providing protection to employees of all organisations through its Protected Disclosures Act of 2000.

Whistleblower Protection Act does not exist in India despite recommendations by various quarters. Whistleblower Protection Act coupled with the Right to Information Act, 2005 could act as a potent tool for promoting good governance. The desirability of an act for the protection of whistle-blowers had been recommended by Veerappa Moily Commission on Administrative Reforms II. Chief Justice Y.K. Sabharwal stoutly pleaded for the enactment of a whistle-blower's law in India. The Law Commission favoured a whistle-blower's law, called Public Interest Disclosure (Protection) Act in 2001.

The whistle-blowers (Protection of Public Interest Disclosures) Bill, 2006 was introduced in the Rajya Sabha on the 3 March 2006 to provide for protection from criminal or civil liability, departmental inquiry, demotion, harassment and discrimination of whistle-blowers, that is, the persons who bring to light specific instances of illegality, criminality, corruption, miscarriage of justice, any danger to public health and safety, in any government, public or private enterprise, to an authority designated for the purposes and matters connected therewith.

26.7 CONCLUSION

As Rothschild and Miethe have demonstrated, not only is whistle-blowing a form of political behaviour in its intention of effecting systemic change in organisations, but management often responds in a political fashion by trying to discredit the whistle-blower. It is therefore important to investigate ways in which organisations could be transformed in ways that would obviate the need for whistle-blowing. Lalitha Ravishankar has suggested a few steps for creating a whistle-blowing culture in organisations that include:

1. creating a policy after finding out employee's opinions about the organisation's culture vis-à-vis its commitment to ethics and values;
2. clear communications about the policy that bans on retaliation;
3. getting endorsement from top management;
4. Publicising the organisation's commitment;
5. investigation and follow-up and
6. assessing the organisation's internal whistle-blowing system periodically.

Suggested Questions

1. Explain the meaning of the term 'whistle-blowing'.
2. State the theory of whistle-blowing.
3. What are the types of whistle-blowing? Enumerate the names of any three famous whistle-blowers and the scandals they exposed to the public.
4. Are whistle-blowers protected? State the measures needed to protect whistle-blowers in India.
5. What measures can be taken by management to prevent scandals in organisations?

Bibliography

Beauchamp, T. L. and N. E. Bowie (1993). *Ethical Theory and Business* (USA: Prentice-Hall).

Joan, R. B. (2005). *Ethics and the Conduct of Business* (USA: Pearson Education).

Manuel, G. V. (2006). *Business Ethics, Concepts and Cases* (Prentice-Hall).

Nader, R., P. J. Petakas and K. Blackwell (eds.) (1972). *Whistle-Blowing: The Report of the Conference on Professional Responsibility* (New York: Grossman).

Peters, C. and T. Branch (1972). *Blowing the Whistle: Dissent in the Public Interest* (New York: Praegar).

Tina Uys, (2000) The politicization of whistle-blowers: A case study, *Business Ethics: A European Review*.

Chapter 27

Insider Trading

Tanusree Jain

> 'In a classical theory framework, market makers who provide liquidity to a market with informed and uninformed investors do not possess superior information. However, the model implications are not entirely consistent with some recent empirical evidence.'
>
> Jinghua Yan

LEARNING OUTCOMES

This chapter tells us about various aspects of Insider Trading. It would help you in various ways:

- to understand the concept of insider trading.
- for knowing the various dimensions of insider trading.
- to be able to identify the tests of insider trading.
- for classifying an insider.
- also to determine the legal status of insider trading in India.

27.1 INTRODUCTION

The practice of insider trading has generated a lot of interest and debate in recent times across the globe. Companies such as Enron, Worldcom and Imclone systems have been in the news for exactly the same reason. When hearing news stories about insider-trading activity, investors usually take notice because it is an activity that affects them. Also insider trading raises questions that have moral, economic and legal concerns. More Indians are investing in the stock markets than ever before. Such an increase in interest and investment in the securities market would continue when the investors are able to place their trust and confidence in the fairness and integrity of the market exchanges as well its regulatory authorities. This calls for strict regulation of the market to make it free, fair and open.

27.2 INSIDER TRADING DEFINED

Insider trading as a term is subject to many definitions and connotations and encompasses both legal and prohibited activity. In other words, not all insider trading is illegal. Company executives — generally, officers, directors and employees — trade in their own securities and report these to the Securities Exchange Board (SEB). As long as these 'insiders' act on publicly disclosed information — there is no problem. It is when they act on non-public information, that the so-called 'insider trading'[1] becomes illegal.

[1]For the purpose of this chapter, hereinafter IT will be used in the illegal context.

Illegal insider trading generally occurs when securities are bought and sold based on privileged possession of information that is material and not yet publicly available.

Thus, IT takes place when someone having access to unpublished price sensitive information deals in a company's securities for a personal benefit, thereby gaining an unfair advantage over the rest of the market. The private benefit may be either in terms of an increase in the profit or avoidance of loss. Insider trading violations may also include 'tipping'[2] such information, securities trading by the person 'tipped'[3] and securities trading by those who misappropriate such information.

According to Post, Fredrick and Lawrence, 'Insider Trading is an illegal practice of buying and selling shares of a corporate based on fiduciary information, which is known to only a small group of persons, such as executives and their friends ('insiders'), and which enables them to make profit at the expense of other investors who do not access to the inside information.'

27.3 THE INSIDER TRADING DEBATE

Insider trading occurs when a trade has been influenced by the privileged possession of corporate information that has not yet been made public. Since the information is not available to other investors, it compromises market transparency as well as integrity. Applying the consequentialist approach to moral reasoning, referred to in Chapter 13, insider trading can be considered as an act that has bad consequences. Because of ethical and moral considerations, the prevention of insider trading is widely treated as an important function of securities regulation. In India, the prohibition of insider trading is an important function of the Securities and Exchange Board of India (SEBI). In spite of this, there is no unanimous agreement on the implication and consequences of IT. The following discussion lays out arguments in favour and against insider trading on several economic, ethical and legal grounds.

27.3.1 INSIDER TRADING AND MORAL REASONING

Moral theory (as discussed earlier in Chapter 13) has two parts. One part of moral theory deals with 'what should be done' or 'what should not be done' which is in other words, the theory of right the other part deals with the 'what is good' or 'what is bad' which is the theory of value. While the theory of right determines whether an action is right or wrong, the theory of value establishes the nature of an action in terms of its consequences being good or bad. The ordinary understanding is that IT is wrong when seen in this perspective can be considered as a wrong activity irrespective of its consequences. However, the opponents of regulation of insider trading believe that if allowed, insider trading may in fact lead to some good consequences. Essentially, it is argued that it makes markets more efficient. This makes it pertinent for us to discuss the arguments in favour and against regulation of insider trading. The debate it must be pointed out is about whether or not there should be any regulation on insider trading.

27.3.2 ECONOMIC DIMENSION

27.3.2.1 Arguments in Favour

- Insider trading makes the market more efficient

  Most proponents of insider trading defend it as being economically efficient. A market is said to be efficient when the market price of each security reflects accurately its future risk and return. In addition, the price fixing of the securities is considered efficient when all information has been absorbed and used

[2]Tipping is a process wherein a person, known as the tipper, breaks his fiduciary duty by consciously revealing price-sensitive inside information.

[3]The person who is tipped is also known as the tippee. A tippee is the person who knowingly uses such information to make a trade (in turn also breaking his confidentiality).

in the process. In the absence of insider trading, some material, but non-public information, remains unutilised. This implies that the prices so fixed do not reveal the true state of affairs of the company and hence are not efficient. IT uses real and not fictitious information and is more likely to make the market efficient.

Insider trading is often equated with market manipulation, yet the two phenomena are completely different. Manipulation is intrinsically about making market prices move away from their fair values; manipulators reduce market efficiency. Insider trading brings prices closer to their fair values; insiders enhance market efficiency.

- Beneficial to the economy

  When insiders, armed with real information, trade on securities it accelerates the movement of share prices and furthers the resolution of wealth transfers. This enhances market efficiency to a greater extent and benefits all traders — insiders and outsiders.

  Insider trading appears unfair, especially to speculators outside a company. However, the interests of the economy and the interests of these professional traders are not congruent. So while one class of economic agent suffers the economy at large benefits.

- Motivation of executives

  Company executives with inside information can utilise the first mover's advantage for mutual gains. They are motivated to improve the performance of the company by putting together new deals, launching new and improved products, entering new markets, thereby benefiting the company and consequently using this inside information for personal gains. In this manner, they can club their personal interests with those of the company and its shareholders.

- Reduction in company cost

  Some argue that insider trading is a legitimate form of compensation for corporate employees, permitting lower salaries that, in turn, results in reduced corporate costs and increased benefits to shareholders.

- Perfect competition situation

  Some theorists believe that unregulated insider trading can be compared to a perfect competition situation wherein the market will find its own equilibrium at the optimum point. This is based on the 'invisible hand' theory of Adam Smith. [4]

27.3.2.2 *Arguments Against*

- Against free competition

  IT appears to be based on the principle of free market with no restrictions imposed on the activities of insiders as well as outsiders. In reality, IT leads to regulation of the market by insiders, that is, people holding confidential information. Now if the assumption that free competition provides the best economic results holds good, IT being against free competition cannot make the market more efficient, as argued.

- No perfect competition

  Proponents compare IT to a perfect competition situation. Actually, perfect competition hardly ever exists. In any case, such a market requires the participants to have perfect knowledge. The presence of IT makes people unequal in terms of access to vital information and hence is against the very principle.

[4]This phrase was used by Scottish economist Adam Smith (1723–1790) in explaining his belief that the actions of individuals, although taken for their own economic benefit, are guided in such a manner as to benefit society as a whole.

Further, there is no evidence that the 'invisible hand' can deal with the excesses of IT.

- Lowers market liquidity

  A consistent price manipulation by insiders deters investor confidence and trust. The market gets a reputation as an unlevel playing field and investors stay away as also it increases the spread of rumours. Such loss of trust creates problems for companies by eroding their market values, hampering their future capital-raising capacity and lowering market liquidity in general.

- Anti-company practice

  The real and significant hazard of IT is that it creates an incentive for corporate insiders to enter into risky or ill-advised ventures for short-term personal gain, as well as to put off the public release of important corporate information so that they can capture the economic fruits at the expense of shareholders. Thus, executives with inside information can benefit from it whether the news is positive or negative. Therefore, IT does not automatically guarantee improved executive and company performance. Besides, employees tend to spend more time, attention and concentration on gaining through insider trading which further restrains them from their respective managerial duties. Using IT as compensation can be equated, therefore, to stealing and cheating from outsiders in order to lower company costs.

- Dangerous activity

  Considering that every market has both buyers and sellers, the profit of one investor is the loss of the other. With insider trading possible, insiders generally would always be at a profit and the overall net result would be negative for outsiders and for the market overall.

- Against morality

  For efficient operation of markets, the presence of people who put morality and reason ahead of their self-interest is a prerequisite. The very motive of IT is personal gain and hence people engaging in the same cannot exhibit such moral behaviour.

- Violation of property rights

  'Inside' information about any company — its trade secrets, strategies, etc. — are assets that belong solely to shareholders. Only a firm's owners have the moral right to exclusively profit from it as well as decide how their employees can use such information. From this viewpoint, insider trading by executives of a company can be considered as violation of property rights equivalent to theft.

- Source of unfairness and inequality

  Using non-public information for making a trade violates transparency, which is the basis of a capital market. Information in a transparent market disseminates in a manner by which all market participants receive it at more or less the same time. Under conditions of IT, when one person trades with non-public information, he or she, better equipped with information, gains an advantage that is impossible for the rest of the public. This is not only unfair but also leads to loss of confidence of investors in the market and consequently lower market liquidity.

- Violation of fiduciary relationship

  Every executive has a relationship of utmost good faith with his/her company. This fiduciary relationship has strong moral and legal justification. It is, at the same time, the fundamental concept behind modern capitalism which is characterised by a separation of ownership and control. The diffusion of ownership and control calls for trust between the executives (controlling the company) and their owners (scattered shareholders). Involvement of the executives in activities such as insider trading (solely for private benefit) can be considered as a breach of their fiduciary duty to the company.

27.4 THE PRESENT STATUS OF INSIDER TRADING

Laws are the formal seal of approval to the current state of ethics in society. They are the consensus on what society considers as ethical or unethical. The several arguments posed in favour of insider trading do not really hold water. Almost all economically developed nations, including India, have given their verdict on insider trading. Government as well as the industry do not view it favourably and consider it undesirable. Laws have been enacted to curb and prohibit it. Companies have drawn up a code of conduct for themselves and investor education is being taken up seriously by the government.

27.4.1 Test of Insider Trading

The offence of insider trading or dealing requires three ingredients to qualify as such:

1. involvement of insiders,
2. presence of unpublished price-sensitive information and
3. use of such information for dealing in securities.

27.4.1.1 Who Is an Insider?

Corporate insider is someone who is privy to information that is yet to be publicly released. Broadly speaking, it includes the following people:

- corporate officers, directors and employees who traded the corporation's securities after learning of significant, confidential corporate developments;
- friends, business associates, family members and other 'tippees' of such officers, directors and employees, who traded the securities after receiving such information;
- employees of law, banking, brokerage and printing firms who were given such information to provide services to the corporation whose securities they traded;
- government employees who learnt of such information because of their employment by the government and
- other persons who misappropriated, and took advantage of, confidential information from their employers.

A common misconception is that only directors and upper management can be convicted of insider trading. Actually, anybody who has material and non-public information can commit such an act. This means that nearly anybody — including brokers, family, friends and employees — can be considered an insider (Table 27.1).

Table 27.1 Examples of Illegal Trading.

• The director of a company sells a stock after discovering that the company will be losing a big contract next month.
• The CEO's relative sells the company stock after hearing from him that the company will be losing the big government contract.
• A government official realises that the company will lose a big government contract, so the official sells the stock.

27.4.1.2 Price-Sensitive Information

Price-sensitive information is likely to affect the price of a security. As per SEBI, any information that pertains to the subjects mentioned below and was not generally known or was not published by the company concerned for general information but, which if published or known is likely to affect the prices of the securities in the market is price sensitive. However, speculative reports in print or electronic media shall not be considered as published information.

As per SEBI in its amended Insider Trading Rules, 2002, the following seven subjects have been listed as price sensitive:

1. periodical financial results;
2. intended declaration of dividends (interim and final);
3. issue of securities or buy-back of securities;
4. any major expansion plans or execution of new projects;
5. amalgamation, mergers or takeovers;
6. disposal of the whole or part of the undertaking and
7. significant changes in policies, plans or operations.

27.5 PENALTIES FOR INSIDER TRADING

The first country to tackle insider trading effectively, by declaring it illegal, was the United States way back in the 1930s. In almost all the other world markets, it went virtually unregulated up to the 1980s. The United States empowered the Securities and Exchange Commission (SEC) to impose civil as well as criminal penalties on people engaging in insider trading.

In the Indian context, however, it was only in the 1970s that insider trading was first officially recognised as undesirable. A series of committee reports recommended its strict regulation. Consequently, the SEBI issued regulations in 1992 to prohibit IT. Section 15 G of the SEBI Act, 1992 provides for penalties for the offence of insider trading. This section is preventive as well as punitive as it puts the penalty for insider trading extraordinarily high at Rs. 25 crores or three times the amount of profit made, whichever is higher. In addition, Section 24 provides for imprisonment up to a maximum of 10 years or a fine up to Rs. 25 crores in case of any of violations of the act and its regulations.

27.6 CONCLUSION

Insider trading is an extraordinarily difficult crime to prove. The underlying act of buying or selling securities is perfectly legal; however, it is the motive of the trader that can make it a prohibited activity. Almost all economically developed nations agree that insider trading is unethical and should be banned and severely penalised.

Despite all this effort, there have been several cases of IT in Indian markets as well as in international markets. The difficulty of the situation lies in the fact that IT promises huge economic benefits to insiders making them willing to take the risks. On the other hand, no law is without loopholes and there is a certain limit to the severity of laws. In addition, insider trading has assumed international significance since a foreign national may engage in insider trading in the domestic market while nationals may effect insider trading through foreign accounts making it all the more difficult to detect. Successful policing, investigations and prosecutions of such cases require international cooperation. The solution also lies in the introduction of sophisticated IT detection and prevention technologies and efficient and continuous communication of its unethical aspect.

Suggested Questions

1. Explain the meaning of 'insider trading'? Why is there an increasing interest in the same?
2. Comment briefly on the following:
   (a) Insider and
   (b) Price sensitive information.
3. What is meant by insider trading? "Insider trading is a matter of debate." Would you defend it?
4. Who is an insider and how can he/she benefit from insider trading?
5. Is insider trading ethical? Discuss.
6. What is the legal status presently accorded to insider trading?
7. "Insider trading could make the markets more efficient." Comment.

Bibliography

Fishman, M. J. and Hagerty, K. M. (1992). Insider trading and the efficiency of stock prices. *The RAND Journal of Economics*, 23(1) (Spring): 106–122.

Manne, H. (1966). *Insider Trading and the Stock Market* (New York: The Free Press).

McGee, W. R. (2007). Two approaches to examining the ethics of insider trading. *Working Paper*. http://papers.ssrn.com/.

Chapter 28

Employment Discrimination

Sonia

'Education is important because, first of all, people need to know that discrimination still exists. It is still real in the workplace, and we should not take that for granted.'

Alexis Herman

LEARNING OUTCOMES

After going through the chapter, students will be able to:

- understand the meaning and kinds of discrimination.
- get familiar with various kinds of discriminatory policies adopted at the workplace.
- define the concept of 'affirmative actions' and evaluate their pros and cons.
- establish a relationship between Utilitarian approach and affirmative action.

28.1 INTRODUCTION

Discrimination remains a significant ethical issue in business despite nearly 43 years of legislation to outlaw it. Once dominated, workforce today includes significantly more women, lower class, farmers and other minorities, as well as disabled and older workers. This chapter describes how workers and non-workers have suffered due to various substantial and prolonged discriminatory policies. But, nowadays, to help build workforces that reflect their customers base, many companies have initiated affirmative action programmes, which involve efforts to recruit, hire, train and promote qualified individuals from groups that have traditionally been discriminated against on the basis of race, gender or other traits.

The aim of this chapter is to analyse the nature and forms of discrimination in workplace and focus on the other aspects of discrimination, that is, affirmative action programmes

28.2 CONCEPT OF DISCRIMINATION

Discrimination refers to unequal treatment. Discrimination is contrary to the basic principle of equality. The root meaning of the term discrimination is to distinguish one person from other based on prejudice or some other immoral traits. Discrimination has both positive and negative aspects associated with it. When we look at the negative aspects, it is referred as wrongful act of differentiating illicitly among people. On the contrary, discrimination may be justified by saying that it benefits the least advantaged class, more so, when the discriminated classes have been neglected for a long time.

28.3 FORMS OF DISCRIMINATION

A helpful framework for analysing different forms of discrimination can be formulated by distinguishing the extent to which a discriminatory act is intentional and isolated and the extent to which it is unintentional and institutionalised. The common forms of employment discrimination are individual or isolated discrimination and institutional discriminations.

28.3.1 INDIVIDUAL OR ISOLATED DISCRIMINATION

A discriminatory act may be part of the isolated behaviour of a single individual who intentionally (or unintentionally) and knowingly (or unknowingly) discriminates out of personal prejudice, for example, personnel department might assign best paying jobs to males and worst paying jobs to women in an organisation, on the assumption that women are fit for certain jobs only.

28.3.2 INSTITUTIONAL DISCRIMINATIONS

A discriminatory act may be part of the routine behaviour of an institutionalised group, that intentionally (or unintentionally) and knowingly (or unknowingly) discriminates out of the personal prejudice towards its members, for example, the Ku Klux Klan (KKK) is a white supremacist organisation that was founded in 1866. With its characteristic white robes and masks, the secret fraternal organisation has used acts of terrorism — including murder, rape and bombing — to oppose the granting of civil rights to African-Americans and others. This type of discrimination can be explicit and intentional.

28.4 DISCRIMINATORY PRACTICES AT WORKPLACE

When employment opportunities, public contracts etc. are not given on merit but on basis of sex, race, age, colour etc., there is discrimination. It is usually referred as wrongful act of distinguishing illicitly among people based on race, sex, age and non-job-related factors.

According to Prof. Manuel G Velasquez, 'to discriminate in employment is to make an adverse decision against employees based on their membership in a certain group'. Thus, discrimination in employment must involve three basic elements; they are discussed below.

1. It is a decision against one or more employees that is not based on the merits of the case.
2. The decision drives solely from racial reasons, sexual prejudice or some other kind of morally unjustified attitude against members of a class or group.
3. The decision has a harmful impact on the interests of the employees, perhaps costing them their jobs.

Regardless of the arguments against discrimination, it is still prevalent everywhere. There has been a growing recognition of the various forms of discrimination in employment. Among the practices now widely recognised as discriminatory are recruitment practices, screening practices, condition of employment and discharge.

28.4.1 RECRUITMENT PRACTICES

Business firms that depend primarily on the references of present employees to recruit new employees tend to recruit only from those racial and sexual groups that are already represented in their force, for example, dominance of white males in the workforce.

28.4.2 Screening Practices

Job qualifications are discriminatory when they do not match with the job requirements. Aptitude and other screening tests tend to become discriminatory when they serve some particular person group. Similarly, job interviews are discriminatory if interviewer routinely disqualifies women and minorities by relying on sexual racial stereotypes.

28.4.3 Condition of Employment

Wage policies also became discriminatory when equal pay is not given for a same work. There is a need to look into cases where compensation had been lower due to discriminatory compensation policy in the past.

28.4.4 Discharge

Firing employees based on sex or race is a clear form of discrimination. Layoff policies that rely on seniority system tend to become discriminatory particularly when some people have lowest seniority because discriminatory practices existed in the past as well.

28.4.5 Promotion Practices

Promotion and transfer practices are also discriminatory when favour is done to a particular group. When promotion relies on the subjective judgements of the immediate supervisors, promotion policy will be discriminatory to the extent they rely on racial or sexual basis and not on merit.

28.5 AFFIRMATIVE ACTIONS

Affirmative action is an effort to develop a systematic approach to open the doors of educational, employment and business development opportunities to qualified individuals who have experienced long-standing and persistent discrimination. All of the equal opportunities policies ignore the fact that as a result of past discrimination, women and minorities do not have the same skills.

To rectify the effects of past discrimination, many employers have initiated affirmative action programmes to obtain a more representative distribution of minorities and woman within the firm by giving them preference. For this purpose, usually, firms appoint an officer to coordinate and administer the affirmative action programmes to increase the recruitment of disadvantaged class.

Infosys has taken a lead in affirmative action in employing backward class to its workforce. For doing so, the company trained 76 engineers from government-owned institutes. The first batch of trained engineers has got employment in Infosys as well as other enterprises. In this first attempt of training engineers, the company upgraded the soft skills and behavioural skills of engineers for confidence building in order to improve their employability in the industry.

28.5.1 Arguments Against Affirmative Action Programmes

Without question, the principle objection to affirmative action and the reason it has become and remained controversial is due to reverse discrimination. The concept holds that when any sort of preference is given to minorities and women, discrimination may occur against those in majority. This may lead to the situation of chaos and demonstration by the majority class. Like medical students conducted a nationwide strike against the quota system for minority classes.

These programmes have been attacked and mainly on the grounds that, in attempting compensate for past discrimination, these programmes have become racially or sexually discriminatory. These programmes violate the principles of equality and equal opportunities, and sometimes, benefit only few people from disadvantaged class.

28.5.2 Arguments for Affirmative Actions

The arguments used to justify affirmative action programmes in the face of the objections mentioned above are categorised into two main groups:

1. as a form of compensation for past injuries and
2. as an instrument for achieving social goals.

28.5.2.1 Affirmative Action as Compensation

According to this concept, people have an obligation to compensate those whom they have intentionally/unintentionally caused some harm. It is assumed that it is their moral duty to compensate the underprivileged class. The difficulties with the arguments that defend affirmative actions are that:

- This principle requires that compensation should come only from those specific individual who has inflicted a wrong and it is to be given to those specific individual whom they wronged.
- Affirmative action programmes are unfair because the beneficiaries of affirmative actions are not the same individuals who were injured by past discrimination.

28.5.2.2 Affirmative Action as an Instrument for Achieving Social Goals

This is the second justification in favour of affirmative action programmes. These programmes are justified because they promote social welfare. It has been argued by utilitarian philosophers that discrimination has produced a high correlation between race and poverty during the past. As minorities were excluded from better paying jobs, their members became impoverished. Impoverishment in turn has led to unmet needs, lack of self-respect, resentment, social discontent and crime. Therefore, the position of these impoverished persons could only be improved by giving them special educational and employment opportunities.

28.6 UTILITARIAN VIEWPOINT

The most important element of consequentialist ethics is utilitarianism. As we have already studied the utility principle is that in any given case, we ought to choose that course of action which will produce 'the greatest happiness of the greatest number'. At first glance, affirmative actions satisfy this principle by generating greater happiness to greater number but some difficulties are also encountered with respect to this utilitarian view. Therefore, a kind of dilemma occurs between practising affirmative action and reverse discrimination.

28.6.1 Arguments in Favour of Affirmative Actions

Although utilitarian arguments in favour of affirmative action programmes are quite convincing, the most elaborate and persuasive array of arguments advanced in support of affirmative action have proceeded in two steps.

Firstly, the end envisioned by affirmative action programmes is equal to justice.

Secondly, affirmative action programmes are morally legitimate means for achieving this goal because they raise the living standard of the society.

28.6.2 Arguments Against Affirmative Actions

Some opponents believe that cost of these social programmes is more than their benefits. It may be inconvenient and expensive to identify the needy directly. However, the costs might be small compared to the gains that would result from having a more accurate way to identify the needy.

It further leads to dissatisfaction among people, for example, medical students have conducted a serious nationwide strike against quota system.

Opponents to utilitarian view have questioned the assumption that race is an appropriate indicator of need. It may be inconvenient and expensive to identify the needy directly. However, the costs might be small when compared to the gains that would result from having a more accurate way to identify the needy.

28.7 CONCLUSION

In the end, what affirmative actions are supposed to achieve is to distribute benefits and burdens emanating from the society in consistence with the principles of distributive justice. Further, they are expected to neutralise various competitive disadvantages with which minorities are suffering. Thus, we can conclude by saying that the basic end that these programmes seek to achieve is a more just society — a society in which an individual's opportunities are not limited by his/her race or sex.

Suggested Questions

1. Define the concept of 'discrimination'.
2. What are the various forms of discrimination?
3. Explain the dilemma between practising affirmative action and reverse discrimination.
4. What is the moral implication of affirmative actions?
5. What is employment discrimination? Explain various discriminatory practices used by employers against their workers.
6. What is affirmative action? Describe arguments in favour of and against affirmative action.
7. What kinds of arguments are imposed by utilitarians regarding affirmative actions?

Bibliography

Donaldson, T. and P. H. Werhane (1983). *Ethical Issues in Business: A Philosophical Approach*, 2nd edition (Englewood Cliffs, NJ: Prentice-Hall).

Frederick, W. C., K. Davis and J. E. Post (1988). *Business and Society* (New York: McGraw-Hill).

Goodin, R. E. and P. Pettit (Ed.) (1993). *A Companion to Contemporary Political Philosophy* (UK: Oxford University Press).

Richard, T. De George (1990). *Business Ethics*, 3rd edition (New York: Macmillan).

Velasquez, M. G. (2001). *Business Ethics: Concepts and Cases*, 5th edition (India: Prentice-Hall).

Weiss, J. W. (2003). *Business Ethics: A Stakeholder and Issues Management Approach*, 3rd edition (Australia: Thomson South-Western).

Chapter 29

Ethical Issues in Advertising

Dr Savita Hanspal

'Never write an advertisement which you wouldn't want your family to read. You wouldn't tell lies to your own wife. Don't tell them to mine.'

David Ogilvy

LEARNING OBJECTIVES

This chapter proposes to help you:

- by informing you of the various ethical concerns in advertising.
- in understanding how advertising raises important ethical issues.
- in evaluating the impact of these concerns on the society.

29.1 INTRODUCTION

One finds advertisements everywhere — on the roads, television, newspapers, magazines, taxis, trains, in buses and even in hospitals. There is an increase in the number of advertisements that we are exposed to every day. Advertising is not only aimed at consumers but also at manufacturers, wholesalers, retailers and professionals such as doctors, interior decorators and builders.. Further, advertisements relate not only to products but also to services such as health, banking, insurance, security, education and financial services.

It is one of the major devices that business uses to promote sales. However, advertising is not restricted to profit-making organisations. A large number of advertisements are being increasingly released by charitable organisations, such as WWF and UNICEF, advocacy groups, religious institutions, special interest groups, welfare organisations, and even the governments and municipalities.

29.2 ADVERTISING – MEANING

According to the American Marketing Association, advertising is any paid form of non-personal presentation and promotion of ideas, goods and services by an identified sponsor. Advertising is a marketing tool that is used to disseminate information about a brand which is aimed at a large number of people at the same time. It is advertisers' moral duty to depict information about the product honestly and correctly. However, most advertisements are deceptive and misleading. We are discussing these aspects of advertising in the following discussion.

29.3 UNETHICAL ASPECTS OF ADVERTISING

Unethical aspects of advertising have been discussed under the following headings:

- advertising message,
- quantum of advertising,
- inappropriate advertising and
- undesirable influences on the society.

29.4 ADVERTISING MESSAGE OR 'CONTENTS'

The advertising message consists of the content, the way the content is presented and to whom the message is conveyed.

29.4.1 DECEPTIVE MESSAGE

The contents or message of advertisement may include exaggerated product claims. The claims made may be ambiguous, there may be concealment of facts, puffery and insufficient information. The claims may have a bad influence on the children and the society. Some advertisements are charged with the creation of stereotypes, and objectionable language.

29.4.2 MISREPRESENTATION OR OMISSION

When an advertisement for cooking oil says that using the said oil frees the user from heart problems, then such an advertisement is misrepresenting facts. Misrepresentation may occur in any of the following ways:

- Suggesting that a small difference is important, but actually it is not so.
- Using an ambiguous and easily confused phrase such as 'number one', 'leading' and 'top most'.
- Implying a benefit that does not fully or partially exist, such as promising first three services free and then partially charging for the materials and only providing free labour.
- Implying that a product or benefit is unique to a brand, such as the only refrigerator using 'puff' or the only toothpaste using clove oil.

29.4.3 EXAGGERATED CLAIMS

This unethical practice is related to making a claim without substantiation, that is, claims that are not supported by evidence; for example, claiming that a particular toothpaste is 20% stronger than the competitor's brand, without any evidence to support the claim.

Advertisers of anti-ageing creams, complexion-improving creams, weight-loss programmes, anti-dandruff shampoos and manufacturers of vitamins or dietary supplements are usually guilty of making exaggerated product claims. The effect of such claims may be to mislead innocent consumers especially children and vulnerable group into believing in product features or benefits that may not actually exist.

29.4.4 PUFFERY

It means the use of harmless superlatives. The advertisers use them to boast the merits of their products (best, finest, number one etc.).

BMW's claim: 'the ultimate driving machine' involves the highest degree of exaggeration but it is harmless. Similarly, when you see an advertisement where using toothpaste shines your teeth so white that it becomes a source of light, it is simply exaggeration. However, there is a thin line determining the distinction between puffery and deliberate deception. The advertiser's intention and the interpretation of the ad determine whether an advertisement involves puffery or deliberate deception but it nevertheless may mislead the gullible consumers. Advertisements for shampoos are a case in point.

29.4.5 Concealment of Information

This involves suppression of information. The advertiser neglects to mention important information or distracts the consumers' attention away from information, the knowledge of which would probably make their products less desirable.

Ads of financial, housing and other lending institutions emphasise low EMIs suppressing information on the actual cost of loan, and by concealing information on other charges such as processing fees, penalty on early repayment, interest on late payments. Similarly, providing the lure of pre-approved loans without indicating that not many formalities are required. Advertisements for general medicines available over the counter (OTC), never talk of the side effects that may result from their frequent use.

29.4.6 Psychological Appeals

They persuade by appealing primarily to human emotional needs and not to reason. Lifestyle ads for apartments, house locations, hotels, airlines, cars, clothes, mobile phones, etc. appeal to the need of the consumer to desire for status. This results in some cases to a tendency to keep up with the Joneses' and people may be tempted to buy goods and services they are really not able to afford.

29.4.7 Advertisements Directed at Children

Advertising to children is big business. As a result, the brand awareness of children is going up. Advertisements are directed at children both for products aimed at them (e.g. chocolates, ice creams, school bags and children's toys) and also other products (e.g cars and houses). The advertisers rely on the children's pester power on their parents. The ethical issues involved are:

- Young children are naïve and gullible and are vulnerable to advertiser's enticements. They lack independent judgement and experience.
- The line between the children's shows and commercials is fading.
- They may not understand the implications of the money outlay that may be required to get the 'free' gift. Moreover, they have only a passing interest in the goodies advertised leaving the parents down rupees that could have been otherwise spent more wisely.
- Over advertising and advertising on channels telecasting children's programmes are giving rise to the 'brand culture', which is responsible for a fierce desire in children to match up the wealthier counterparts.

29.4.8 Creating Stereotypes

The stereotypical images of women are presented in settings such as family illness, looking after children, cooking, doing housework and always seeking approval of mother-in-law; or they are shown as dependent on men, subservient to them or less intelligent. The stereotypical images of young men and women overly concerned with fairness or with high priced brands of mobiles are another example. Such advertisements generate social pressure to conform and prescribe self-imposed penalties and complexes on others.

29.4.9 USE OF SEX APPEALS

Sex appeal is used explicitly to sell all kinds of things. It is used to gain consumer attention. It is used where it is not even appropriate to the product or service being advertised, for example, men's cosmetics, technical products such as equipment and machinery. Women are shown as decorative objects or as sexually provocative figures for advertisements for products and services where women are not required. The corporate sector should be encouraged to eliminate the violation of women's rights online and the Internet service providers to undertake efforts to minimise pornography, trafficking and all forms of gender-based violence.

29.4.10 BAIT ADVERTISING

It is concerned with announcing the sale of goods that later prove not to be available or to be defective. Once the consumer is lured into the store, he or she is pressured to purchase another more expensive item. You may have seen advertisements by retailers announcing sales at heavy discounts. On visiting such stores, you may find a handful of outdated products on the discount announced and other better products as 'fresh stock'. The advertisement by Big Bazaar, to sell the junk of your house and buy new goods is an example of bait advertising. Similarly, advertisements announcing 'sale' at 50% + 45% or advertisements for discount up to 70% are examples of such practices.

29.5 QUANTUM OF ADVERTISING

Two major issues involved in the quantity or numbers of advertisements are excessive advertising and intrusion in the privacy of individuals by arousing unnecessary feelings and needs.

Advertising has increased in all media, be it newspapers, radio or television. This shows that too much money is being spent in advertising. There is a lot of repetition that can be avoided and the resources put to better use. The posters and billboards spoil the look of the landscape and give the city a dirty look. Moreover, it does have a nuisance value so much so that the people devise ways and means to avoid exposure to advertisements by fast-forwarding the advertisements or switching channels, further resulting in waste of financial resources.

29.6 INAPPROPRIATE ADVERTISING

Advertising is not restricted to products that are good for people. Advertisements for cigarettes, liquor, paan masala and other products that are harmful to the public continue to find a place despite the ban imposed by the government in private channels, cable and through the use of surrogates. Examples include McDowell's Soda and Wills Lifestyle stores which are seen as surrogate advertising for McDowell's Whiskey and Wills cigarettes, respectively. The issues involved are:

- Whether such products should be advertised or not?
- If they should be advertised, and they will need to be advertised so long as their production is not banned, in what media should they be advertised?
- At what time should they be advertised?
- Further, if they are permitted to be advertised, whether the warning signs on the packages of these products really serve any purpose?

The role of in-film and in-serial advertising and surrogate advertising in promoting the sale of these products also needs to be examined more closely. Advertisers pay film producers to place their products in certain scenes by integrating the products in the film scripts and screenplays. When children and other vulnerable groups watch these advertisements, they get carried away by the ambience surrounding their use and the hype created in the scenes that they are attracted to use them at the first opportunity.

29.7 UNDESIRABLE INFLUENCES

29.7.1 FOR CONSUMERS

Too much exposure to advertisements also results in certain unwanted influences on the society, people are attracted towards being more materialistic, trying to be one up the others and trying to maintain false standards of living. They do not hesitate in taking debts that are unaffordable to repay. When reasonable means may not be available, they may even resort to crimes at a young age. The advertisements for various contests with large prize amounts encourage strategies for getting rich quickly thus undermining hard work and sincere efforts to do well. There may also be prejudices against the well-to-do classes because of exposure to their lifestyles in media such as television. The cases of financial frauds increase and there is a decline in moral values. These developments have long-term repercussions for individuals, their families and the society at large.

29.7.2 FOR MEDIA

Further, advertising also adversely influences the freedom of the press and the media. The media are dependent upon the advertisers for revenue. The advertisers' pressure may prevent the unscrupulous businessmen from being brought to the book or suppressing information that is in public interest but hurts powerful interests. The media may not expose them for fear of losing revenue.

29.8 CONCLUSION

Advertising has a profound influence on the society. The consumers need to be made aware of the unethical aspects of advertisements. It is the responsibility of business to ensure that in order to promote their products they should behave ethically. The consumers should also be vigilant for challenges posed by unethical ads.

Suggested Questions

1. Define advertising. List the various ethical issues involved in advertising.
2. The quantity of advertising is not an ethical issue because the more an organisation advertises, the more it sells. Do you agree? Give reasons for your answer.
3. Advertisements create stereotypes. Give suitable examples to illustrate.
4. Give three examples to show how advertising influences children. Does it raise any ethical concerns? If so, what are they?
5. Distinguish between puffery and exaggerated claims.
6. Do you think advertising creates some undesirable influences on the society? Give suitable examples to support your answer.
7. What is bait advertising? Explain the concept with an example of your own experience. Do you think it raises any ethical concerns?
8. Sex appeals are used to advertise for products and services. With the help of suitable examples, please discuss the ethical issues involved.

Bibliography

Aaker, D. A. and J. G. Myers (1982). *Advertising Management* (Englewood Cliffs, NJ: Prentice Hall).

Jefkins, F. (2002). *Advertising* (MacMillan India Ltd.).

Khanna, S., H. Savita, *et al.* (2007). *Consumer Affairs* (Universities Press India Private Ltd.).

Kotler, P. (2004). *Marketing Management* (India: Pearson Education), p. 590.

Chapter 30

Consumer Rights

Dr Savita Hanspal

'It is important that new developments take place within a legal framework that can secure a safe and fair consumer market for all consumers.'

The Yearbook of Consumer Law, 2007

LEARNING OBJECTIVES

In India, consumer interests are protected under the Consumer Protection Act, 1986. It is important to be a responsible consumer because it will equip you with skills that are important to help you in spending your money wisely and encourage you to get value for the money already spent. This chapter will:

- enable you to understand who a consumer is.
- help you identify some problems faced by consumers.
- inform you about how the rights of consumers have evolved.
- explain you the basic rights available to consumers in India.
- discuss your responsibilities as a consumer to effectively enforce your rights.

30.1 WHO IS A CONSUMER?

Each one of us is a consumer because we buy goods and services and also make use of public utilities such as electricity, water, telephone and sanitation. According to the Consumer Protection Act, 1986, a consumer is any person who buys, hires or avails of any goods or services for a consideration which has been paid, or promised or partly paid or promised or paid under a system of deferred payment. It also includes any user of such goods or a beneficiary of such services. The term consumer, however, does not include a person who obtains such goods and services for resale or for any commercial purpose. This means that a person who obtains such goods for resale or for any commercial purposes is not a consumer and consequently he/she cannot approach a consumer disputes redressal agency alleging any defect in the goods purchased by him.

The liberalisation of economic policies and the resultant globalisation and privatisation as well as opening up of the media have brought in a number of changes in the marketing environment. Changes are also taking place in the purchasing power of the consumers. Today, they seek greater value for money spent by them.

In the present scenario, though the consumer can exercise more choice in the satisfaction of his/her needs, yet he/she does not always have the necessary skills to make a rational choice or to understand the implications of the offerings made. In addition, the consumers encounter a number of problems related to adulteration, spurious goods, hoarding, use of deceptive and fractional weights, late deliveries, variations in the contents of the pack, defective goods, poor after-sales service, misleading advertising, deficiency in services, cultural invasion, hidden pricing components, price discrimination, ATM and credit card frauds, financial frauds, promotional contests and problems related to public utilities. These problems arise primarily because unscrupulous businesspersons take an unfair advantage of the ignorance and helplessness of the consumers.

30.2 RIGHTS OF CONSUMERS

The basic rights of the consumers were first recognised and defined on 15 March 1962 by John F. Kennedy, the president of the United States of America, in his special message to the Congress on Consumer Protection. Four basic rights were incorporated as human rights in the UN Charter. They are:

1. the right to safety,
2. the right to be informed,
3. the right to choose and
4. the right to be heard.

Later, the International Organization of Consumer Union (IOCU) and the Confederation of Indian Consumers Organization (CICO) added three more rights, they are:

1. the right to healthy environment,
2. the right to consumer education and
3. the right to redressal.

In 1991, the right to boycott was also included in the National Convention of CICO, held at Kolkata. The right to basic needs is the latest addition to the rights of consumers.

30.3 CONSUMER RIGHTS IN INDIA

As per Indian Consumer Protection Act, 1986, the following rights of consumer are safeguarded.

30.3.1 Right to Safety

The right to safety ensures that consumers has right to be protected against the products, the production processes and the marketing of goods and services that are hazardous to their life or property (Consumers International). This implies that the consumers have right to demand products that are safe to use and unadulterated. The use of adulterated mustard oil, milk, khoya, silver foils, Coke or Pepsi containing high level of pesticides, appliances such as cookers that burst or electrical appliances that cause shock or short circuiting, gas cylinders that leak impinge upon a consumers' right to safety. In order to ensure that safe goods are sold to the consumers and safe procedures are followed in the delivery of services, the Government of India has taken an initiative on standardisation and quality control through ISI mark (for appliances), Agmark (for edible items), Hallmark (for gold) and so on.

30.3.2 Right to Information

Each consumer has right to be given factual information so that he/she can make informed choices or decisions on aspects such as quality, quantity, purity, potency, standards and price of a product. This also implies that the consumers have right to be protected against fraudulent, deceitful and misleading advertising, labelling or other unfair trade practices. The consumer has right to full information and not just partial information.

Accordingly, consumers have right to demand that packaging and labelling must provide clear and unambiguous information. The consumers should be informed of the harmful effects of products such as cigarettes and paan masala; they have right to demand information on quality, features, handling, repairs and spare parts of products; and that advertising of products and services is not misleading and false. There is now a mounting pressure on the manufacturers to disclose place of manufacturing; and the conditions under which such manufacturing is being done.

30.3.3 RIGHT TO CHOOSE

Every buyer has right to have access to basic products and services that vary in quality, price, size and design. It implies that the consumers can choose products and services at competitive prices with an assurance of satisfactory quality and safety. He/she should not be forced to purchase products of the same manufacturer if he/she does not wish to as, for example, in case of cable services, where the service providers allocate areas among themselves and restrict the entry of other service providers. Tie in sales wherein, for example, if he/she wishes to purchase one computer he/she must also purchase a printer from the same manufacturer. It restricts the freedom of choice.

30.3.4 RIGHT TO BE HEARD

This means that the consumers have right to be heard or to make a representation against exploitation and unfair trade practices. This means that if they are not satisfied with a product or service, they have right to complain. If laws, rules and regulations are being made then they have right to give their opinion on matters that affect them directly or indirectly.

30.3.5 RIGHT TO CONSUMER EDUCATION

This right means educating and preparing the consumers in a way that they acquire knowledge regarding consumer rights, law and the philosophy of consumer protection. Such education will help them to get the skills needed for taking action to influence factors such as price, advertising and sales promotion, which affect consumer decisions. They must be educated on what they must do in case of dissatisfaction, what agencies to approach for this purpose, the procedure followed, the time and cost involved etc. They must be educated on what points they should keep in mind while making purchases and how and where they should be able to get information about products and services before they purchases them.

30.3.6 RIGHT TO REDRESSAL

This is the right of the consumers to get a fair settlement of just claims. They have the right to be compensated for misrepresentation, defective goods and deficiency in services. The agencies providing such redressal should be in existence and be able to provide redressal within a reasonable time frame. They have right that business organisations set up appropriate dispute handling mechanisms for their consumers.

30.4 RESPONSIBILITIES OF CONSUMERS

All consumers should behave in a responsible manner while exercising their rights. What is expected of the consumers in terms of being responsible is given as follows:

1. In purchasing goods and services, the consumers should evaluate, from the variety available, the price range and the quality that they want and satisfy them as to whether the available range is acceptable to them and meets their needs.
2. They should make all their purchases at the right places such as authorised dealers to avoid unscrupulous traders.
3. While making a purchase, they should make efforts to obtain the information about the details of the product or the service for which they are going to pay a price. Before they accept the goods or services, they should read and decide on the terms and conditions specified by the seller.

4. It is the duty of the consumers to see that the products bought by them are safe and not substandard. They should get assurance about the quality of the products and preferably the products carrying quality marks such as ISI and Agmark.
5. It is the responsibility of the consumers to obtain and keep receipts and other relevant documents for future reference, especially while purchasing durable goods.
6. The consumers should not be indifferent to any malpractice on the part of the seller even if it is of a small value. At the same time, they should not misuse their rights to exploit the seller. They should be honest in their claim regarding the price paid, the time of purchase etc.
7. They should not buy more than their requirements, as this would lead to hoarding, which encourages black marketing. Such practices affect the availability and price of goods and services for other consumers.

It is the responsibility of the consumers not to pollute their environment while using or disposing off the products.

30.5 CONCLUSION

Since the business does not always act responsibly, there is a need to educate and protect the consumers to enable them to look after their own interests and the interests of the society at large whether they are consuming goods or services. Goods are all movable products that are capable of being sold. Service means services of any descriptions made available to the potential users and includes the provision of facilities in connection with banking, financing, insurance, transport, processing and supply of electrical or other energy, boarding, lodging, entertainment, construction (housing), amusement or providing news or other information. It is, therefore, important that each one of us as consumers must know what our rights and responsibilities are. Therefore, a consumer is not only responsible for himself/herself but also equally concerned with the impact that his/her consumption behaviour will have on other consumers.

Suggested Questions

1. 'Consumer awareness is very dismal in India.' Do you agree with the statement?
2. What information should be available to a consumer as his/her right to be informed? Use suitable examples to illustrate.
3. Explain the various responsibilities of a consumer. How are his/her rights affected if he/she does not fulfil his/her responsibilities?
4. 'Consumer rights were not formed in a day.' State the historical perspective of consumer rights?
5. What are the rights of a consumer in India?
6. Why is it necessary for a consumer to be responsible?
7. What do you understand by right to redress?
8. How can a consumer exercise his/her right to healthy environment?

Bibliography

Consumer Protection Act, 1986.

Khanna, S., S. Hanspal *et al.* (2007). *Consumer Affairs* (Universities Press India Private Ltd.).

Index